She Wolf

VOLUME ONE

RICH TOMMASO

IMAGE COMICS
BERKELEY, CA

IMAGE COMICS, INC.

Robert Kirkman — Chief Operating Officer
Erik Larsen — Chief Financial Officer
Todd McFarlane — President
Mark Silvestri — Chief Executive Officer
Jim Valentino — Vice - President

Eric Stephenson — Publisher
Corey Murphy — Director of Sales
Jeff Boison — Director of Publishing Planning & Book Trade Sales
Jeremy Sullivan — Director of Digital Sales
Kat Salazar — Director of PR & Marketing
Branwyn Bigglestone — Controller
Drew Gill — Art Director
Jonathan Chan — Production Manager
Meredith Wallace — Print Manager
Briah Skelly — Publicist
Sasha Head — Sales & Marketing Production Designer
Randy Okamura — Digital Production Designer
David Brothers — Branding Manager
Olivia Ngai — Content Manager
Addison Duke — Production Artist
Vincent Kukua — Production Artist
Tricia Ramos — Production Artist
Jeff Stang — Direct Market Sales Representative
Emilio Bautista — Digital Sales Associate
Leanna Caunter — Accounting Assistant
Chloe Ramos-Peterson — Library Market Sales Representative

IMAGECOMICS.COM

Spell Number

1

Shapeshifting

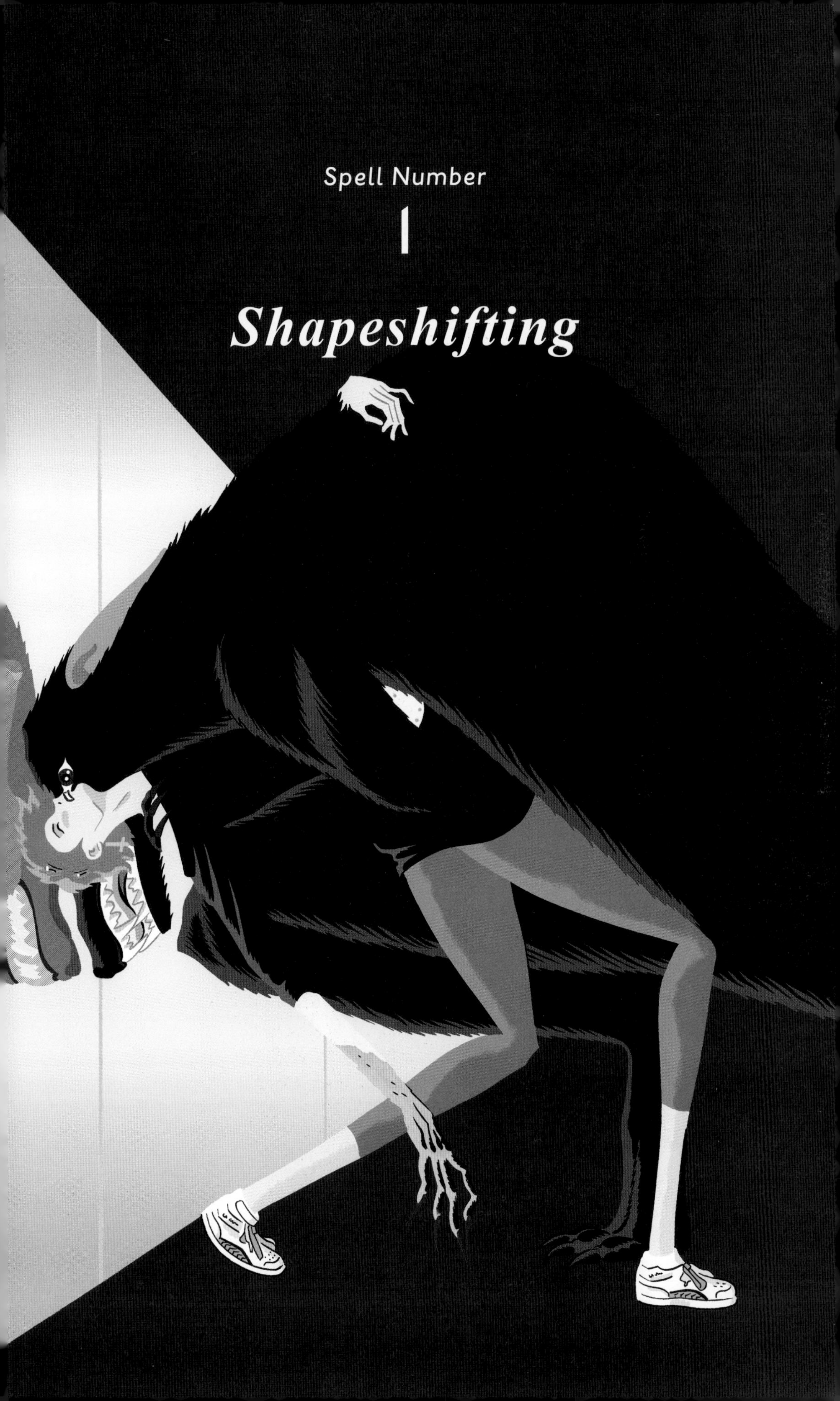

SHE WOLF Vol. 1. First printing. November 2016. Published by Image Comics, Inc. Office of publication: 2001 Center Street, Sixth Floor, Berkeley, CA 94704. Copyright © 2016 Rich Tommaso. All rights reserved. Contains material originally published as SHE WOLF #1-4. "SHE WOLF," its logos, and the likenesses of all characters herein are trademarks of Rich Tommaso, unless otherwise noted. "Image" and the Image Comics logos are registered trademarks of Image Comics, Inc. No part of this publication may be reproduced or transmitted, in any form or by any means (except for short excerpts for journalistic or review purposes), without the express written permission of Rich Tommaso or Image Comics, Inc. All names, characters, events, and locales in this publication are entirely fictional. Any resemblance to actual persons (living or dead), events, or places, without satiric intent, is coincidental. Printed in the USA. For information regarding the CPSIA on this printed material call: 203-595-3636 and provide reference #RICH–712018. For international rights, contact: foreignlicensing@imagecomics.com. ISBN 978-1-63215-905-2.

With illustrations by Brandon Graham (pg. 26), Chuck Forsman (pg. 48), Eraklis Petmezas (pg. 68), Jim Rugg (pg. 70) Brian Level, Tom Neely, and Patrick Dean (pgs. 117-119)

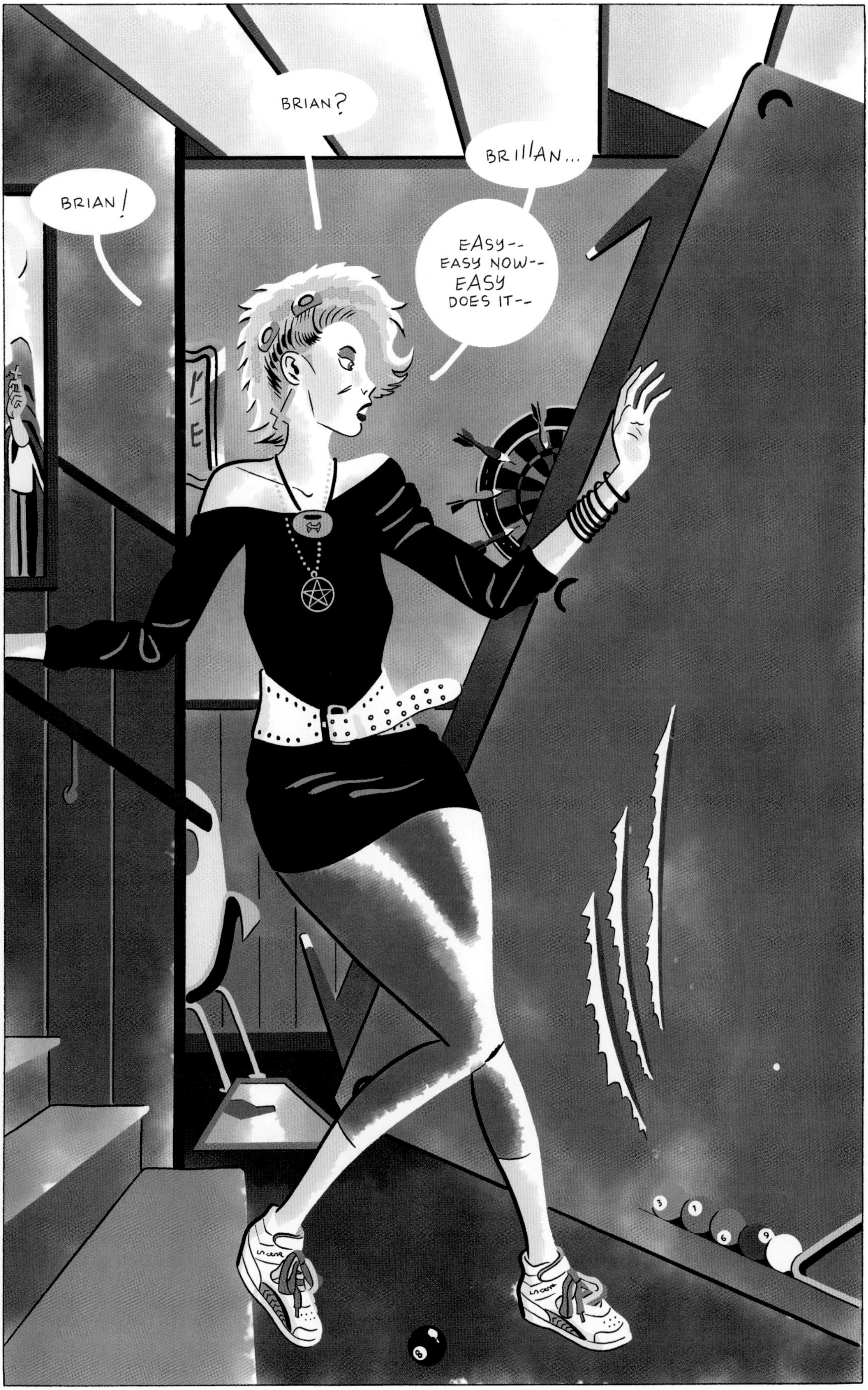
BRIAN!
BRIAN?
BRIIIAN...
EASY--
EASY NOW--
EASY
DOES IT--

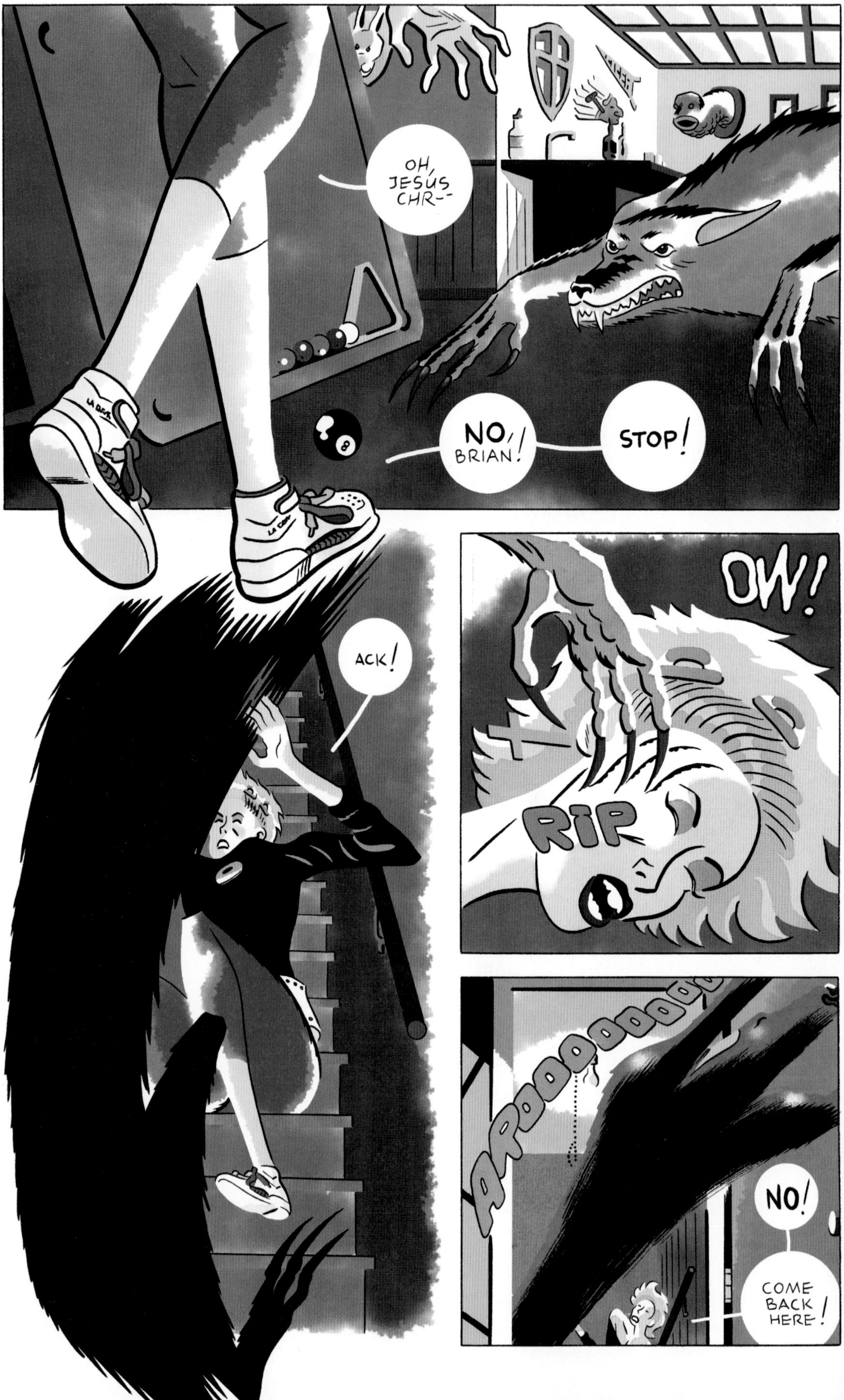
OH, JESUS CHR--
NO, BRIAN!
STOP!
ACK!
OW!
RIP
AROOOOOOOOO
NO!
COME BACK HERE!

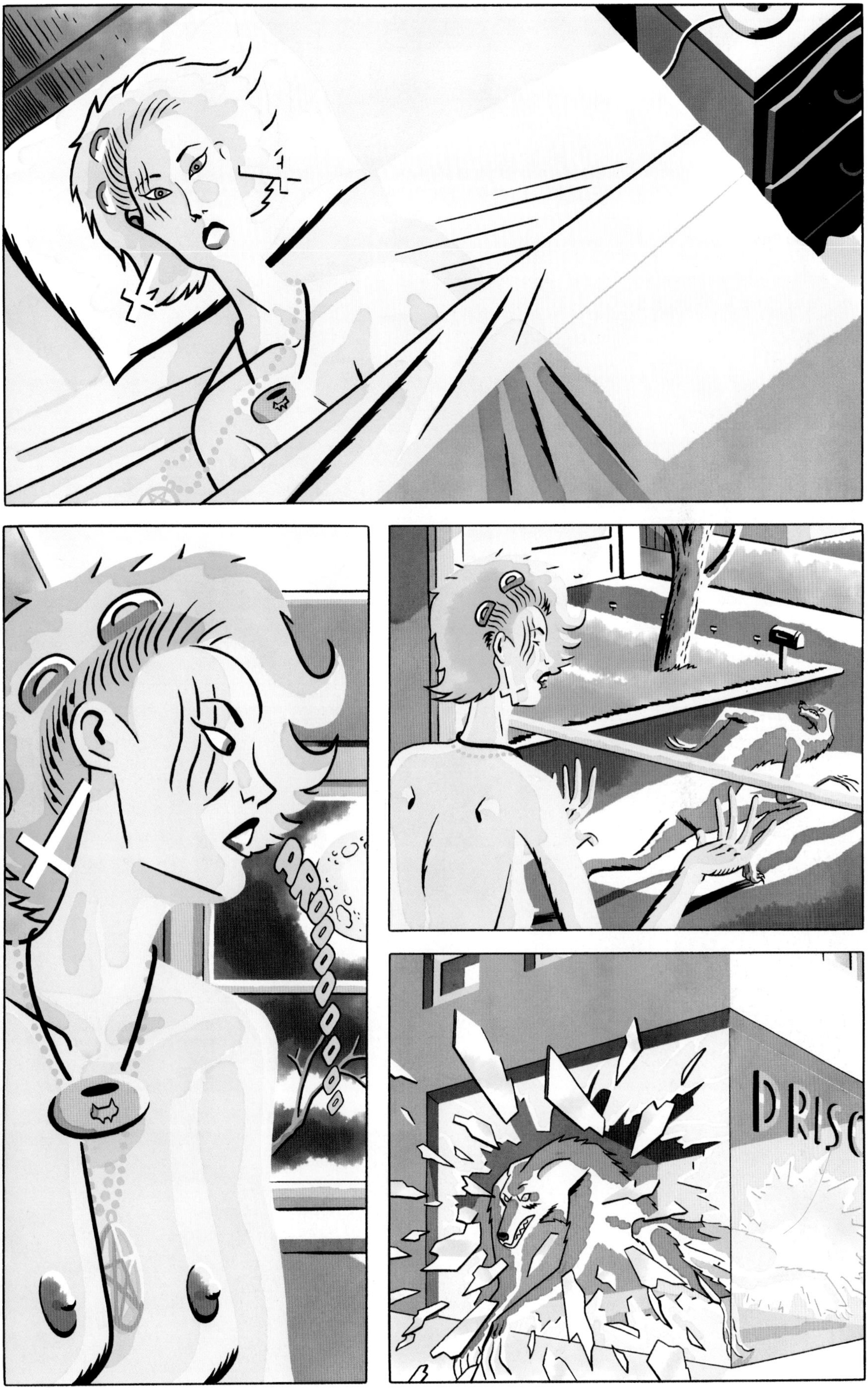
AROOOOOOOO
DRISC

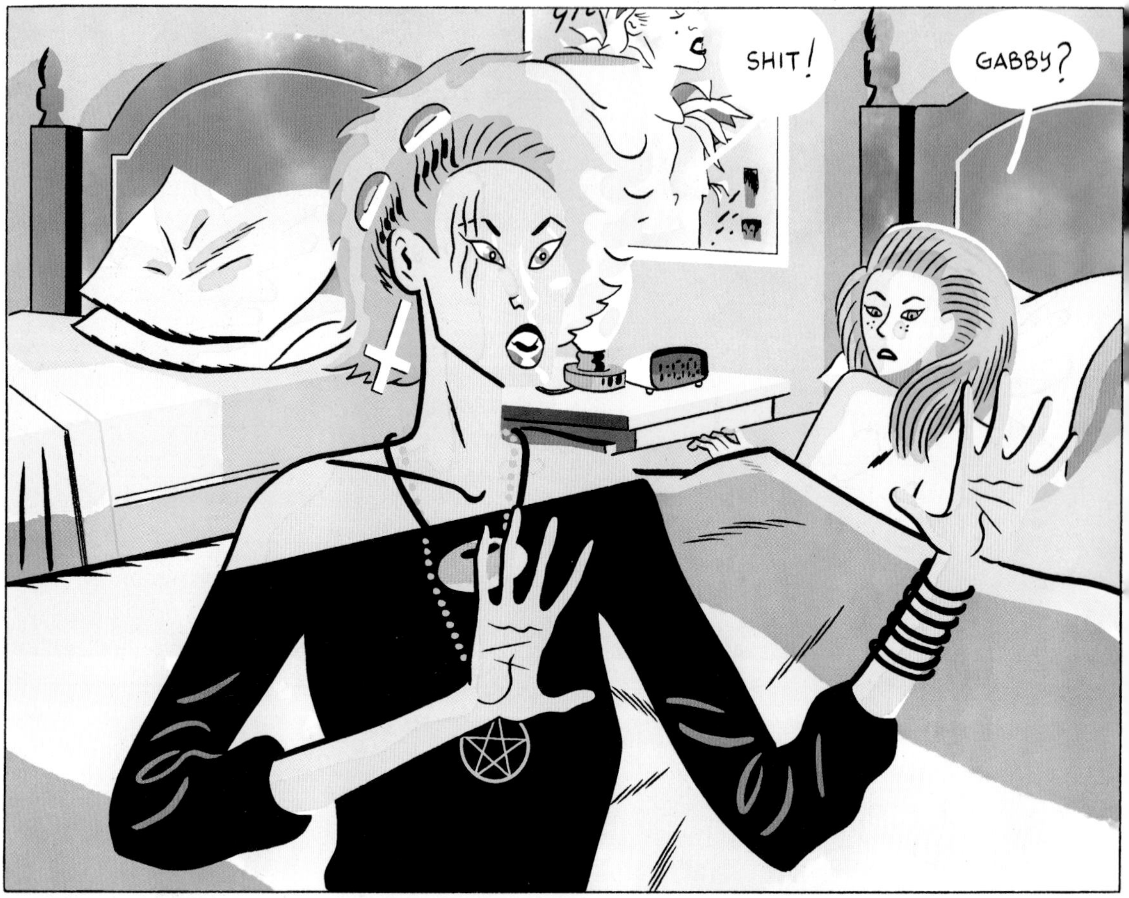
SHIT!
GABBY?

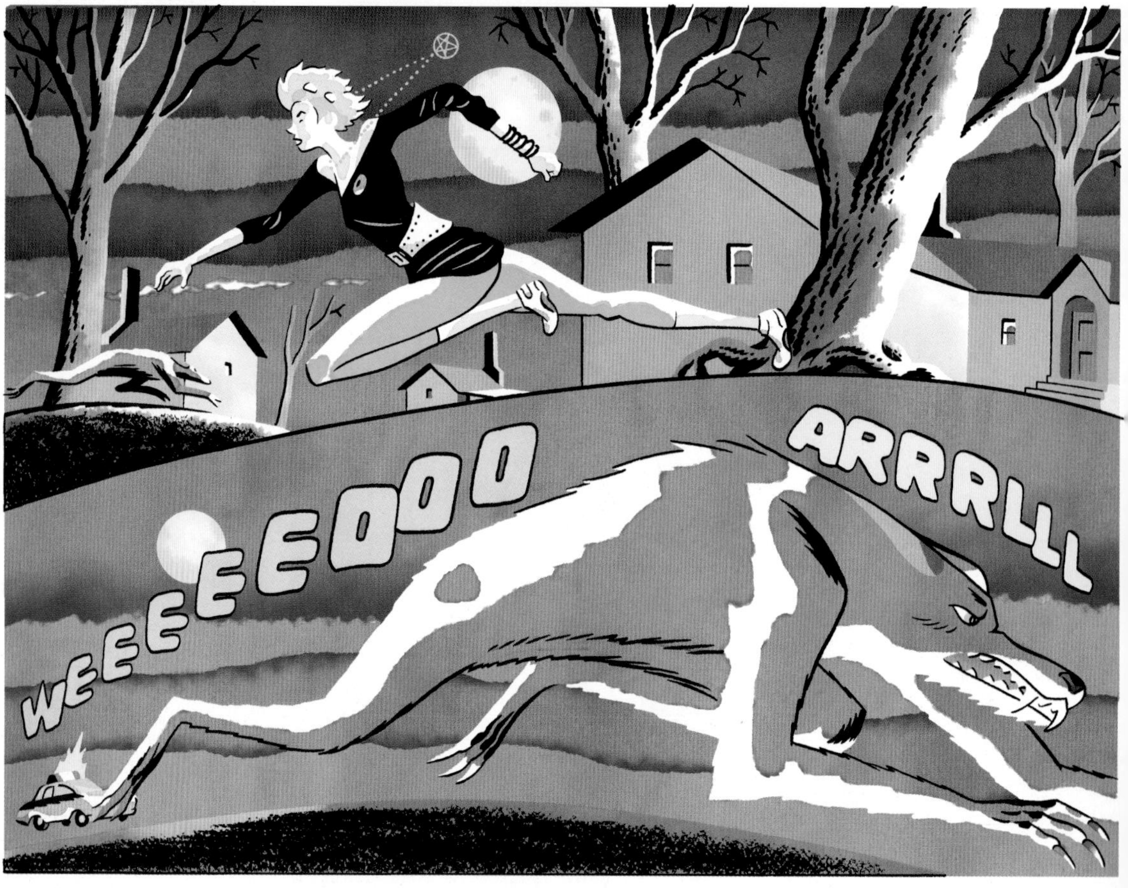
WEEEEEOOOO
ARRRLLL

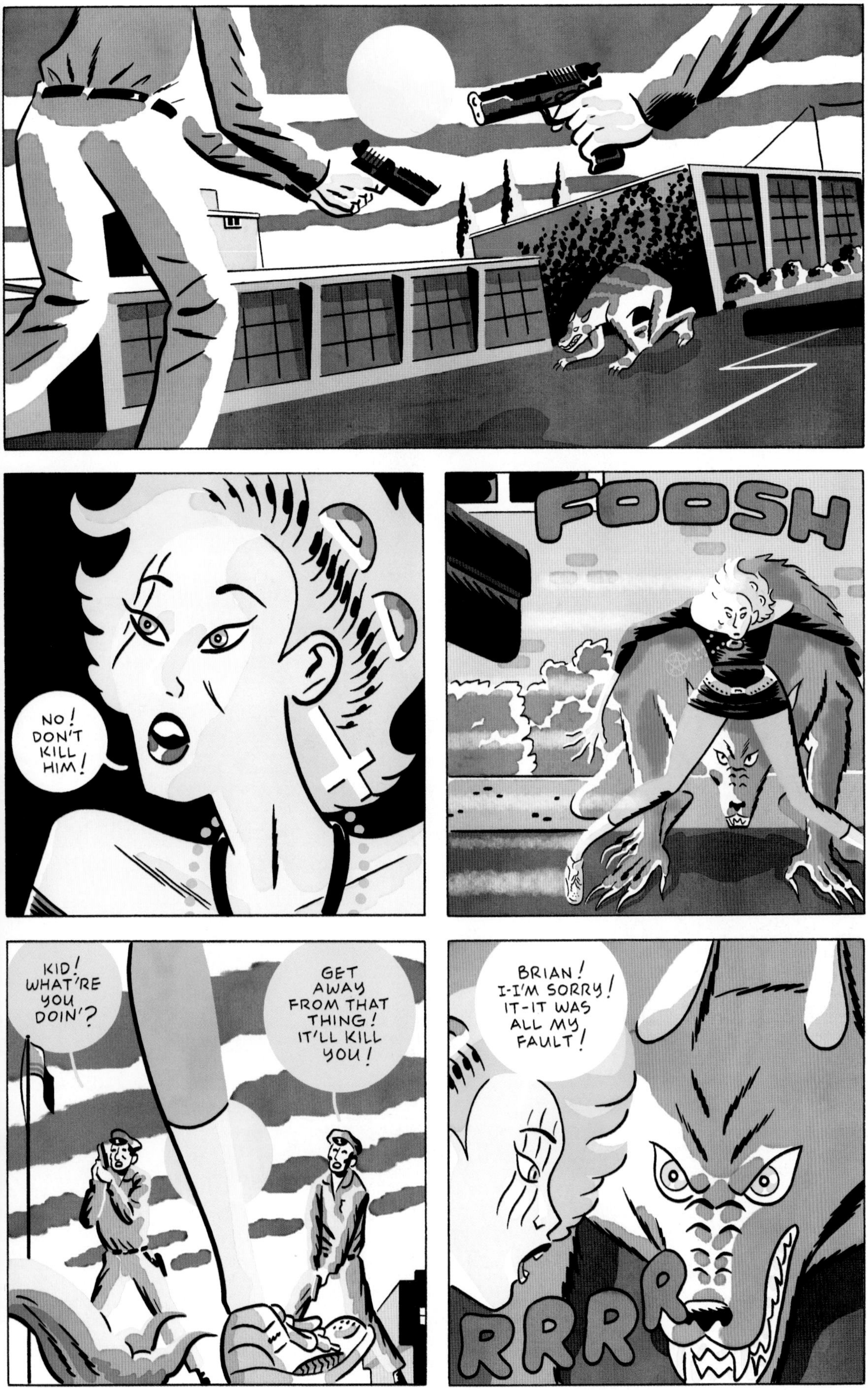
NO! DON'T KILL HIM!
FOOSH
KID! WHAT'RE YOU DOIN'?
GET AWAY FROM THAT THING! IT'LL KILL YOU!
BRIAN! I-I'M SORRY! IT-IT WAS ALL MY FAULT!
RRRR

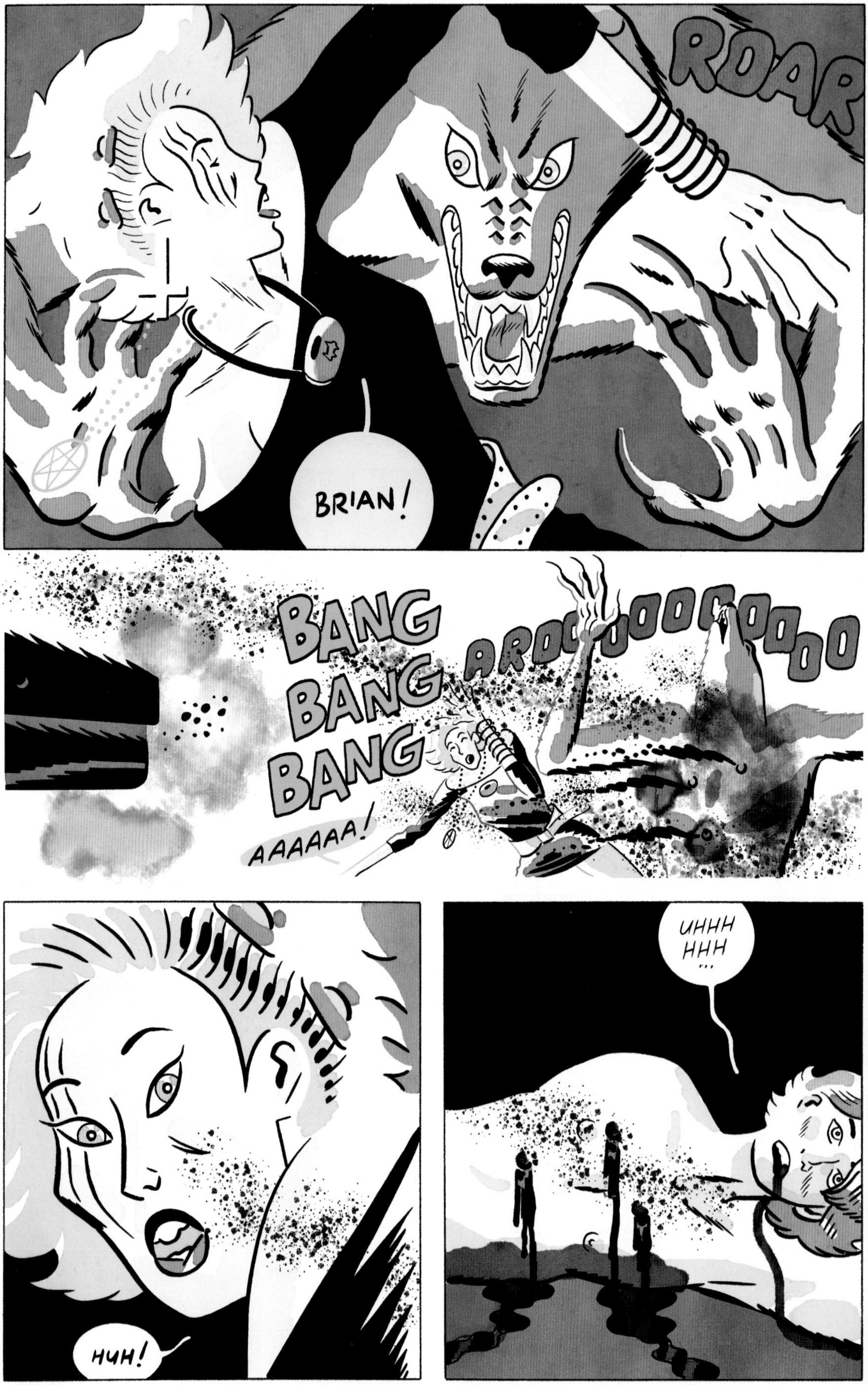

ROAR
BRIAN!
BANG
BANG
BANG
AROOOOOOOOOOOO
AAAAAA!
HUH!
UHHH
HHH
...

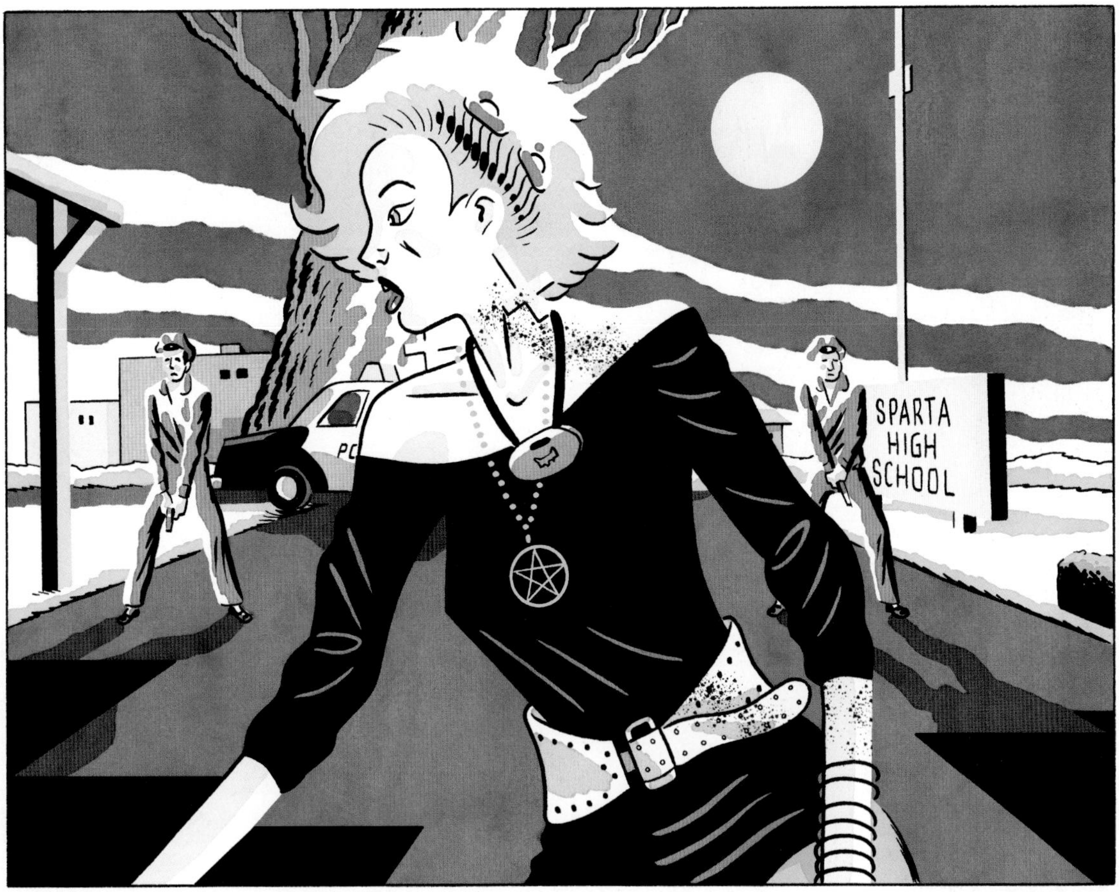
SPARTA
HIGH
SCHOOL

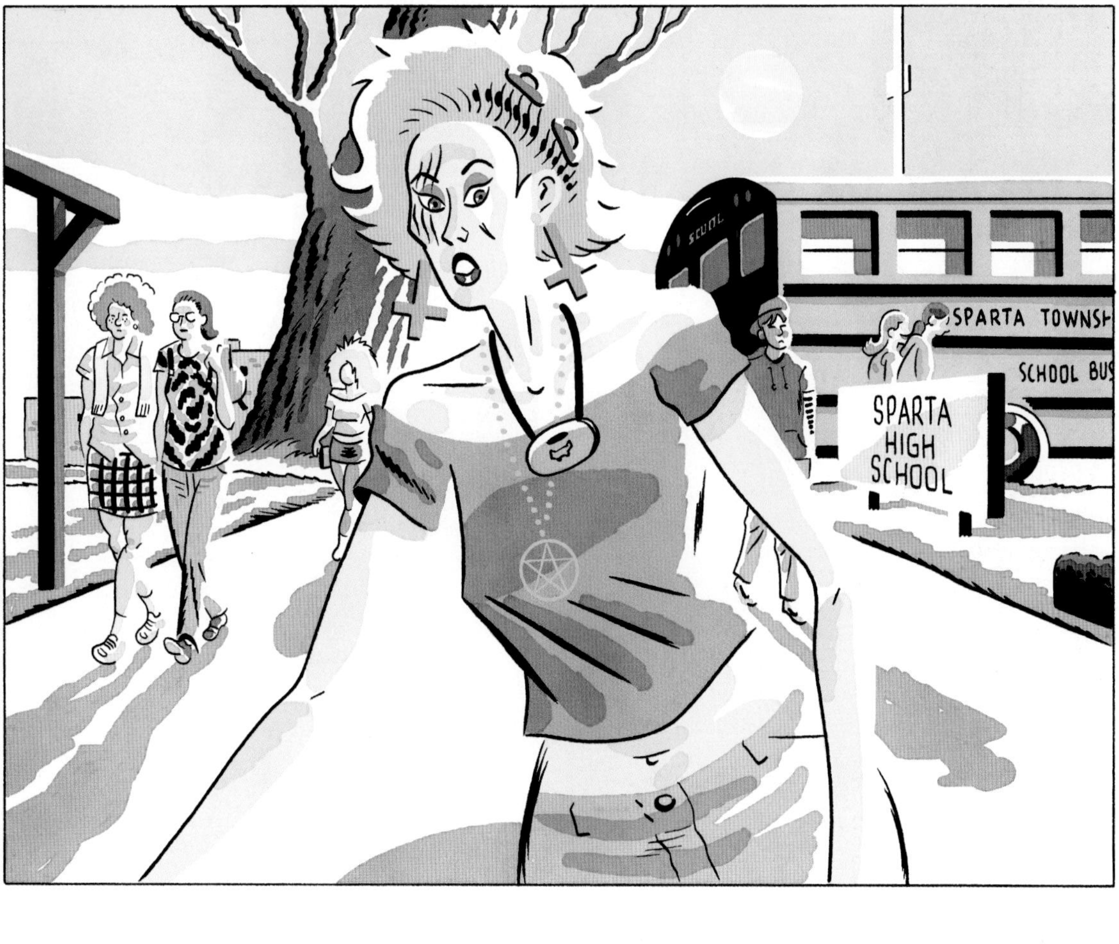
SPARTA
HIGH
SCHOOL

GABRIELLE!

PRINCIPAL CULLEN WANTS TO SEE YOU-- NOW.

OH-- AH!

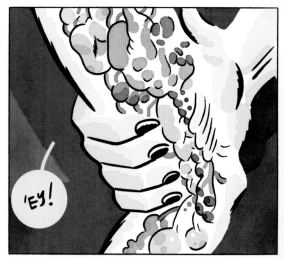

'EY!

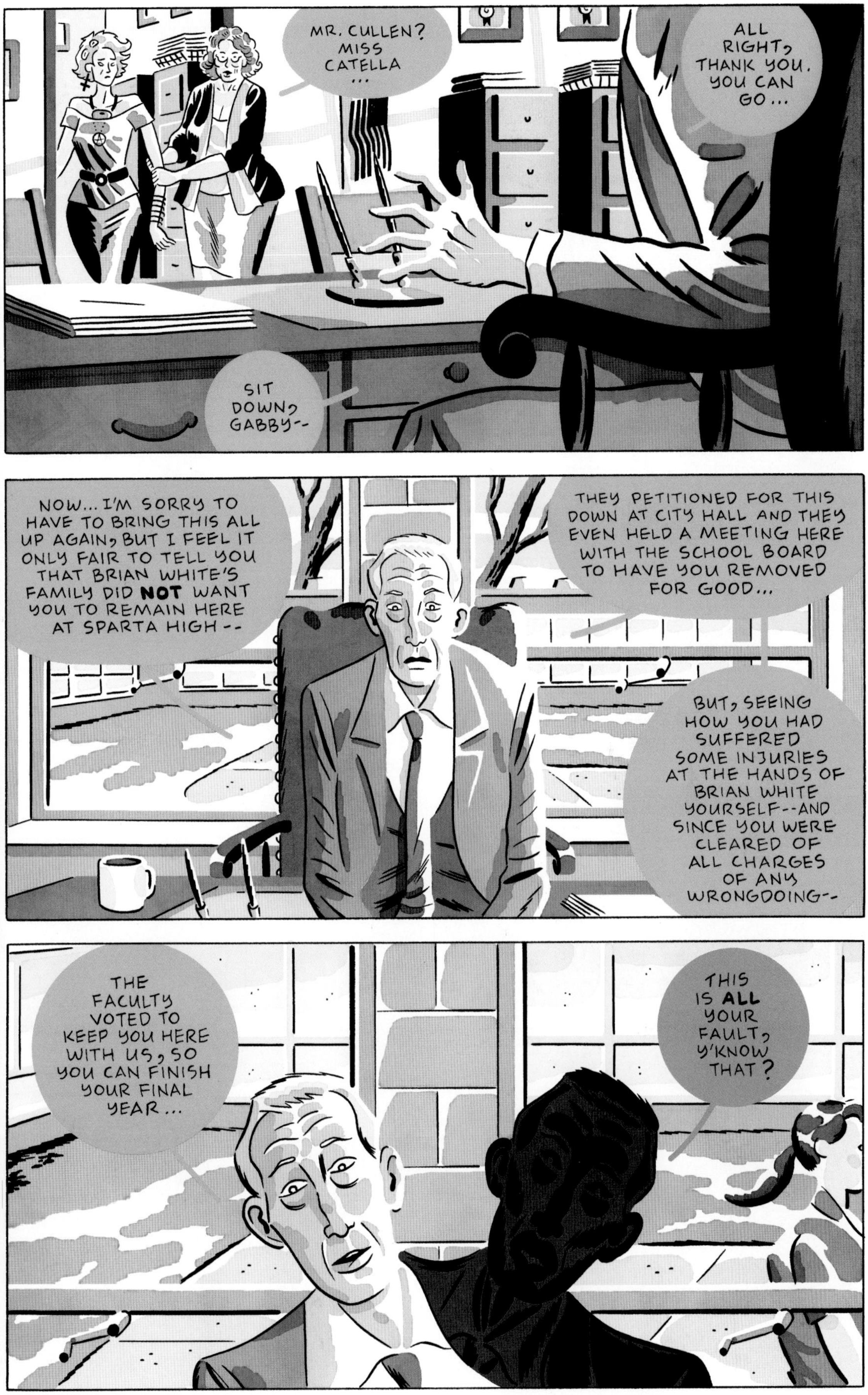

MR. CULLEN? MISS CATELLA ...
ALL RIGHT, THANK YOU. YOU CAN GO...
SIT DOWN, GABBY--
NOW... I'M SORRY TO HAVE TO BRING THIS ALL UP AGAIN, BUT I FEEL IT ONLY FAIR TO TELL YOU THAT BRIAN WHITE'S FAMILY DID **NOT** WANT YOU TO REMAIN HERE AT SPARTA HIGH --
THEY PETITIONED FOR THIS DOWN AT CITY HALL AND THEY EVEN HELD A MEETING HERE WITH THE SCHOOL BOARD TO HAVE YOU REMOVED FOR GOOD...
BUT, SEEING HOW YOU HAD SUFFERED SOME INJURIES AT THE HANDS OF BRIAN WHITE YOURSELF--AND SINCE YOU WERE CLEARED OF ALL CHARGES OF ANY WRONGDOING--
THE FACULTY VOTED TO KEEP YOU HERE WITH US, SO YOU CAN FINISH YOUR FINAL YEAR...
THIS IS **ALL** YOUR FAULT, Y'KNOW THAT?

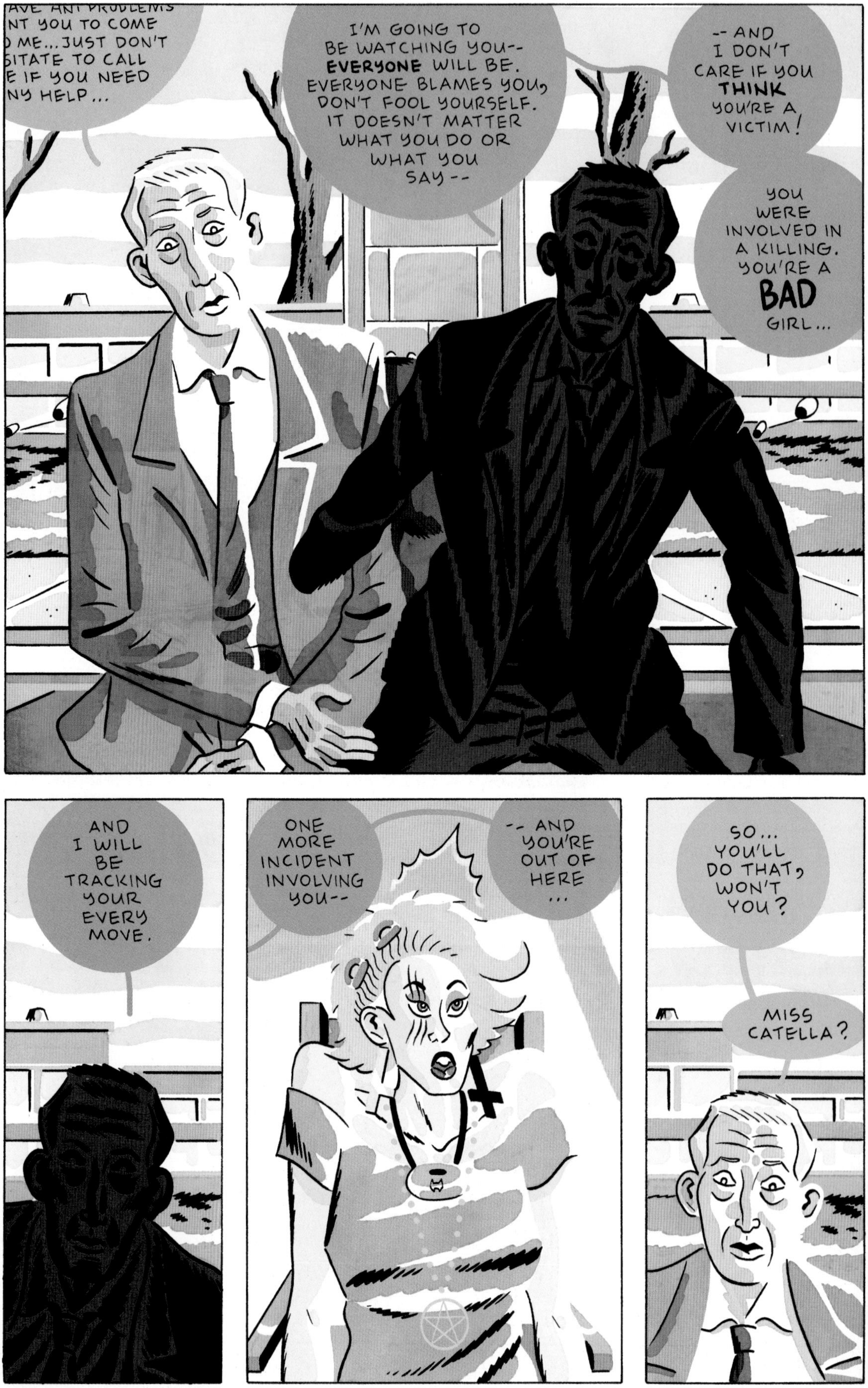
AVE ANY PROBLEMS
NT YOU TO COME
O ME... JUST DON'T
SITATE TO CALL
E IF YOU NEED
NY HELP...
I'M GOING TO BE WATCHING YOU-- EVERYONE WILL BE. EVERYONE BLAMES YOU, DON'T FOOL YOURSELF. IT DOESN'T MATTER WHAT YOU DO OR WHAT YOU SAY --
-- AND I DON'T CARE IF YOU THINK YOU'RE A VICTIM!
YOU WERE INVOLVED IN A KILLING. YOU'RE A BAD GIRL...
AND I WILL BE TRACKING YOUR EVERY MOVE.
ONE MORE INCIDENT INVOLVING YOU--
-- AND YOU'RE OUT OF HERE ...
SO... YOU'LL DO THAT, WON'T YOU?
MISS CATELLA?

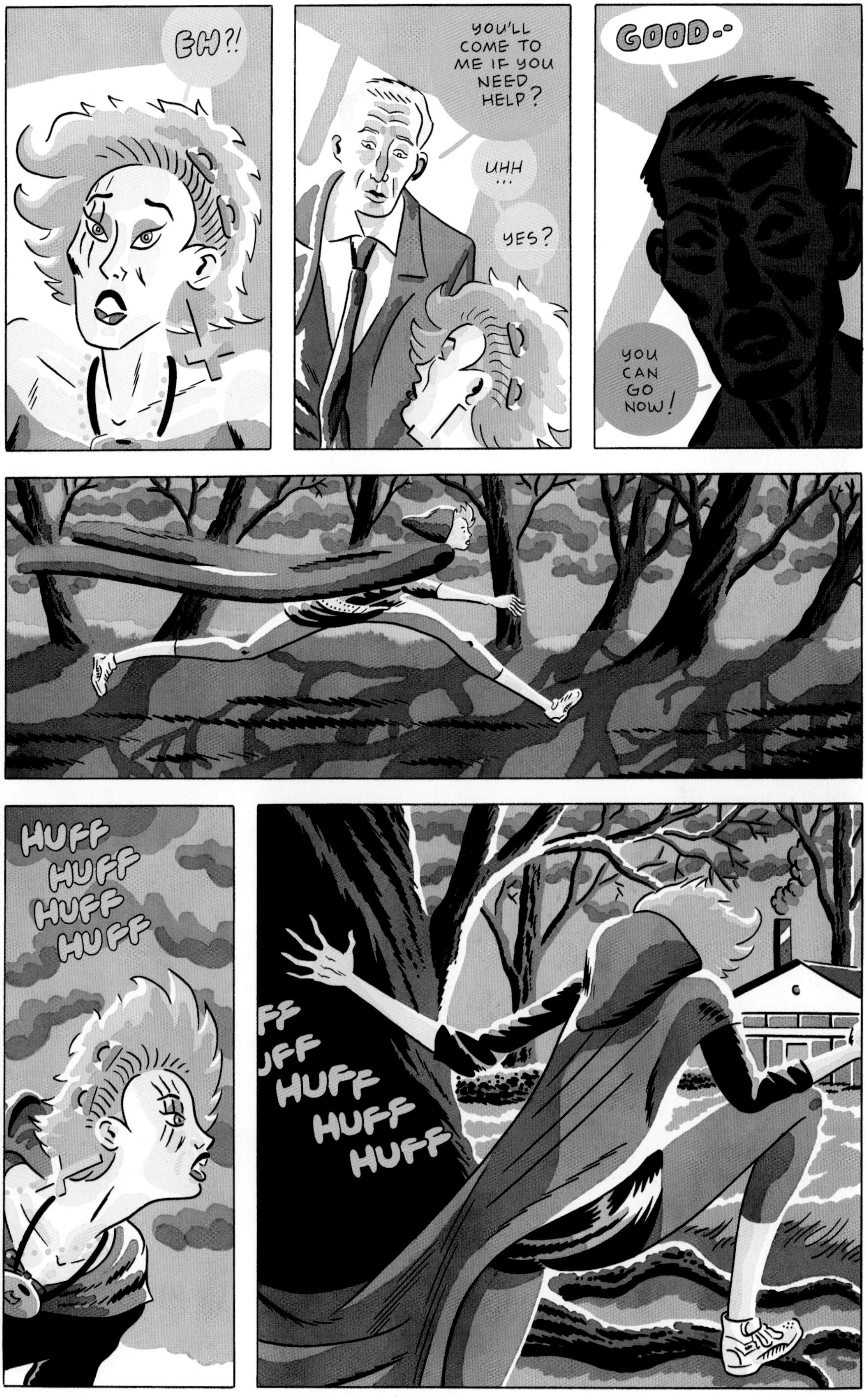
EH?!
YOU'LL COME TO ME IF YOU NEED HELP?
UHH ...
YES?
GOOD..
YOU CAN GO NOW!
HUFF HUFF HUFF HUFF
HUFF HUFF HUFF

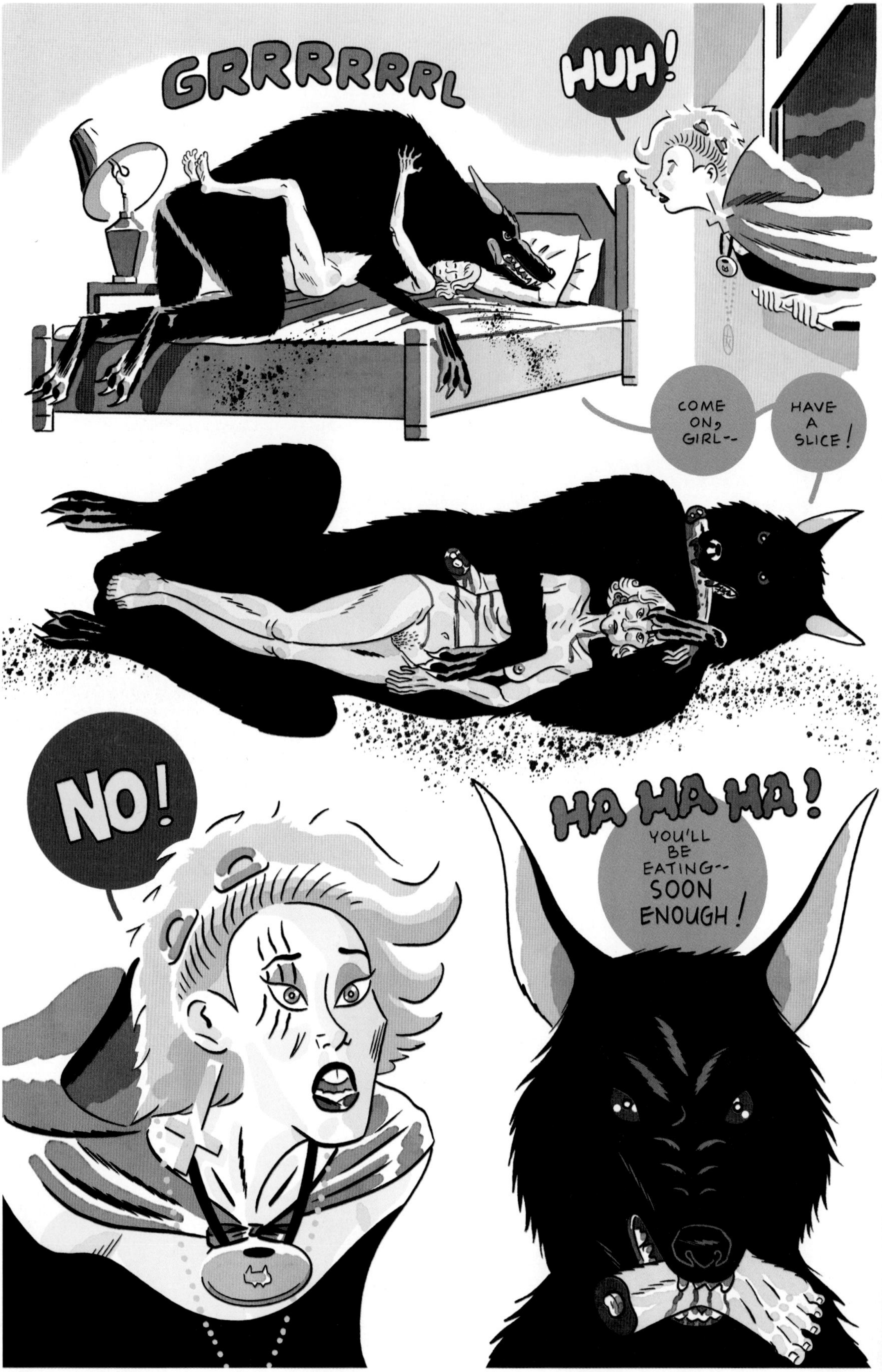
GRRRRRRL
HUH!
COME ON, GIRL--
HAVE A SLICE!
NO!
HA HA HA!
YOU'LL BE EATING-- SOON ENOUGH!

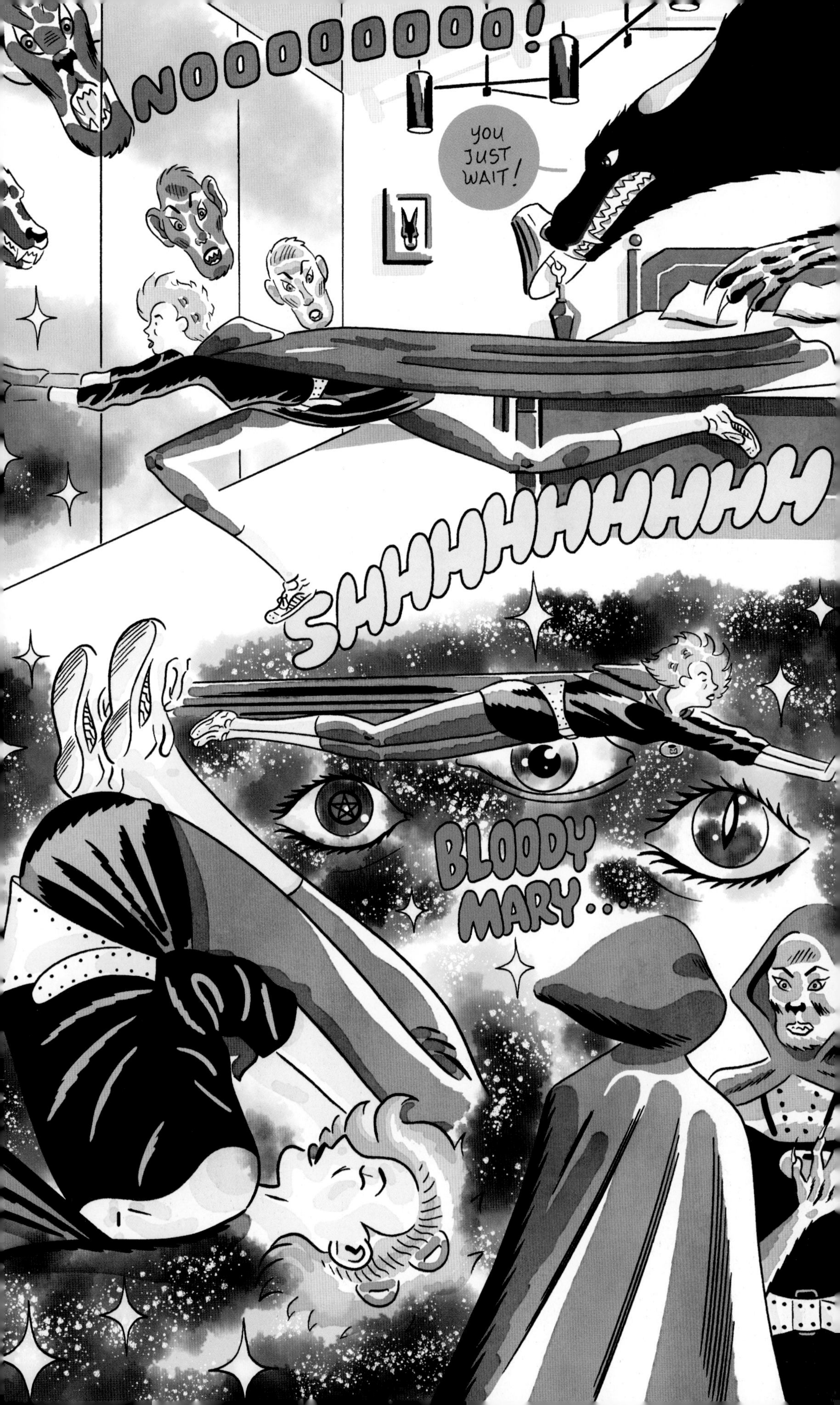
NOOOOOOOO!
YOU JUST WAIT!
SHHHHHHHHH
BLOODY MARY...

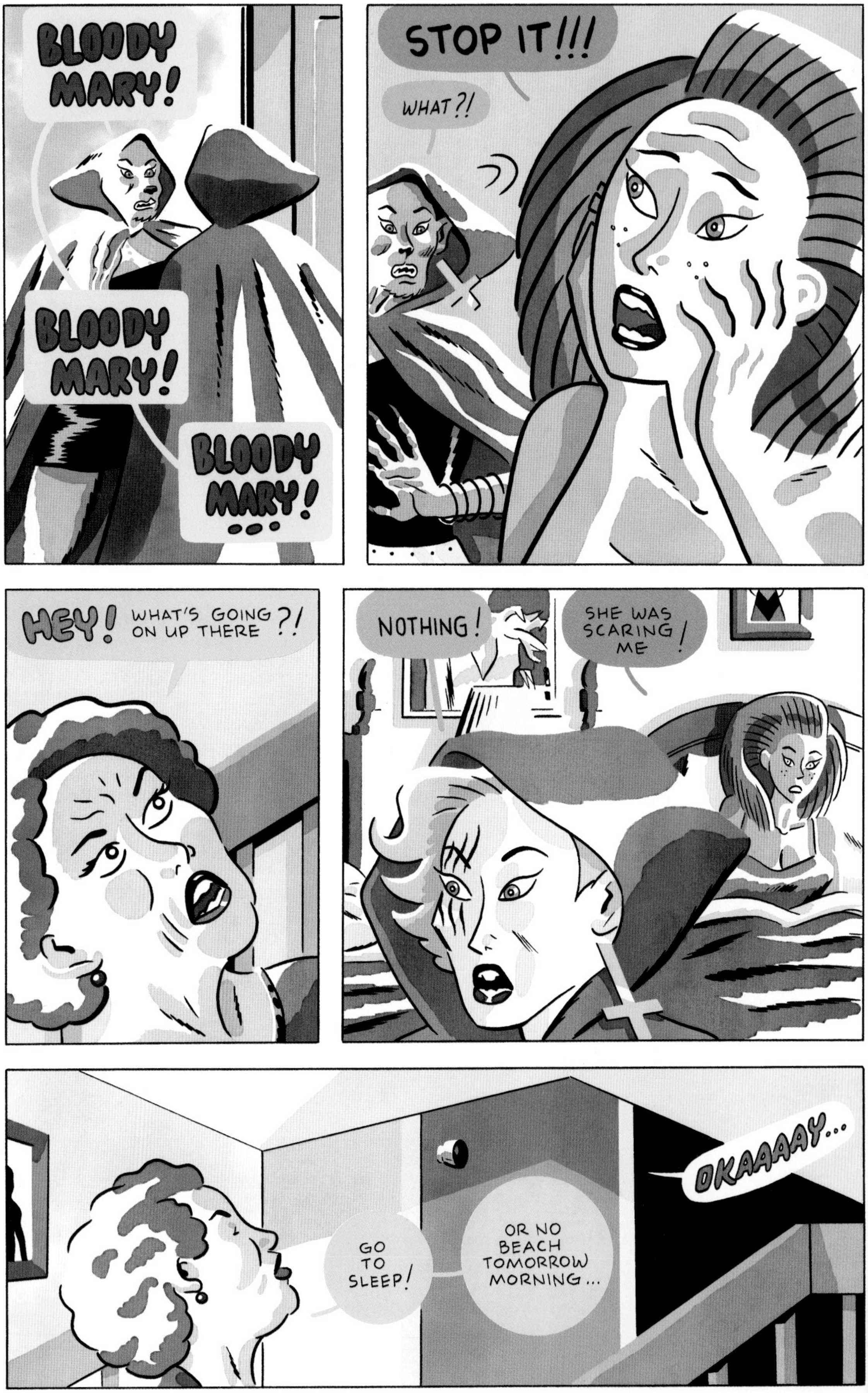
BLOODY MARY!
BLOODY MARY!
BLOODY MARY! ...
STOP IT!!!
WHAT?!
HEY! WHAT'S GOING ON UP THERE?!
NOTHING!
SHE WAS SCARING ME!
GO TO SLEEP!
OR NO BEACH TOMORROW MORNING...
OKAAAAY...

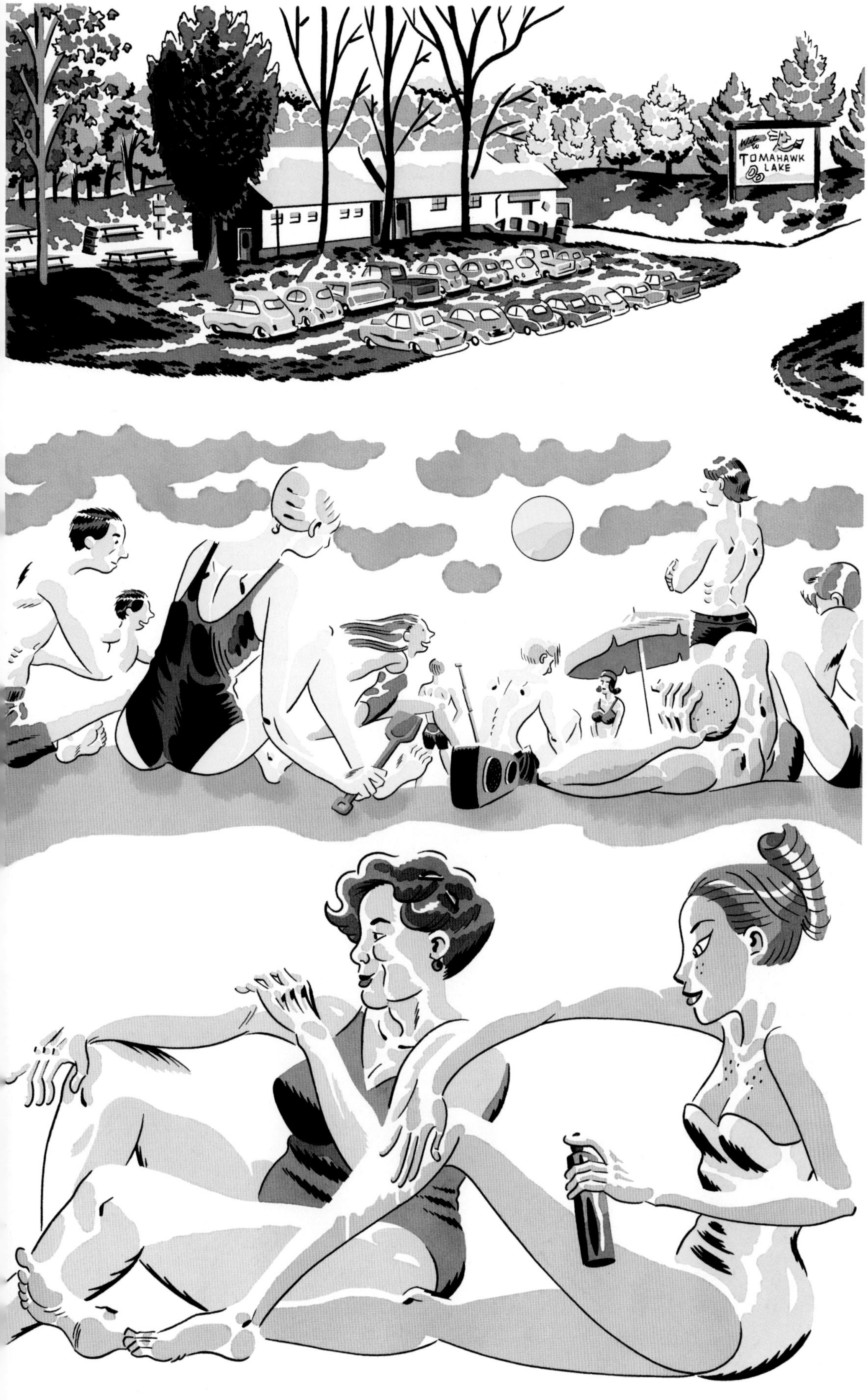
TOMAHAWK
LAKE

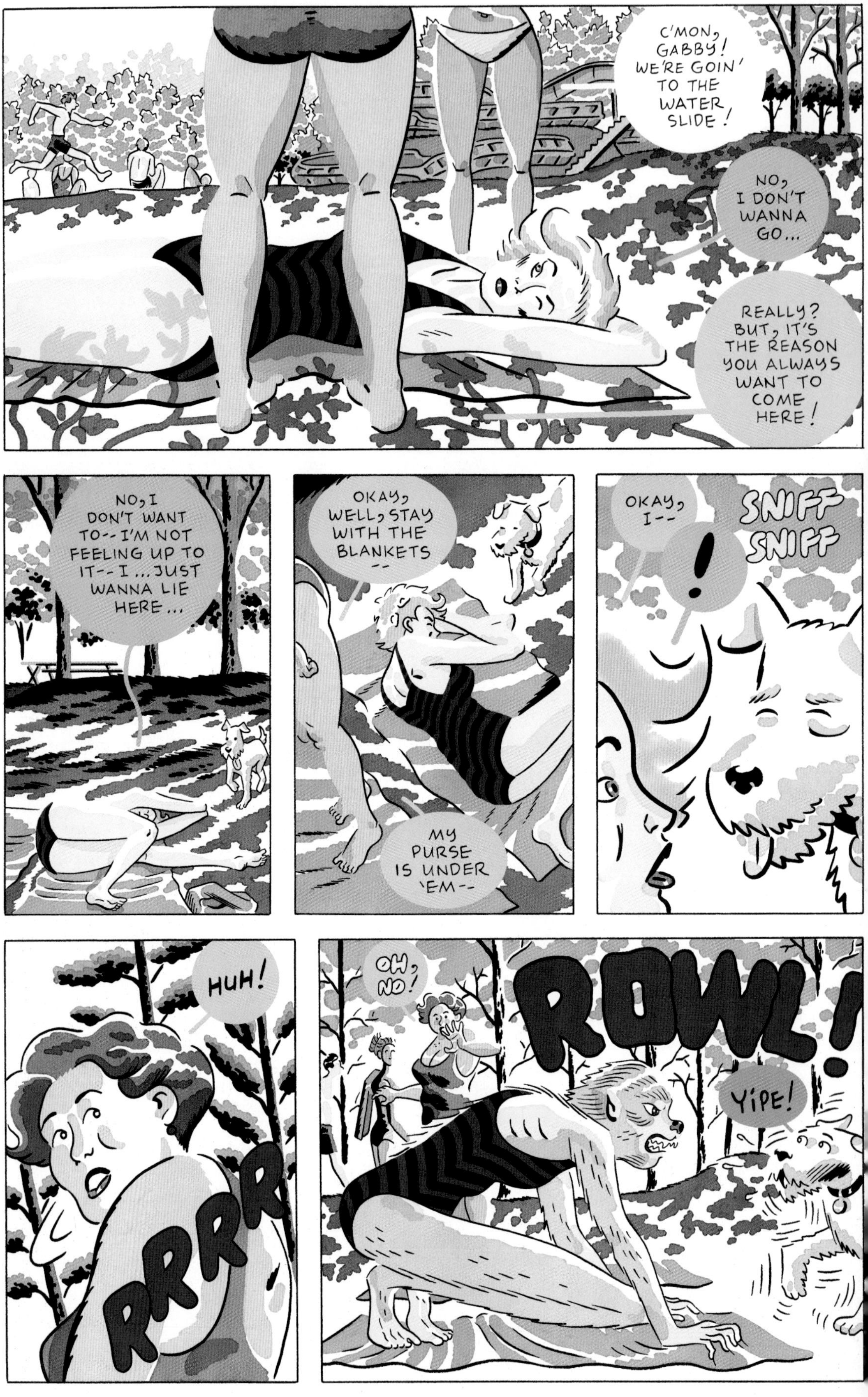
C'MON, GABBY! WE'RE GOIN' TO THE WATER SLIDE!
NO, I DON'T WANNA GO...
REALLY? BUT, IT'S THE REASON YOU ALWAYS WANT TO COME HERE!
NO, I DON'T WANT TO-- I'M NOT FEELING UP TO IT-- I... JUST WANNA LIE HERE...
OKAY, WELL, STAY WITH THE BLANKETS --
MY PURSE IS UNDER 'EM--
OKAY, I--
SNIFF SNIFF
!
HUH!
RRRR
OH, NO!
ROWL!
YIPE!

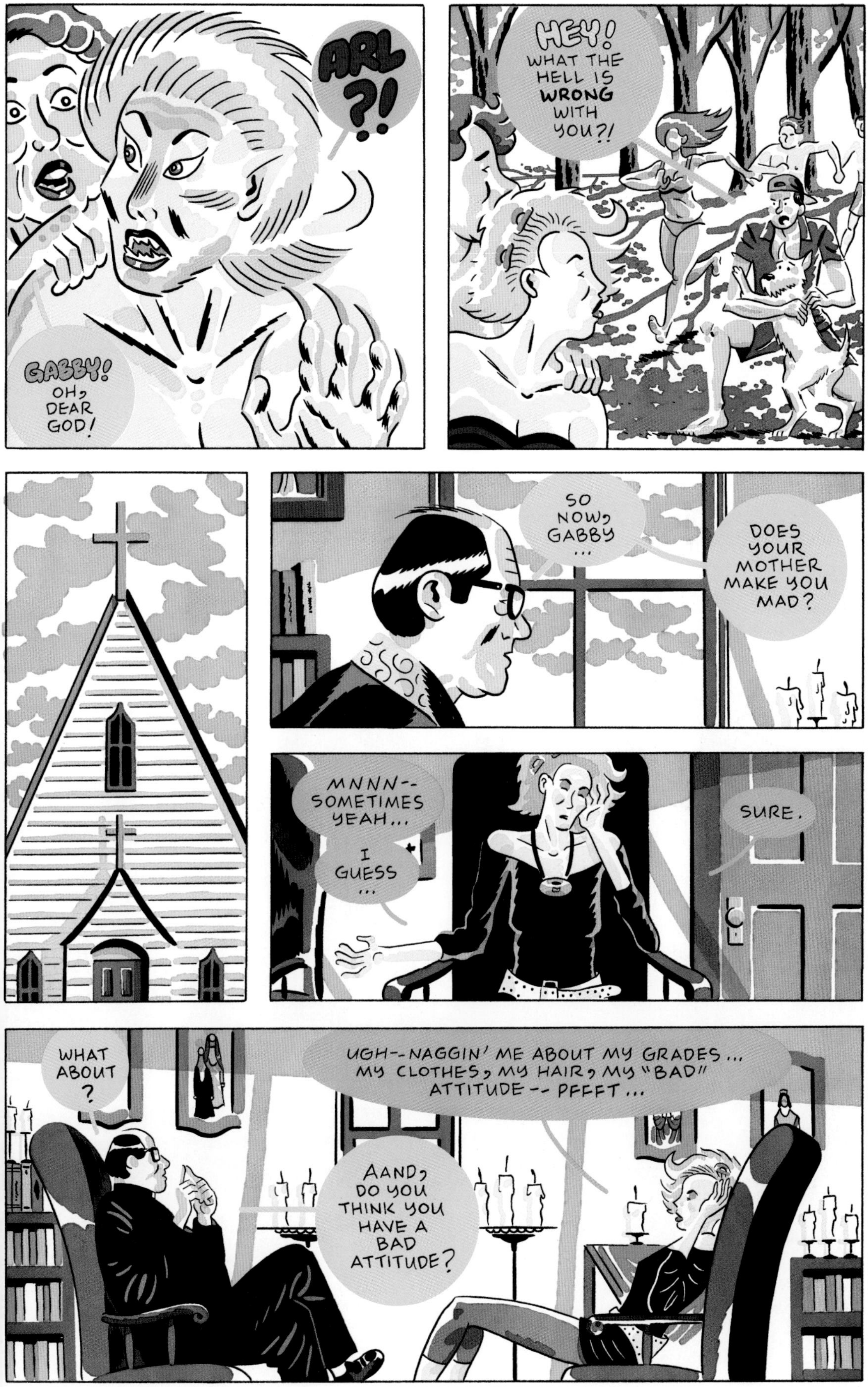
ARL ?!
GABBY! OH, DEAR GOD!
HEY! WHAT THE HELL IS WRONG WITH YOU?!
SO NOW, GABBY ...
DOES YOUR MOTHER MAKE YOU MAD?
MNNN-- SOMETIMES YEAH...
I GUESS ...
SURE.
WHAT ABOUT ?
UGH--NAGGIN' ME ABOUT MY GRADES... MY CLOTHES, MY HAIR, MY "BAD" ATTITUDE -- PFFFT...
AAND, DO YOU THINK YOU HAVE A BAD ATTITUDE?

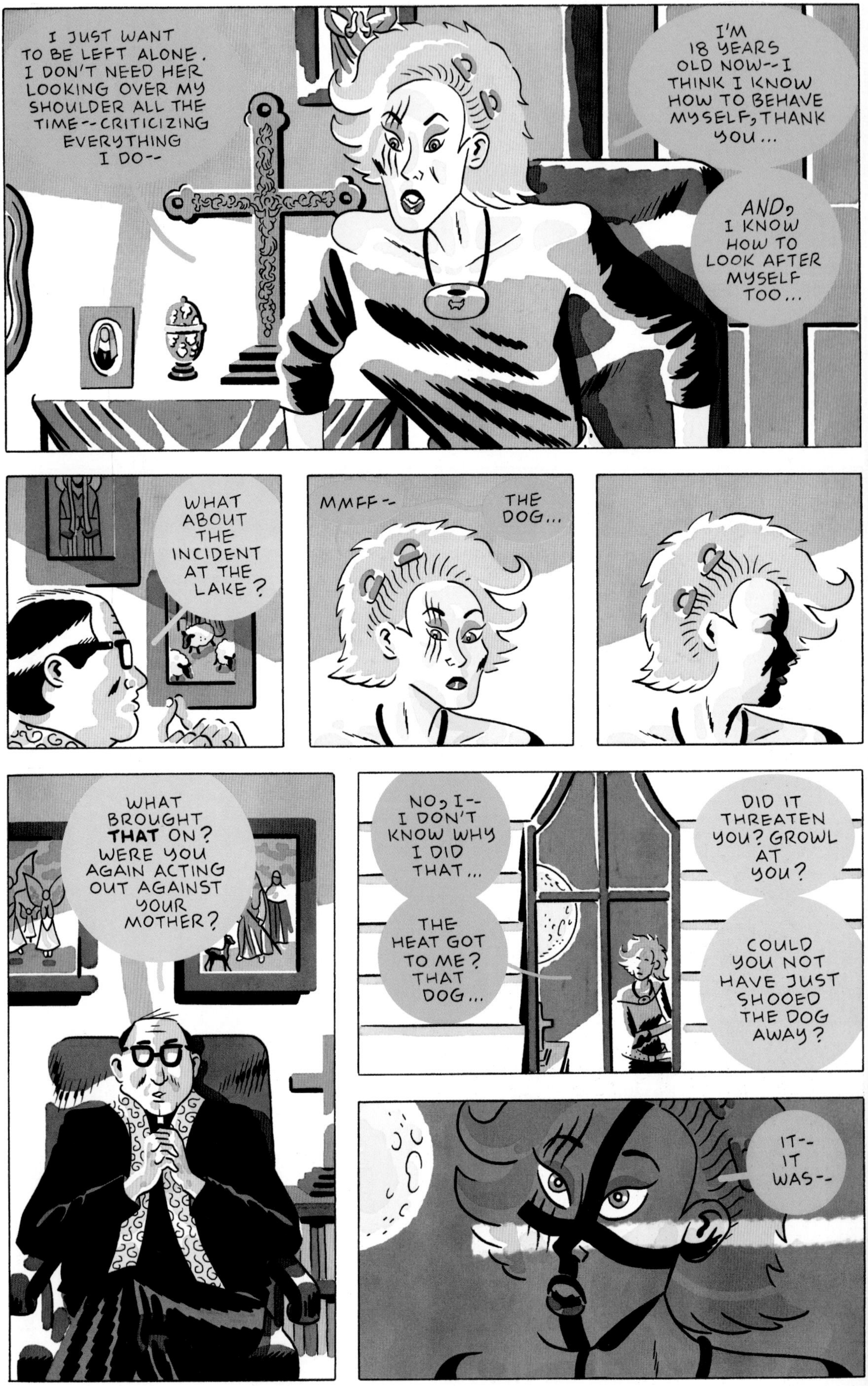
I JUST WANT TO BE LEFT ALONE. I DON'T NEED HER LOOKING OVER MY SHOULDER ALL THE TIME--CRITICIZING EVERYTHING I DO--
I'M 18 YEARS OLD NOW--I THINK I KNOW HOW TO BEHAVE MYSELF, THANK YOU...
AND, I KNOW HOW TO LOOK AFTER MYSELF TOO...
WHAT ABOUT THE INCIDENT AT THE LAKE?
MMFF--
THE DOG...
WHAT BROUGHT **THAT** ON? WERE YOU AGAIN ACTING OUT AGAINST YOUR MOTHER?
NO, I-- I DON'T KNOW WHY I DID THAT...
THE HEAT GOT TO ME? THAT DOG...
DID IT THREATEN YOU? GROWL AT YOU?
COULD YOU NOT HAVE JUST SHOOED THE DOG AWAY?
IT-- IT WAS--

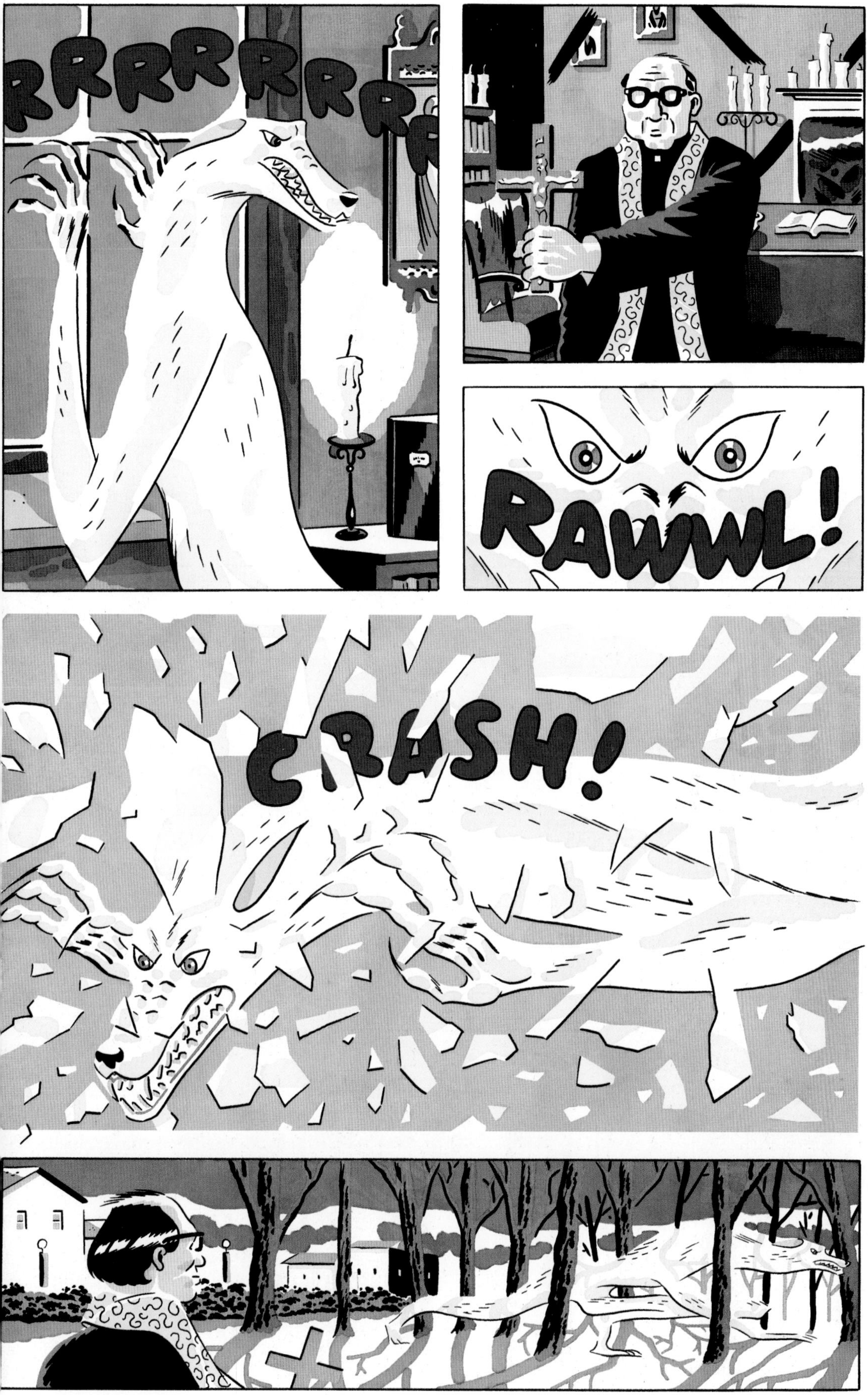

RRRRRRRRRR
RAWWL!
CRASH!

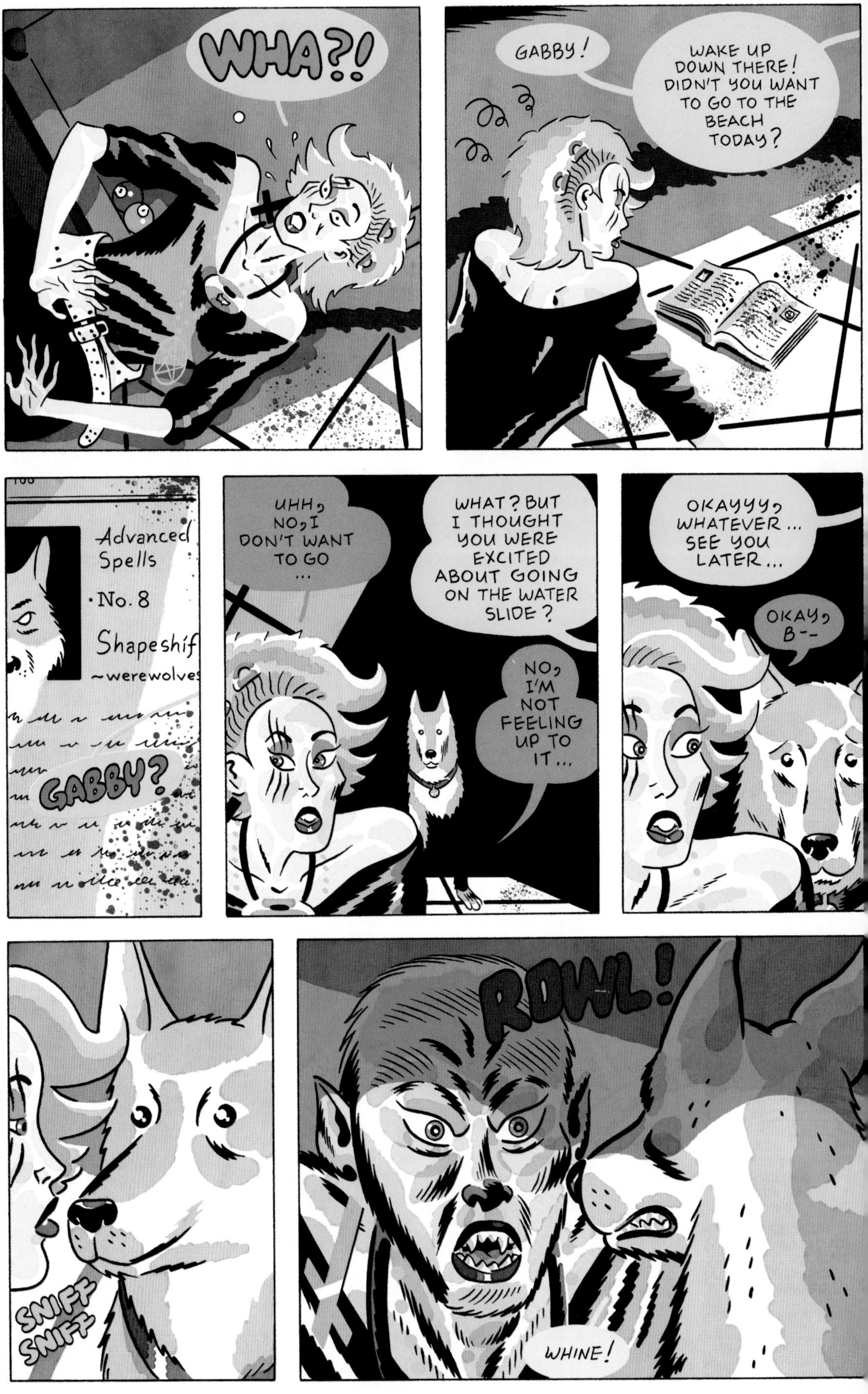

WHA?!
GABBY!
WAKE UP DOWN THERE! DIDN'T YOU WANT TO GO TO THE BEACH TODAY?
Advanced Spells
·No. 8
Shapeshif
~werewolves
GABBY?
UHH, NO, I DON'T WANT TO GO ...
WHAT? BUT I THOUGHT YOU WERE EXCITED ABOUT GOING ON THE WATER SLIDE?
NO, I'M NOT FEELING UP TO IT...
OKAYYY, WHATEVER... SEE YOU LATER...
OKAY, B--
SNIFF SNIFF
RDWL!
WHINE!

Spell Number

2

Mirror Walking

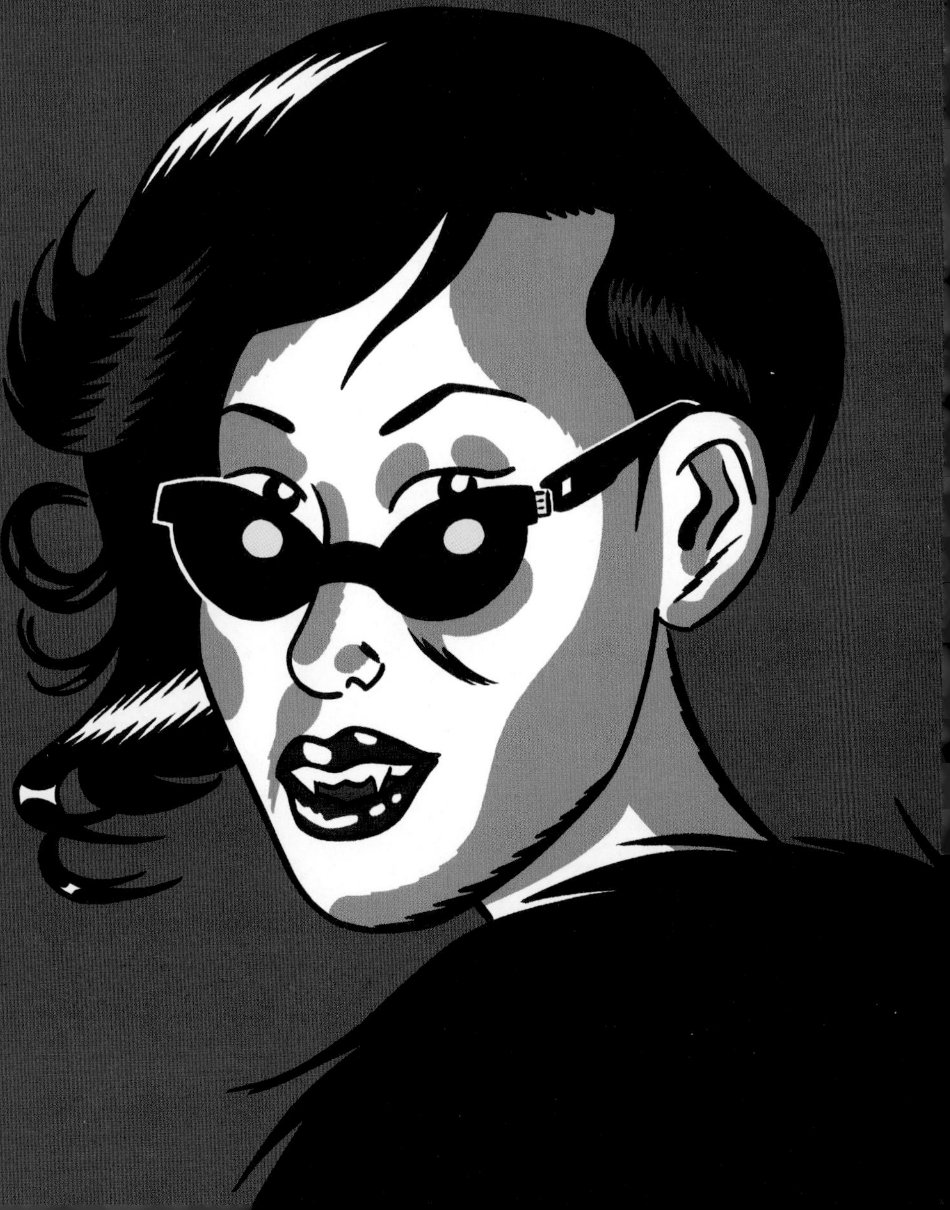

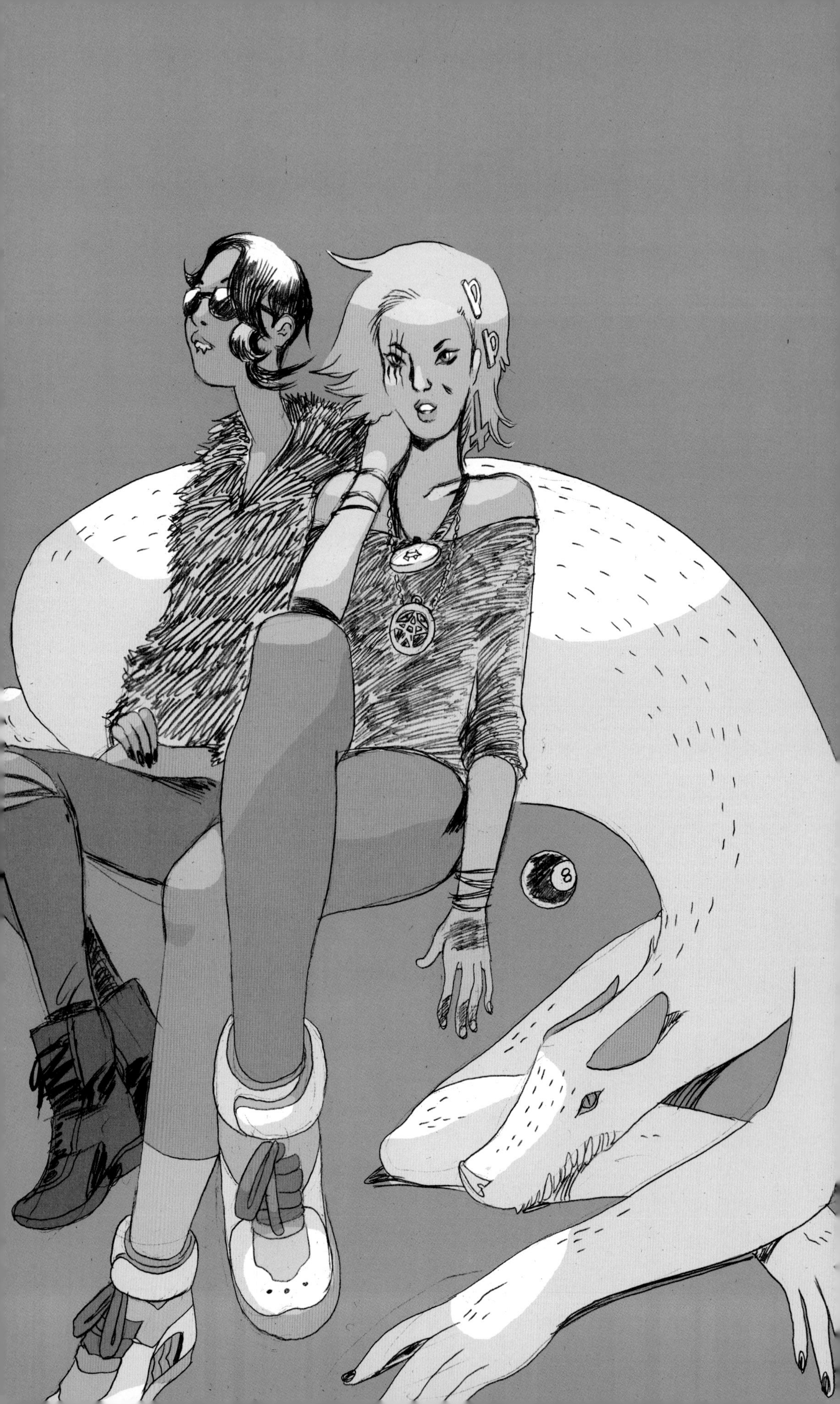

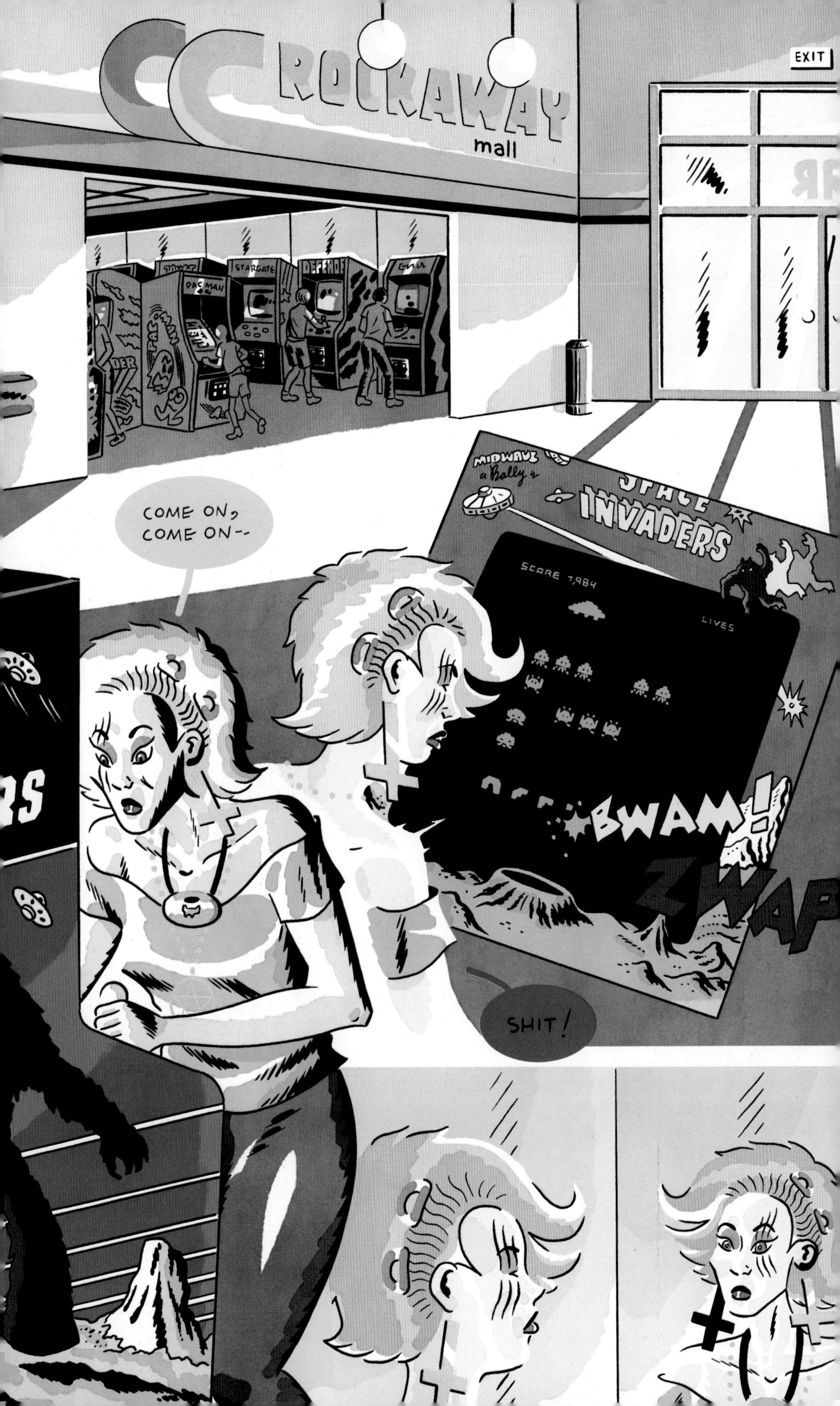
ROCKAWAY
mall
EXIT
STARGATE
DEFENDER
PAC-MAN
MIDWAY a Bally co.
SPACE INVADERS
SCORE 1,984
LIVES
COME ON, COME ON--
BWAM!
ZWAP
SHIT!

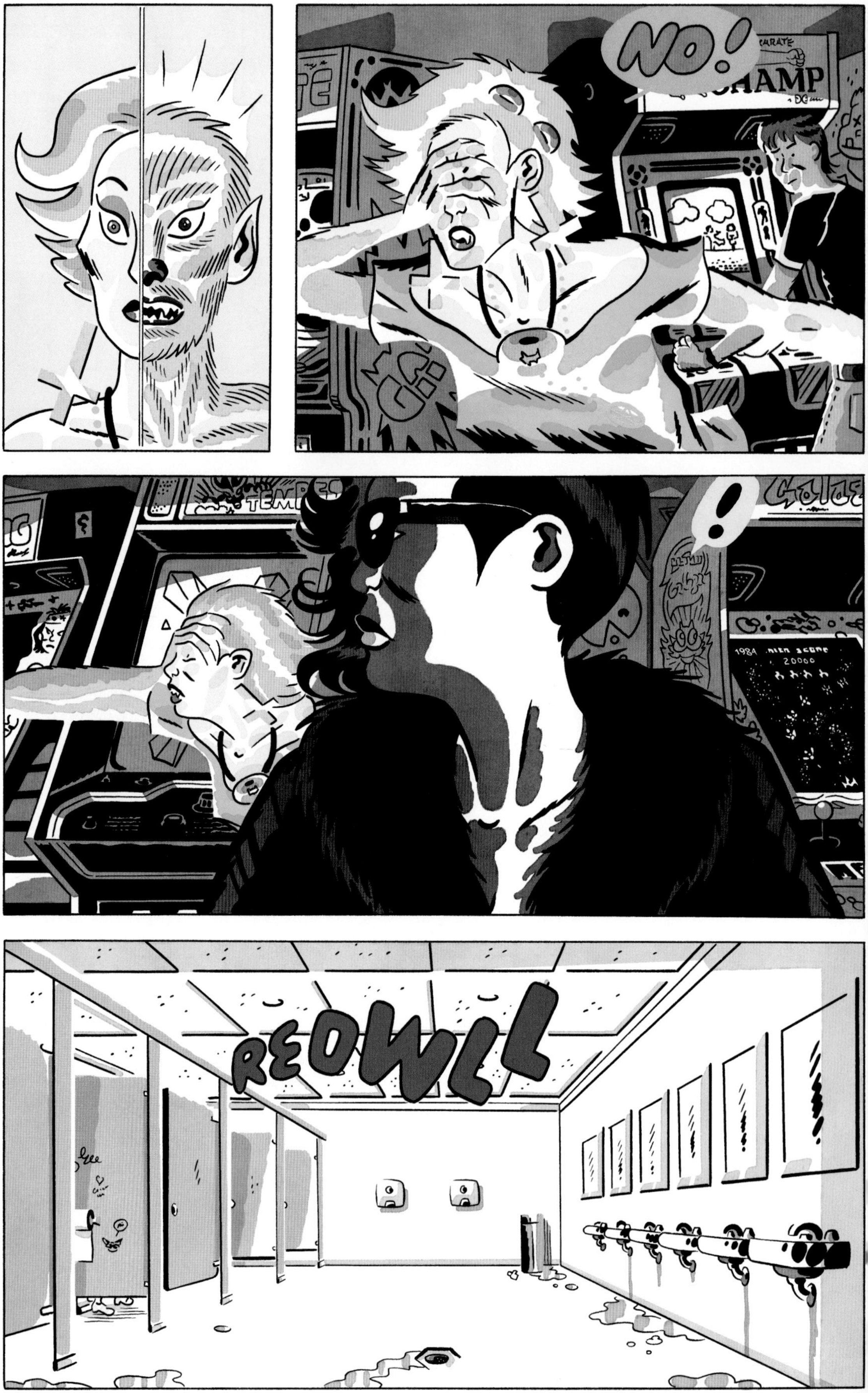
NO!
KARATE
CHAMP
!
1984 HIGH SCORE 20000
REOWLL

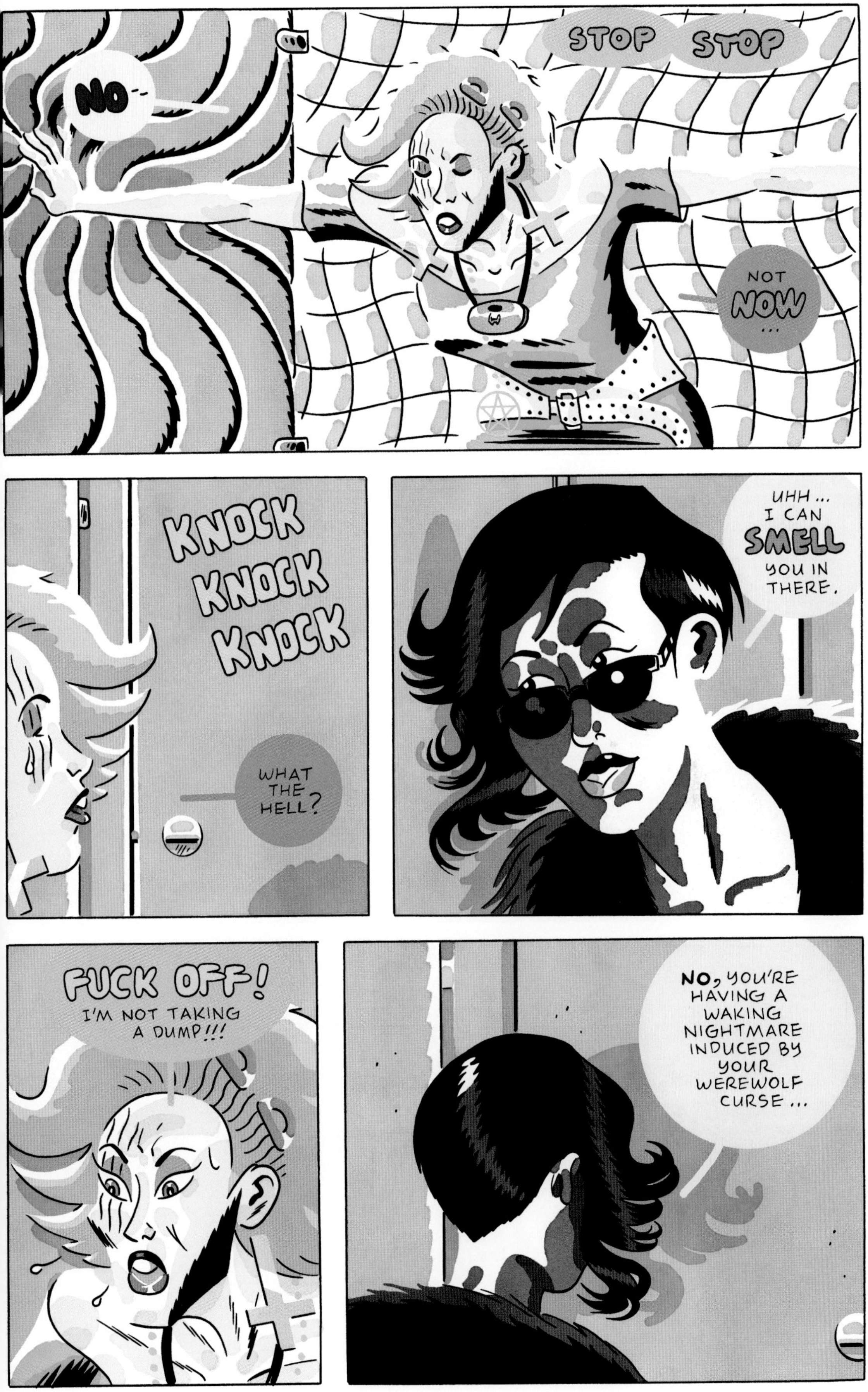
NO
STOP STOP
NOT NOW ...
KNOCK KNOCK KNOCK
WHAT THE HELL?
UHH... I CAN SMELL YOU IN THERE.
FUCK OFF! I'M NOT TAKING A DUMP!!!
NO, YOU'RE HAVING A WAKING NIGHTMARE INDUCED BY YOUR WEREWOLF CURSE...

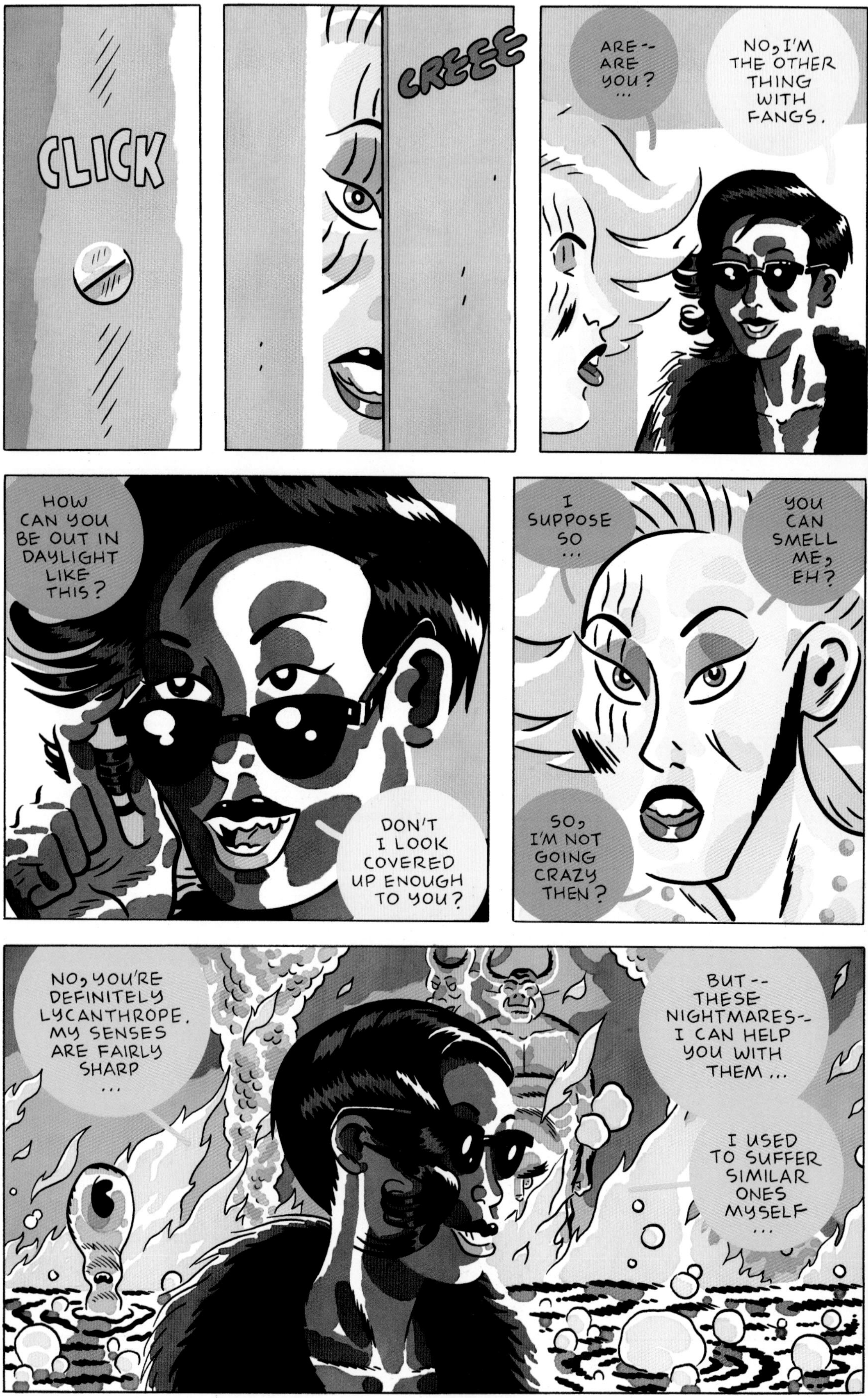
CLICK
CREEE
ARE-- ARE YOU? ...
NO, I'M THE OTHER THING WITH FANGS.
HOW CAN YOU BE OUT IN DAYLIGHT LIKE THIS?
DON'T I LOOK COVERED UP ENOUGH TO YOU?
I SUPPOSE SO ...
YOU CAN SMELL ME, EH?
SO, I'M NOT GOING CRAZY THEN?
NO, YOU'RE DEFINITELY LYCANTHROPE. MY SENSES ARE FAIRLY SHARP ...
BUT -- THESE NIGHTMARES-- I CAN HELP YOU WITH THEM ...
I USED TO SUFFER SIMILAR ONES MYSELF ...

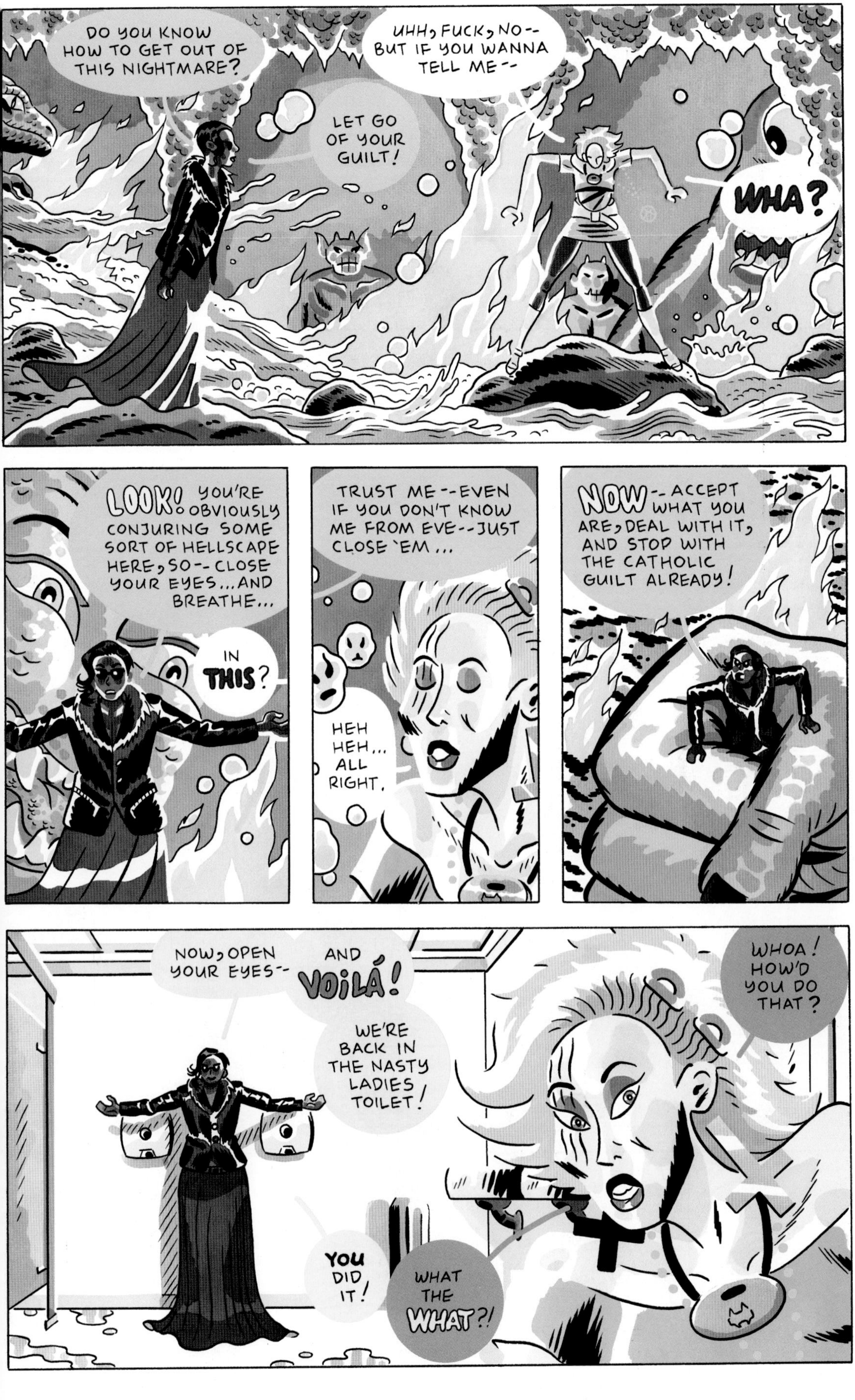

DO YOU KNOW HOW TO GET OUT OF THIS NIGHTMARE?
UHH, FUCK, NO-- BUT IF YOU WANNA TELL ME--
LET GO OF YOUR GUILT!
WHA?
LOOK! YOU'RE OBVIOUSLY CONJURING SOME SORT OF HELLSCAPE HERE, SO--CLOSE YOUR EYES... AND BREATHE...
IN THIS?
TRUST ME--EVEN IF YOU DON'T KNOW ME FROM EVE--JUST CLOSE 'EM...
HEH HEH... ALL RIGHT.
NOW--ACCEPT WHAT YOU ARE, DEAL WITH IT, AND STOP WITH THE CATHOLIC GUILT ALREADY!
NOW, OPEN YOUR EYES--
AND VOILÁ!
WE'RE BACK IN THE NASTY LADIES TOILET!
WHOA! HOW'D YOU DO THAT?
YOU DID IT!
WHAT THE WHAT?!

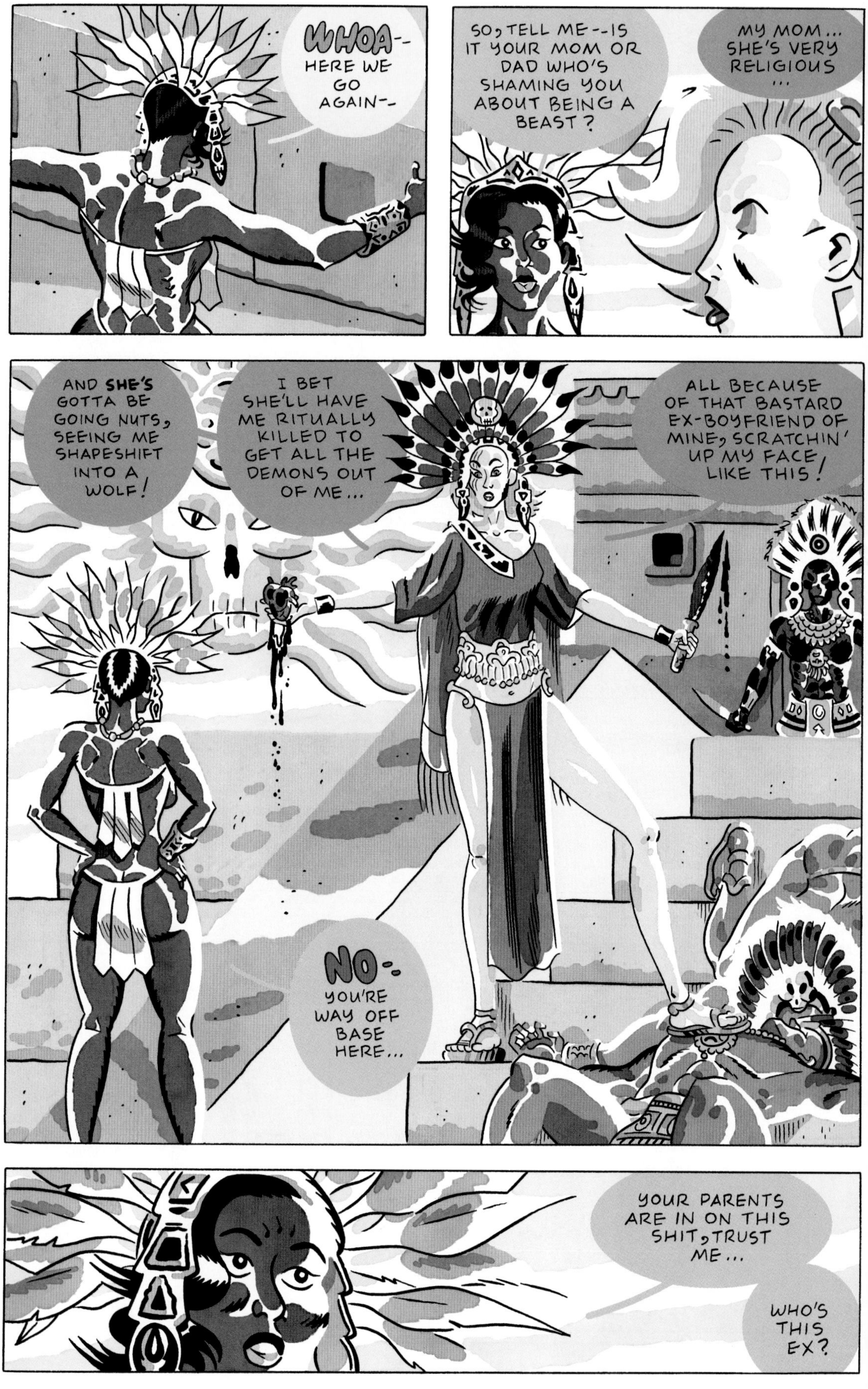
WHOA-- HERE WE GO AGAIN--
SO, TELL ME--IS IT YOUR MOM OR DAD WHO'S SHAMING YOU ABOUT BEING A BEAST?
MY MOM... SHE'S VERY RELIGIOUS...
AND SHE'S GOTTA BE GOING NUTS, SEEING ME SHAPESHIFT INTO A WOLF!
I BET SHE'LL HAVE ME RITUALLY KILLED TO GET ALL THE DEMONS OUT OF ME...
ALL BECAUSE OF THAT BASTARD EX-BOYFRIEND OF MINE, SCRATCHIN' UP MY FACE LIKE THIS!
NO-- YOU'RE WAY OFF BASE HERE...
YOUR PARENTS ARE IN ON THIS SHIT, TRUST ME...
WHO'S THIS EX?

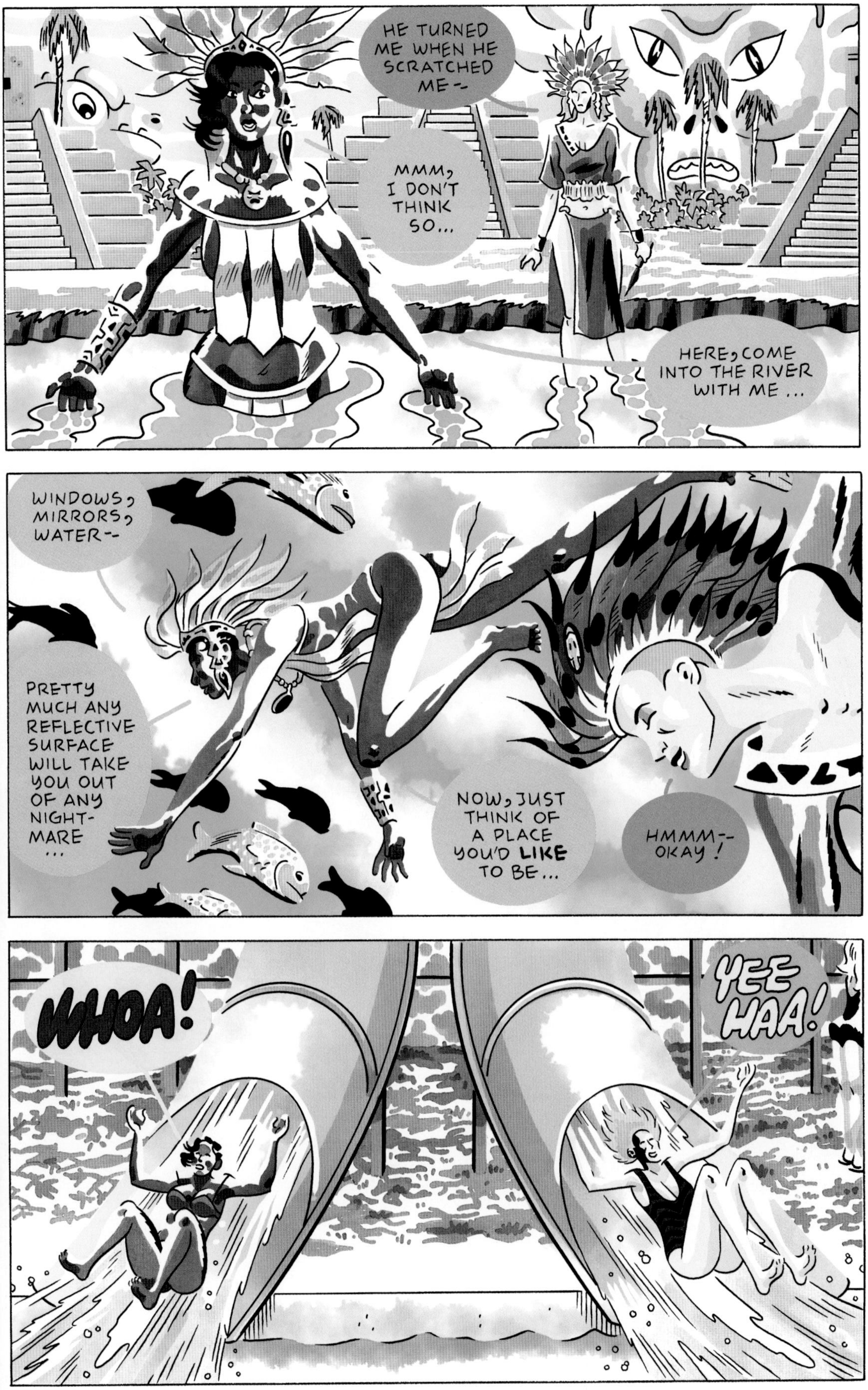
HE TURNED ME WHEN HE SCRATCHED ME--
MMM, I DON'T THINK SO...
HERE, COME INTO THE RIVER WITH ME ...
WINDOWS, MIRRORS, WATER--
PRETTY MUCH ANY REFLECTIVE SURFACE WILL TAKE YOU OUT OF ANY NIGHT-MARE ...
NOW, JUST THINK OF A PLACE YOU'D LIKE TO BE...
HMMM-- OKAY!
WHOA!
YEE HAA!

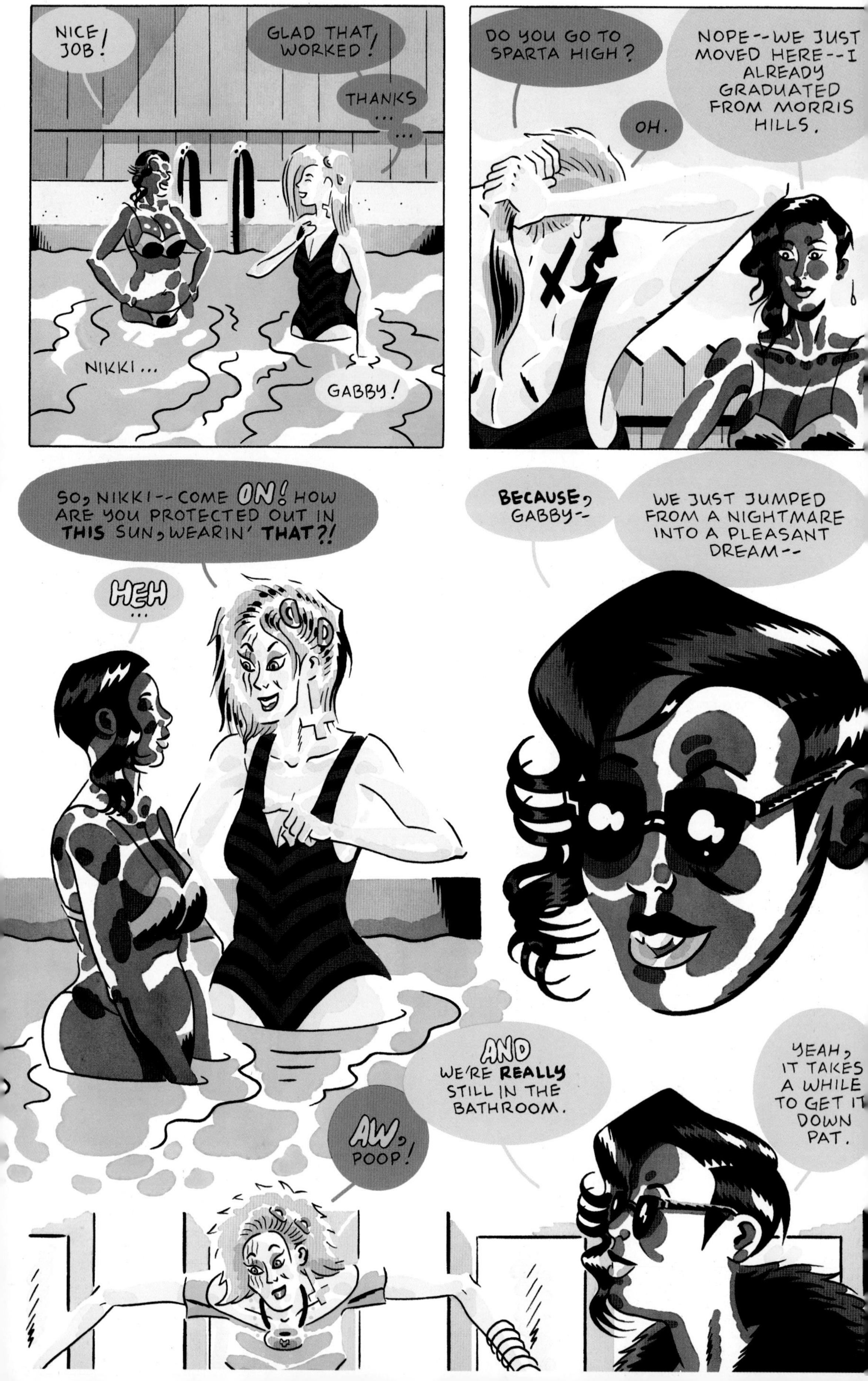
NICE JOB!
GLAD THAT WORKED!
THANKS ... ...
NIKKI...
GABBY!
DO YOU GO TO SPARTA HIGH?
OH.
NOPE--WE JUST MOVED HERE--I ALREADY GRADUATED FROM MORRIS HILLS.
SO, NIKKI--COME ON! HOW ARE YOU PROTECTED OUT IN THIS SUN, WEARIN' THAT?!
HEH ...
BECAUSE, GABBY-
WE JUST JUMPED FROM A NIGHTMARE INTO A PLEASANT DREAM--
AND WE'RE REALLY STILL IN THE BATHROOM.
AW, POOP!
YEAH, IT TAKES A WHILE TO GET IT DOWN PAT.

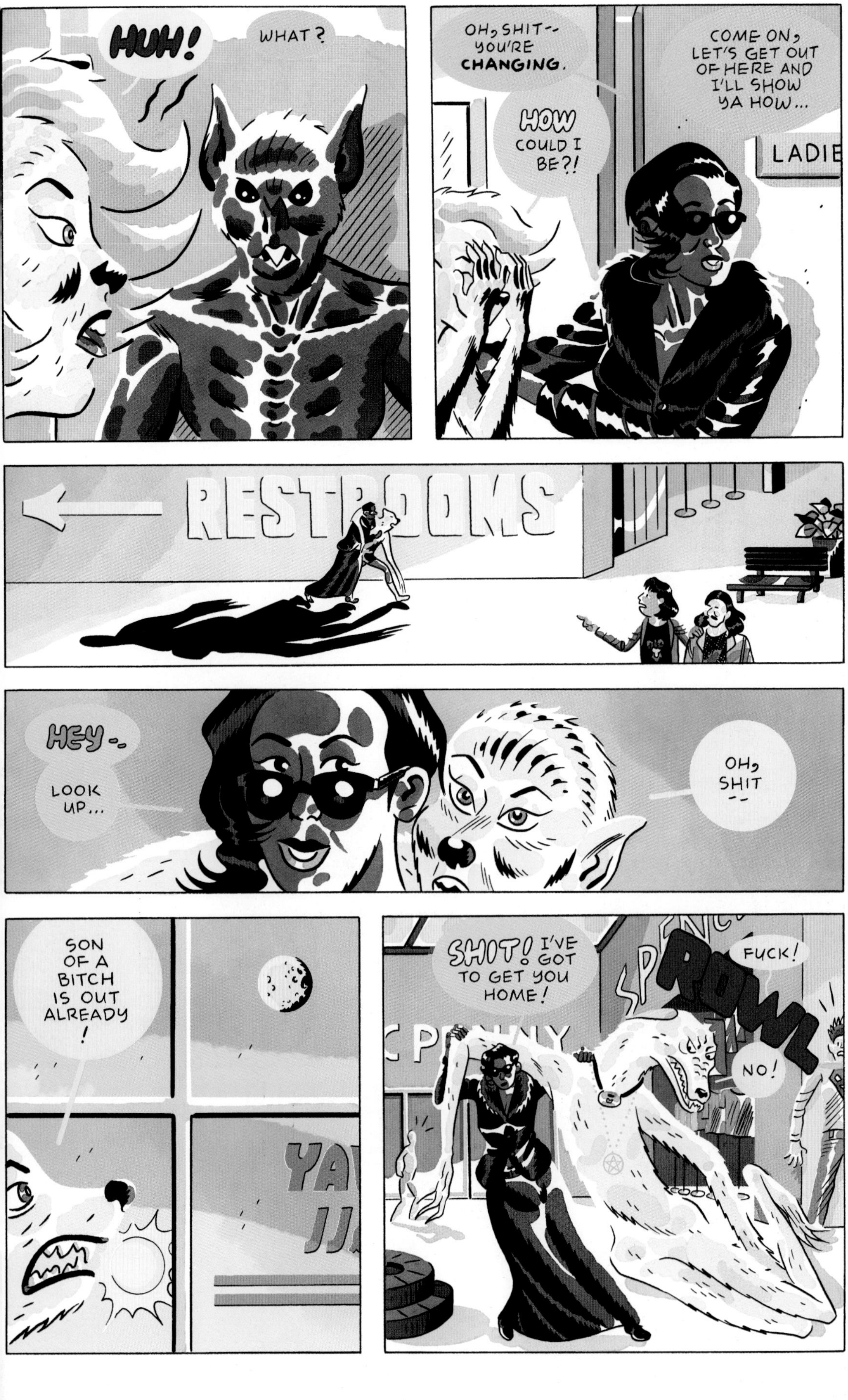
HUH!
WHAT?
OH, SHIT-- YOU'RE CHANGING.
HOW COULD I BE?!
COME ON, LET'S GET OUT OF HERE AND I'LL SHOW YA HOW...
LADIE
RESTROOMS
HEY--
LOOK UP...
OH, SHIT --
SON OF A BITCH IS OUT ALREADY!
SHIT! I'VE GOT TO GET YOU HOME!
FUCK!
ROWL
NO!

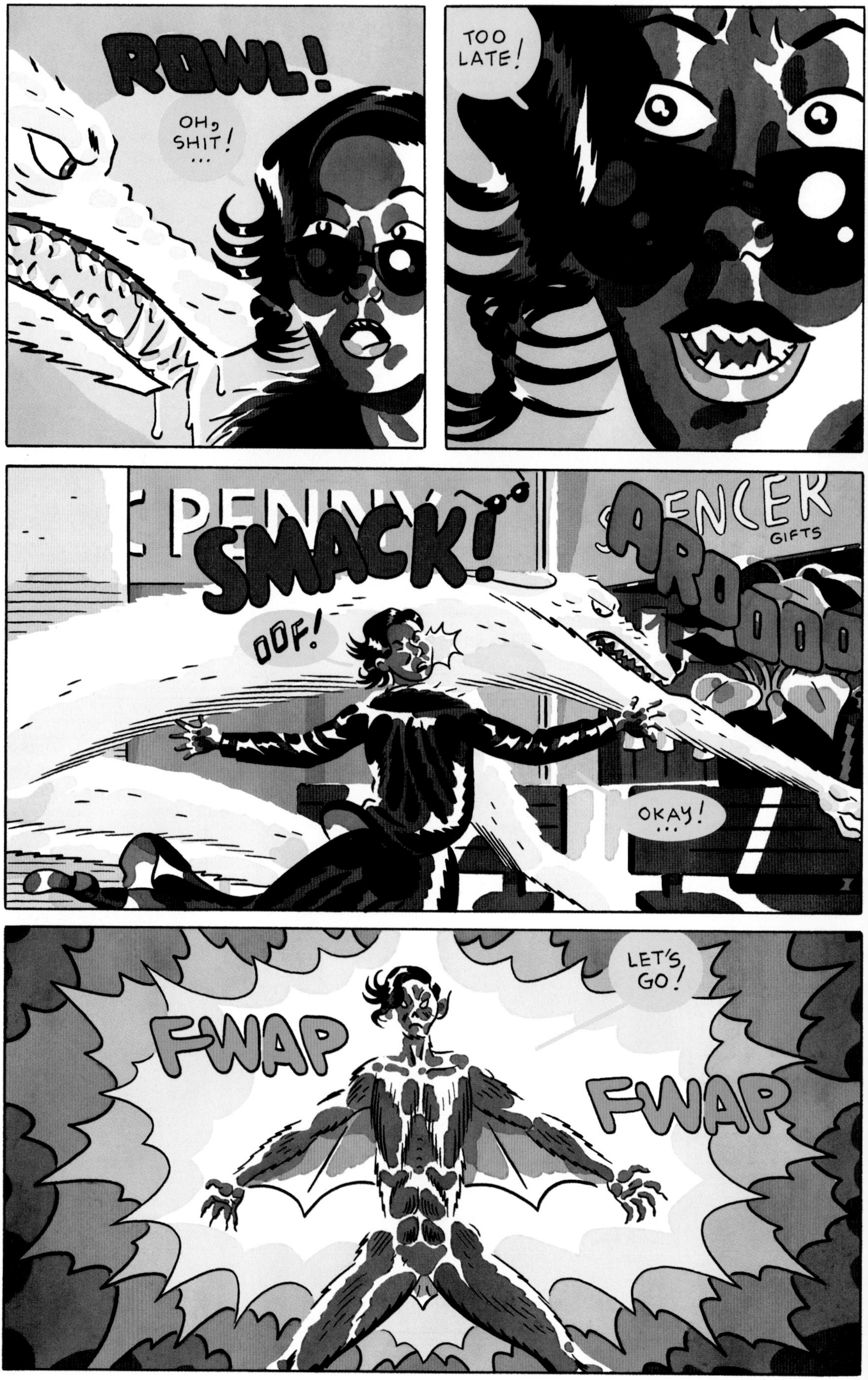
ROWL!
OH, SHIT! ...
TOO LATE!
PENNY
SMACK!
SPENCER GIFTS
AROOOOO
OOF!
OKAY! ...
LET'S GO!
FWAP
FWAP

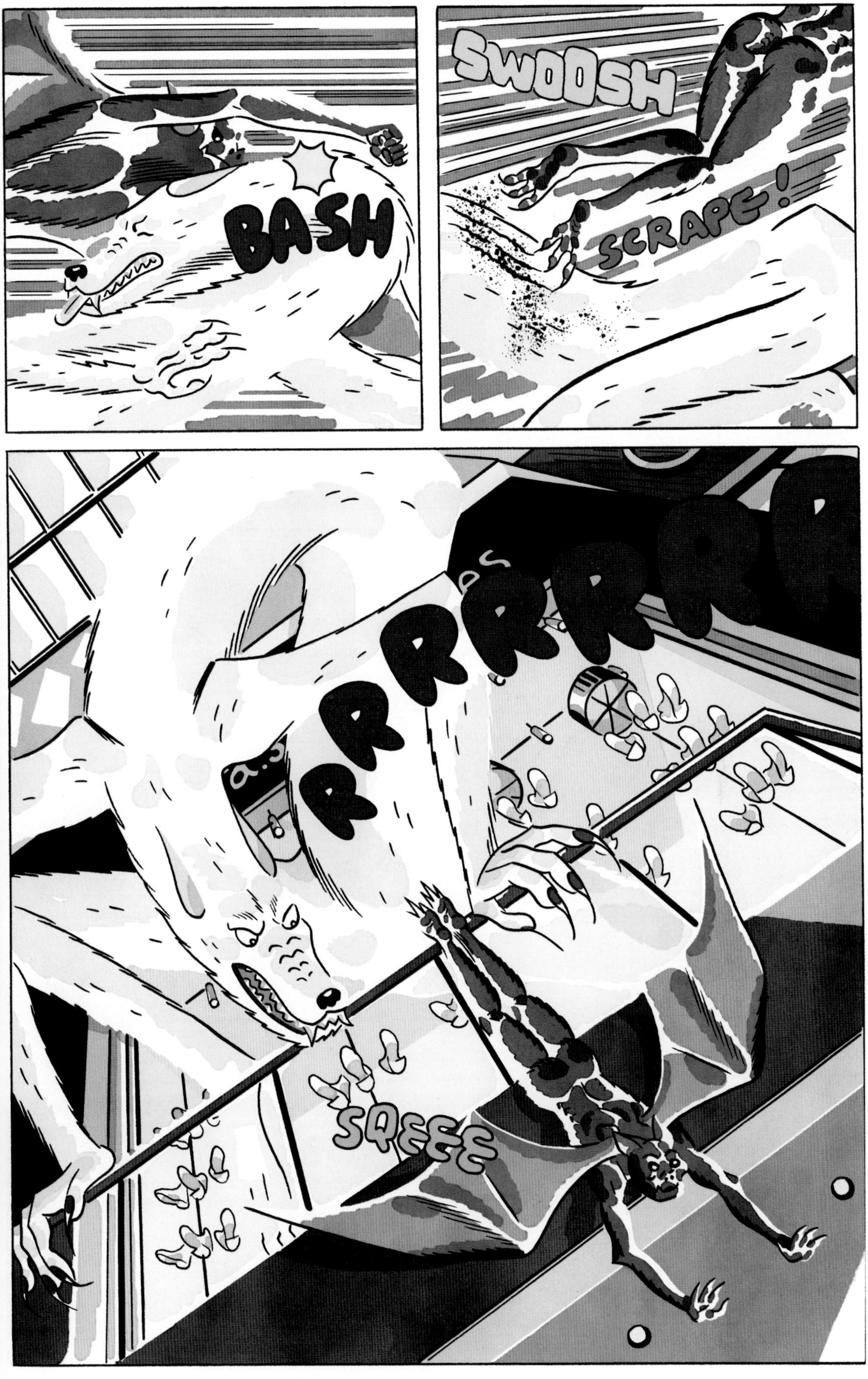
BASH
SWOOSH
SCRAPE!
RRRRRRR
SQEEE

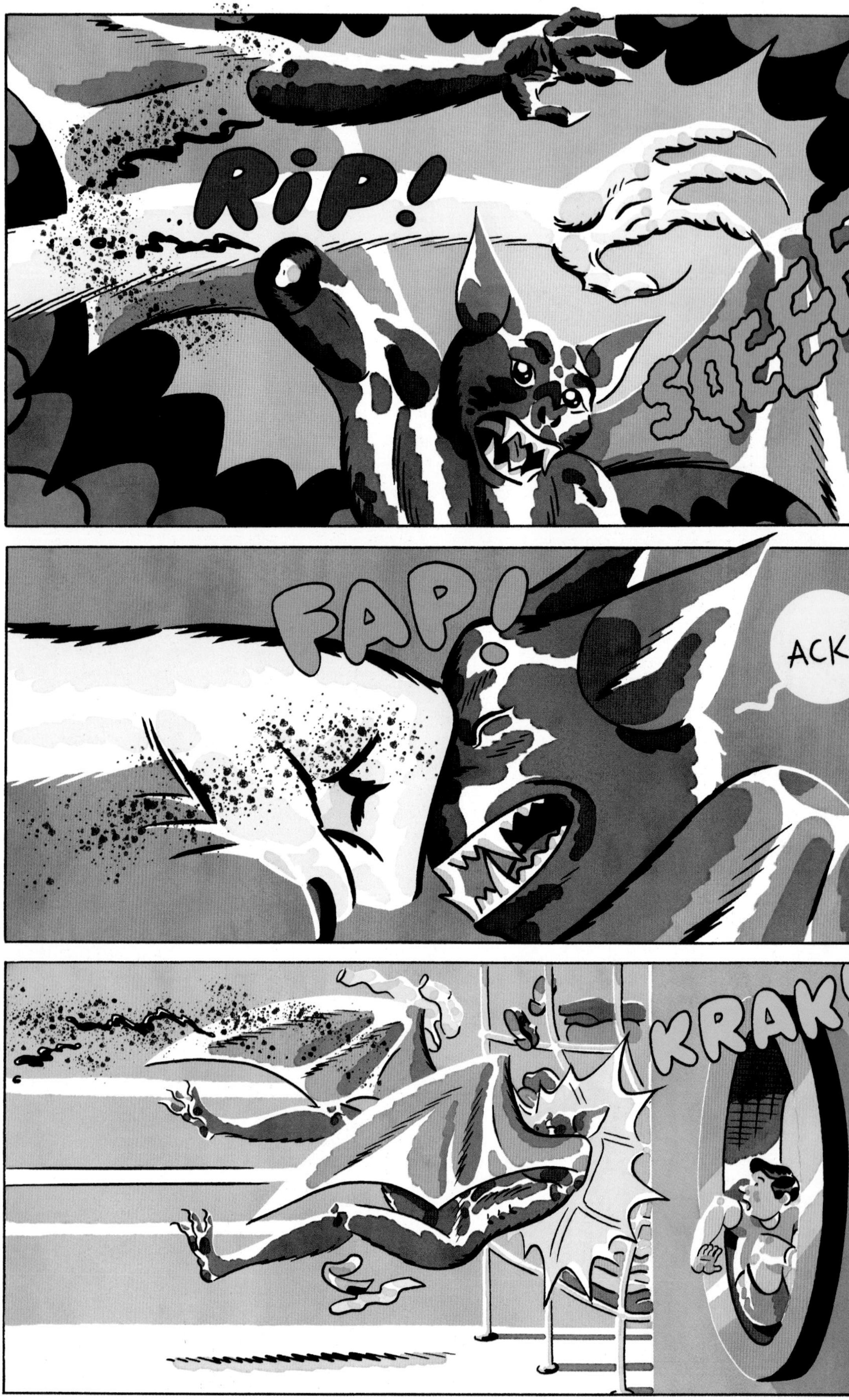
RIP!
SQEEE
FAP!
ACK!
KRAK!

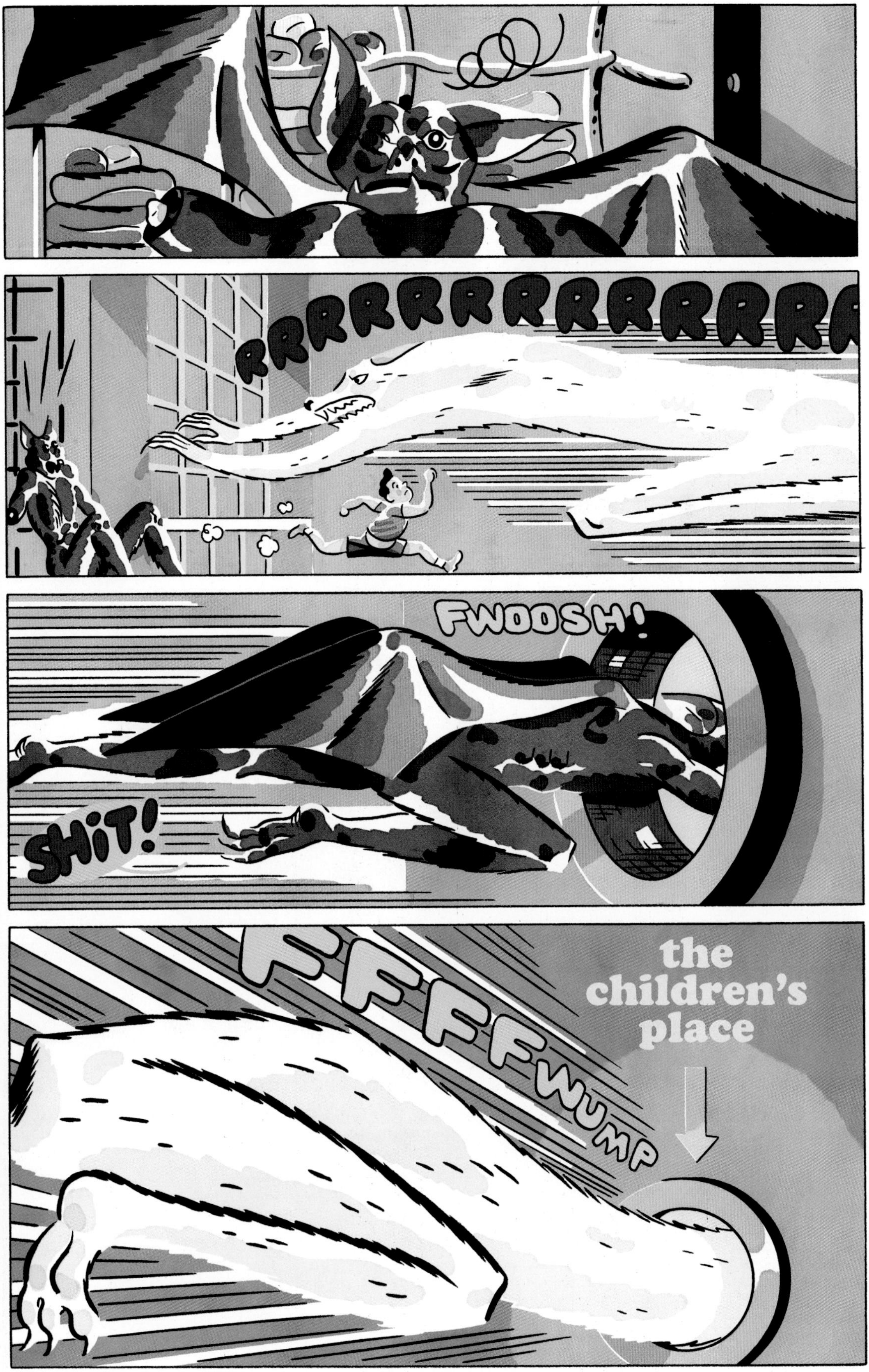
RRRRRRRRRRRRR
FWOOSH!
SHIT!
FFFFWUMP
the children's place

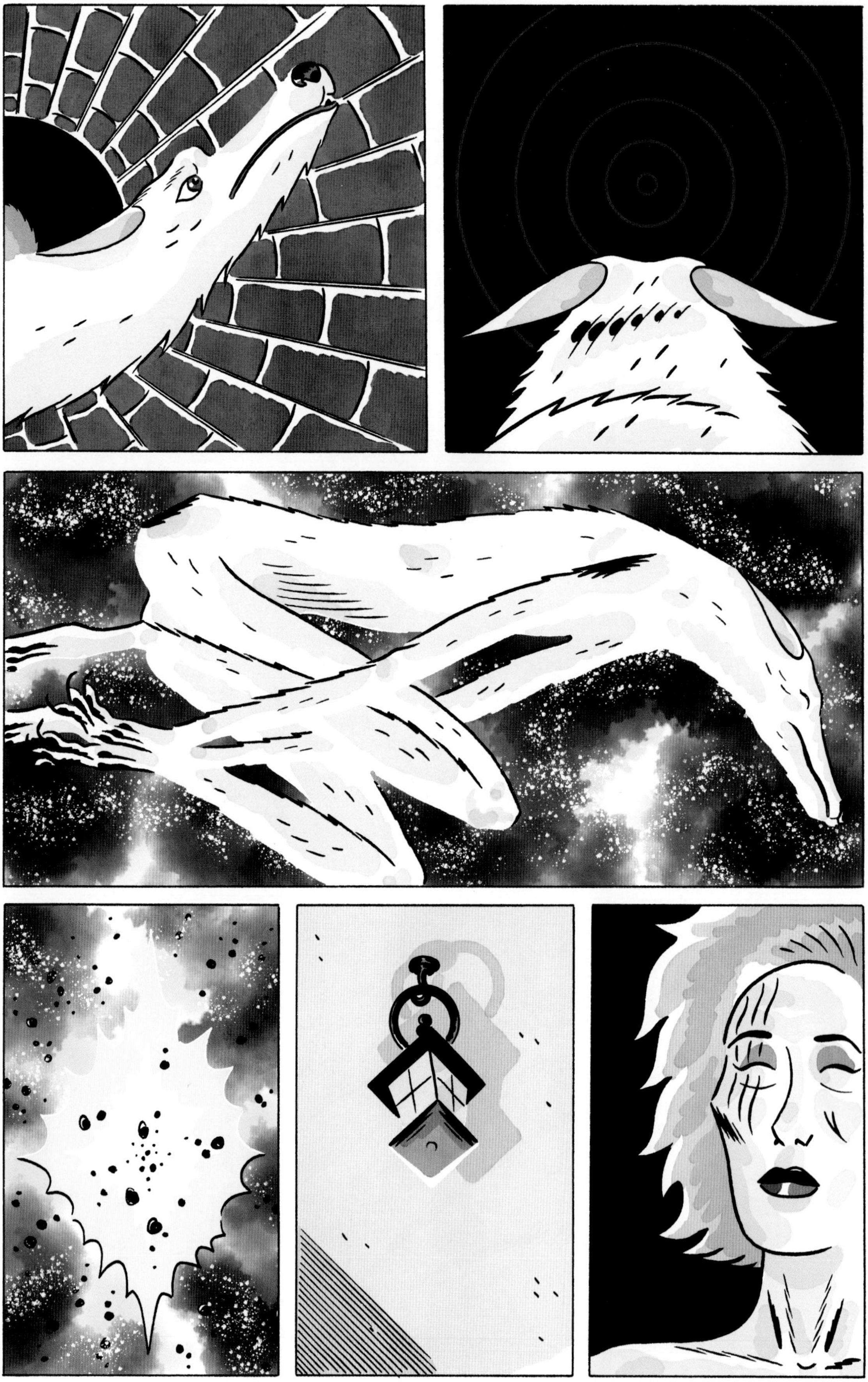

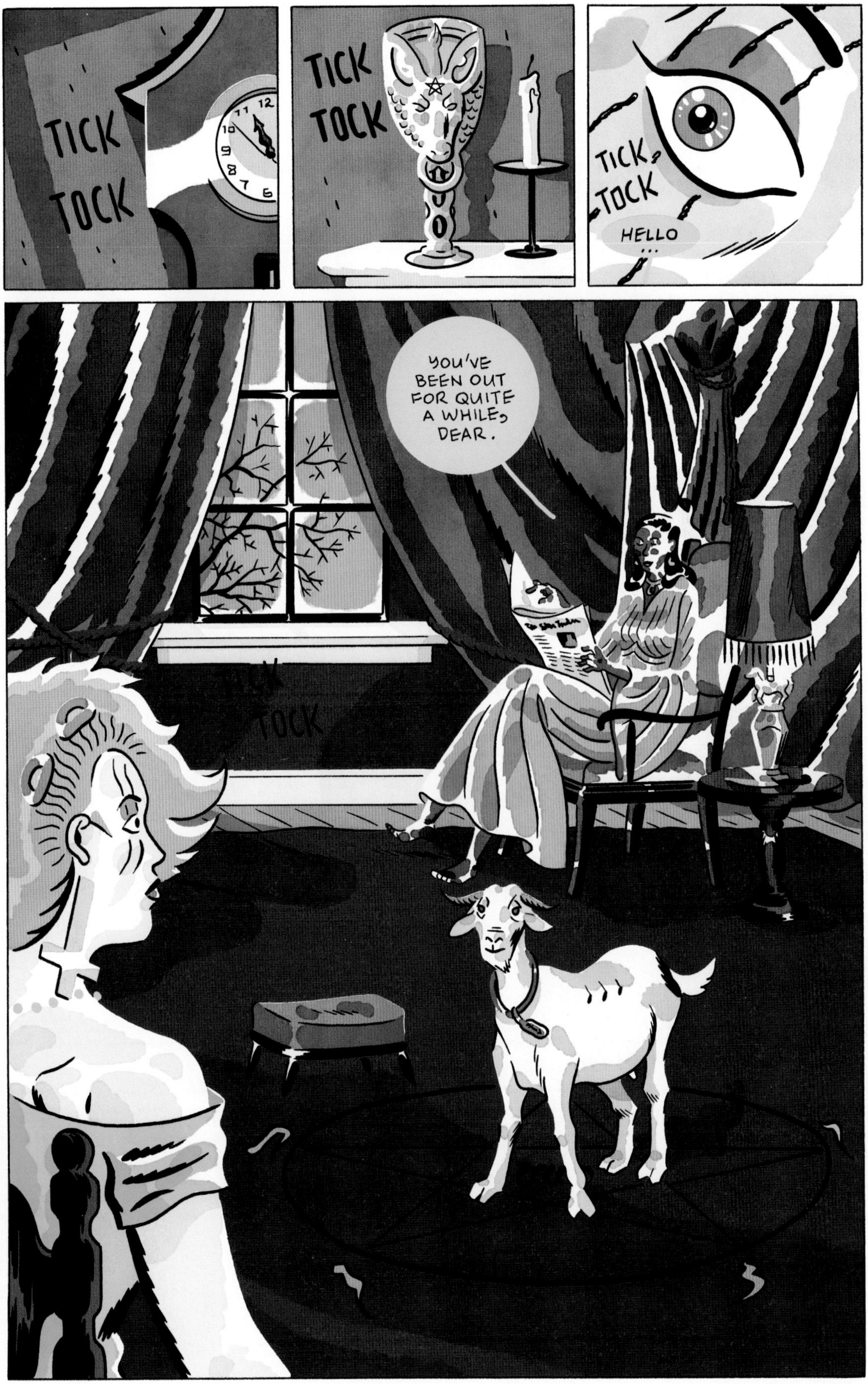
TICK
TOCK
TICK
TOCK
TICK,
TOCK
HELLO
...
YOU'VE BEEN OUT FOR QUITE A WHILE, DEAR.
TICK
TOCK

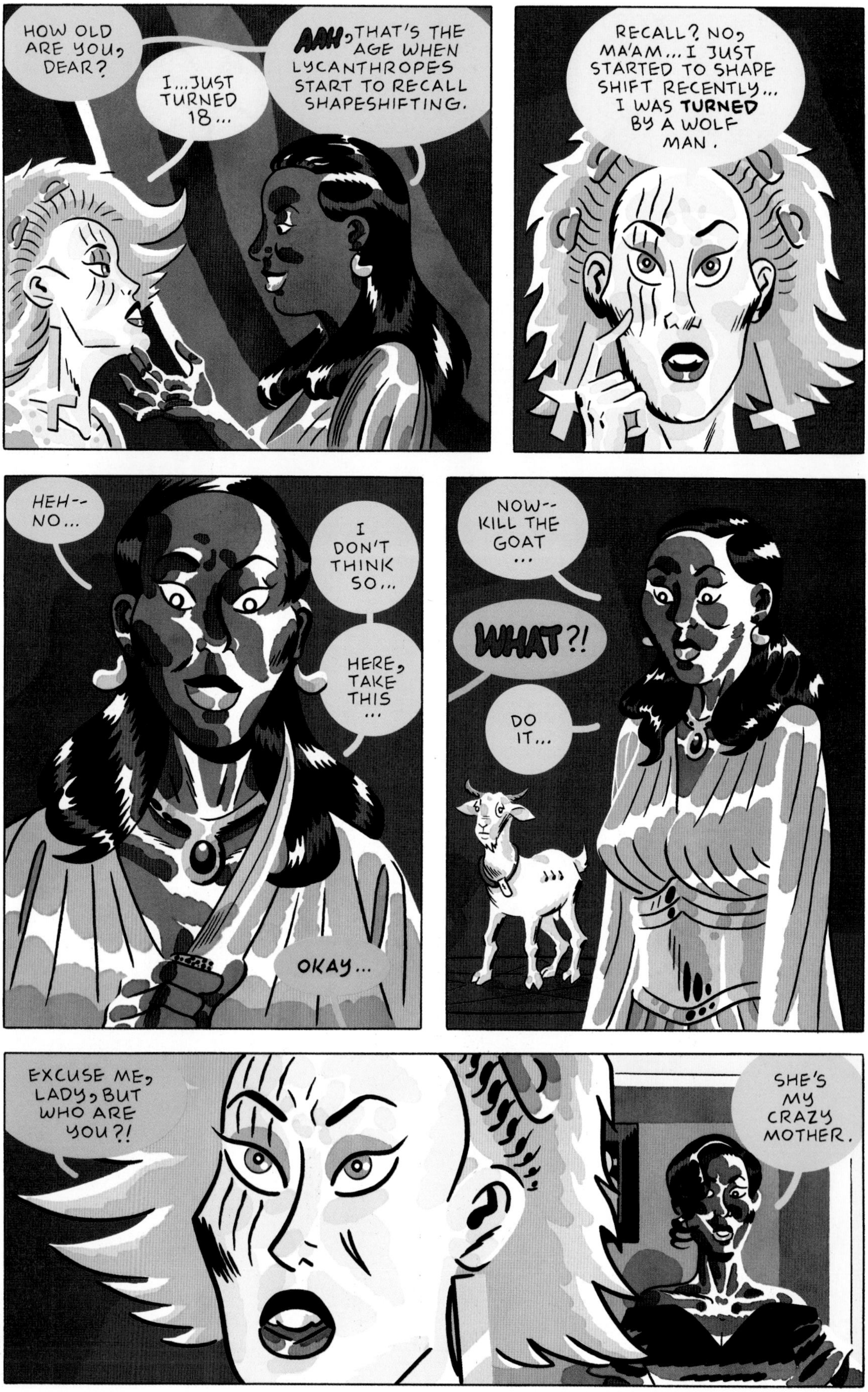
HOW OLD ARE YOU, DEAR?
I...JUST TURNED 18...
AAH, THAT'S THE AGE WHEN LYCANTHROPES START TO RECALL SHAPESHIFTING.
RECALL? NO, MA'AM... I JUST STARTED TO SHAPE SHIFT RECENTLY... I WAS TURNED BY A WOLF MAN.
HEH-- NO...
I DON'T THINK SO...
HERE, TAKE THIS...
OKAY...
NOW-- KILL THE GOAT...
WHAT?!
DO IT...
EXCUSE ME, LADY, BUT WHO ARE YOU?!
SHE'S MY CRAZY MOTHER.

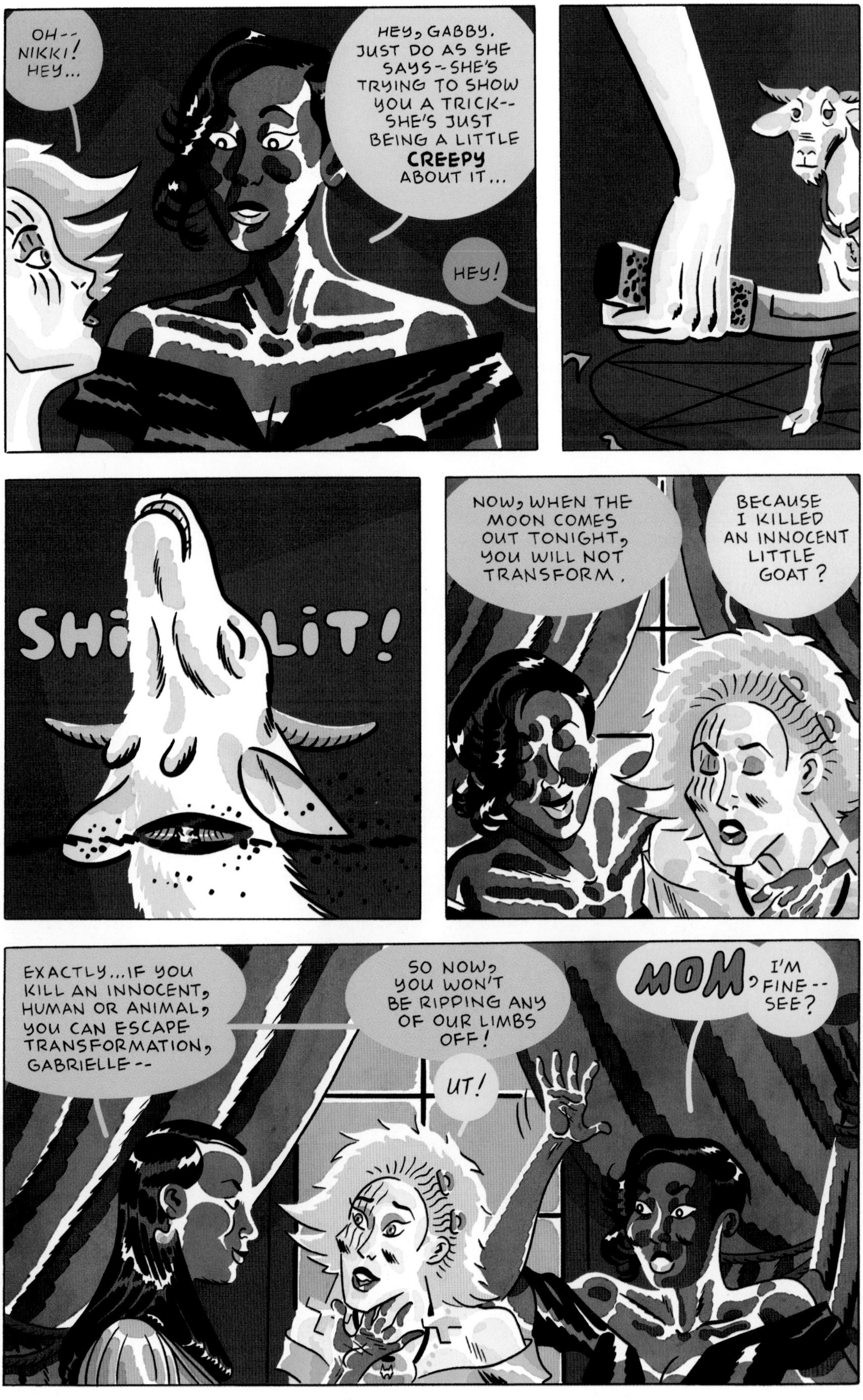
OH-- NIKKI! HEY...
HEY, GABBY. JUST DO AS SHE SAYS--SHE'S TRYING TO SHOW YOU A TRICK-- SHE'S JUST BEING A LITTLE **CREEPY** ABOUT IT...
HEY!
SHI LIT!
NOW, WHEN THE MOON COMES OUT TONIGHT, YOU WILL NOT TRANSFORM.
BECAUSE I KILLED AN INNOCENT LITTLE GOAT?
EXACTLY...IF YOU KILL AN INNOCENT, HUMAN OR ANIMAL, YOU CAN ESCAPE TRANSFORMATION, GABRIELLE--
SO NOW, YOU WON'T BE RIPPING ANY OF OUR LIMBS OFF!
UT!
MOM, I'M FINE-- SEE?

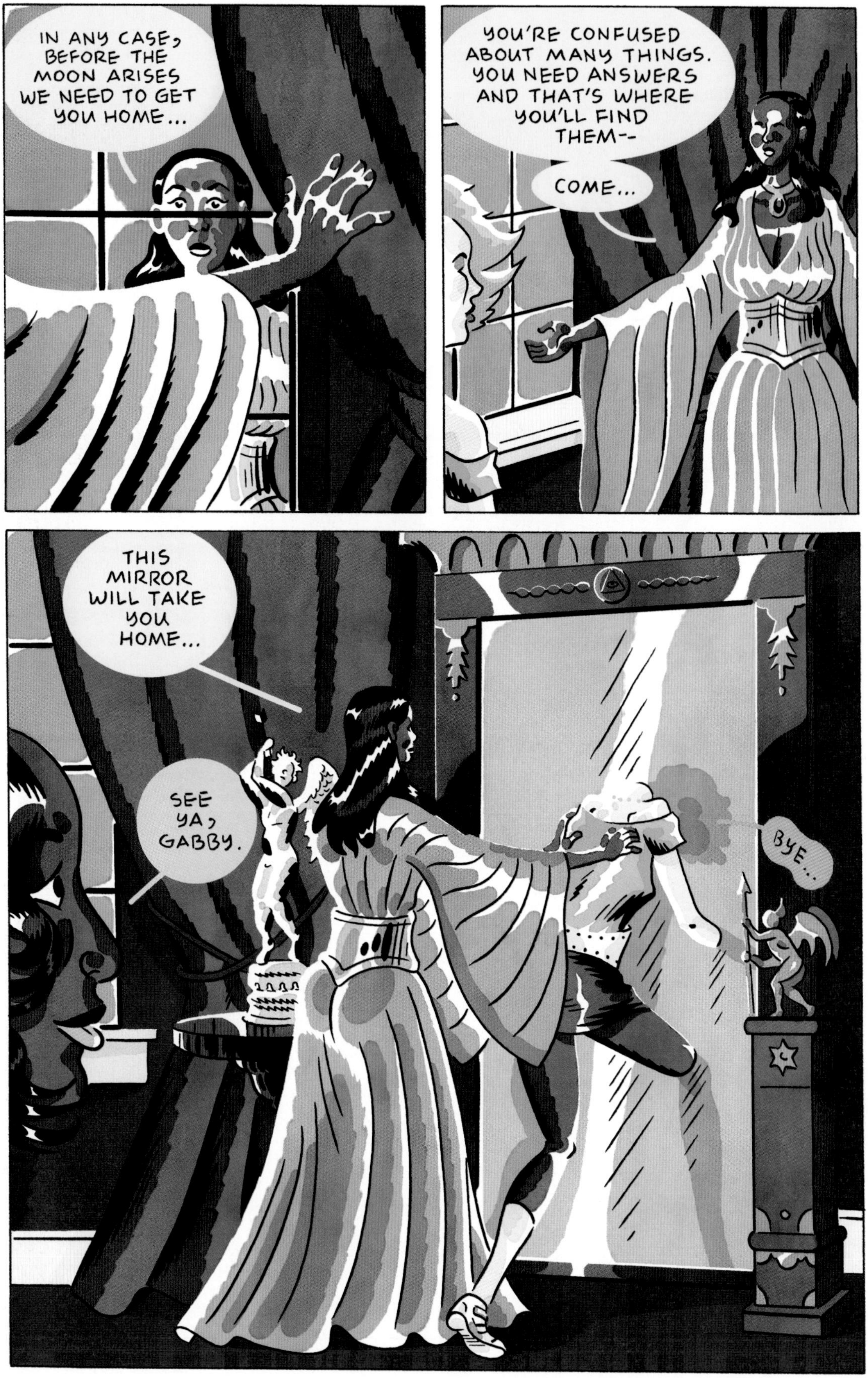
IN ANY CASE, BEFORE THE MOON ARISES WE NEED TO GET YOU HOME...
YOU'RE CONFUSED ABOUT MANY THINGS. YOU NEED ANSWERS AND THAT'S WHERE YOU'LL FIND THEM--
COME...
THIS MIRROR WILL TAKE YOU HOME...
SEE YA, GABBY.
BYE...

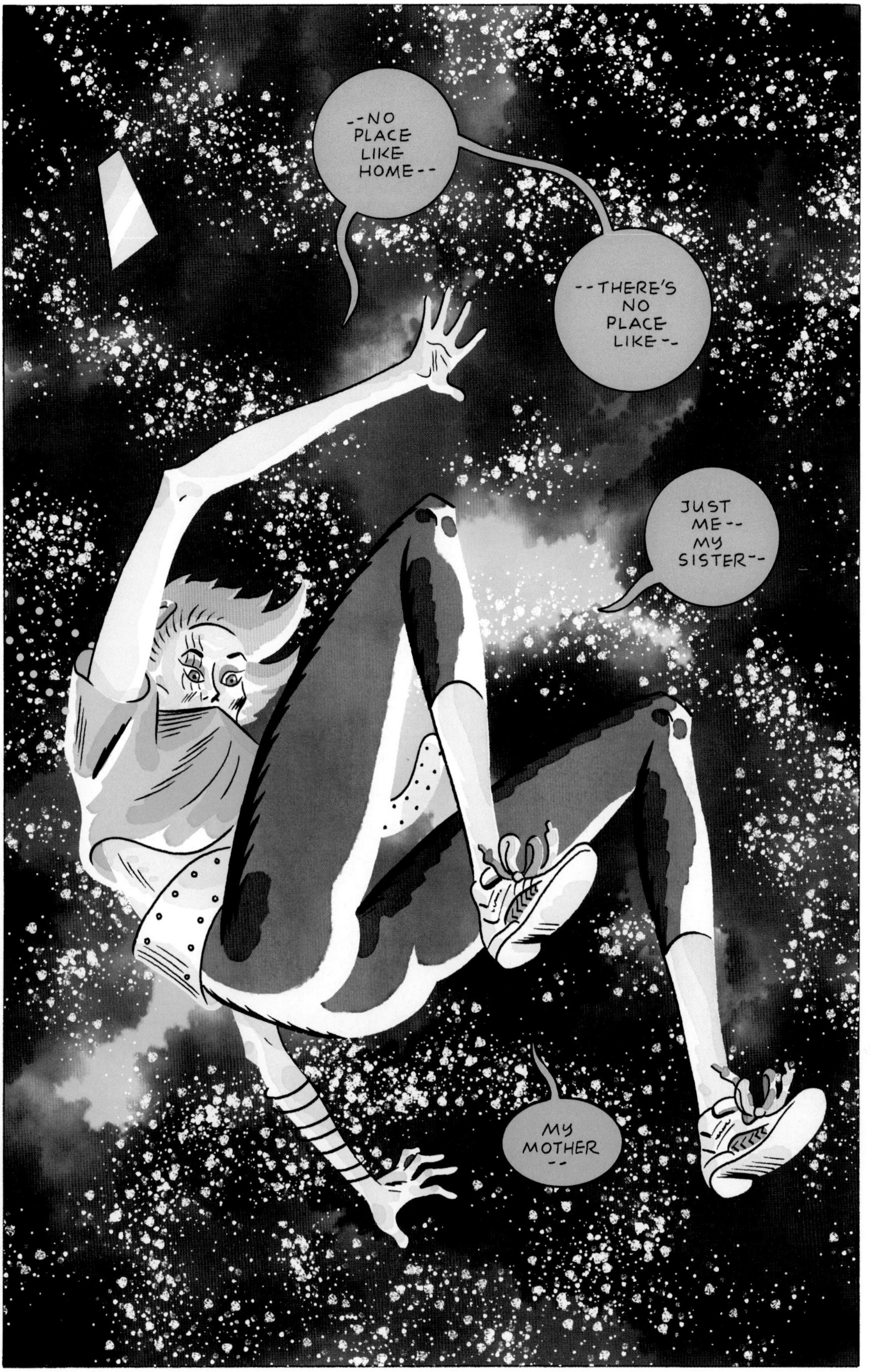
--NO PLACE LIKE HOME--
--THERE'S NO PLACE LIKE--
JUST ME-- MY SISTER--
MY MOTHER --

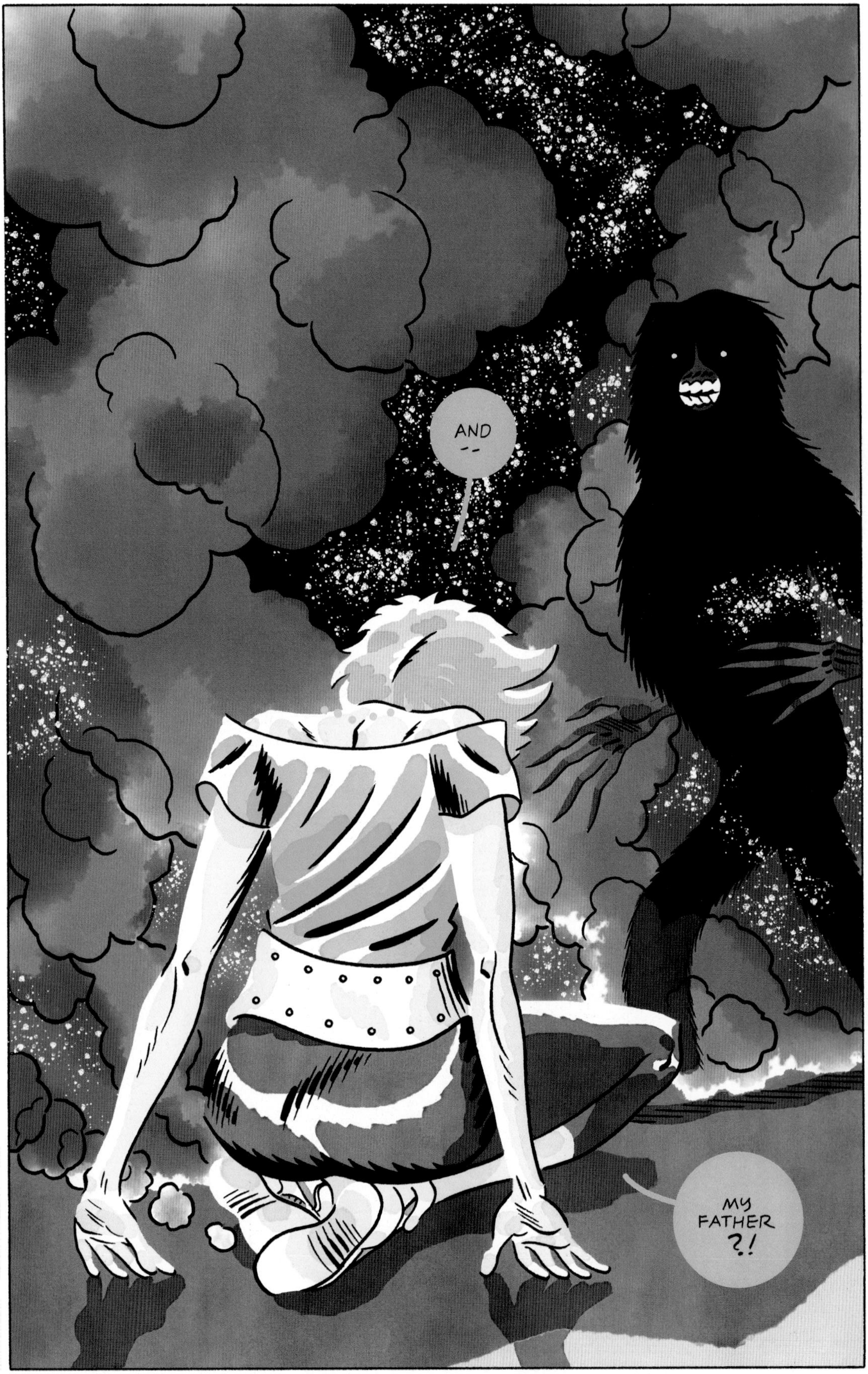
AND --
MY FATHER ?!

Spell Number

3

Ancient Incantations

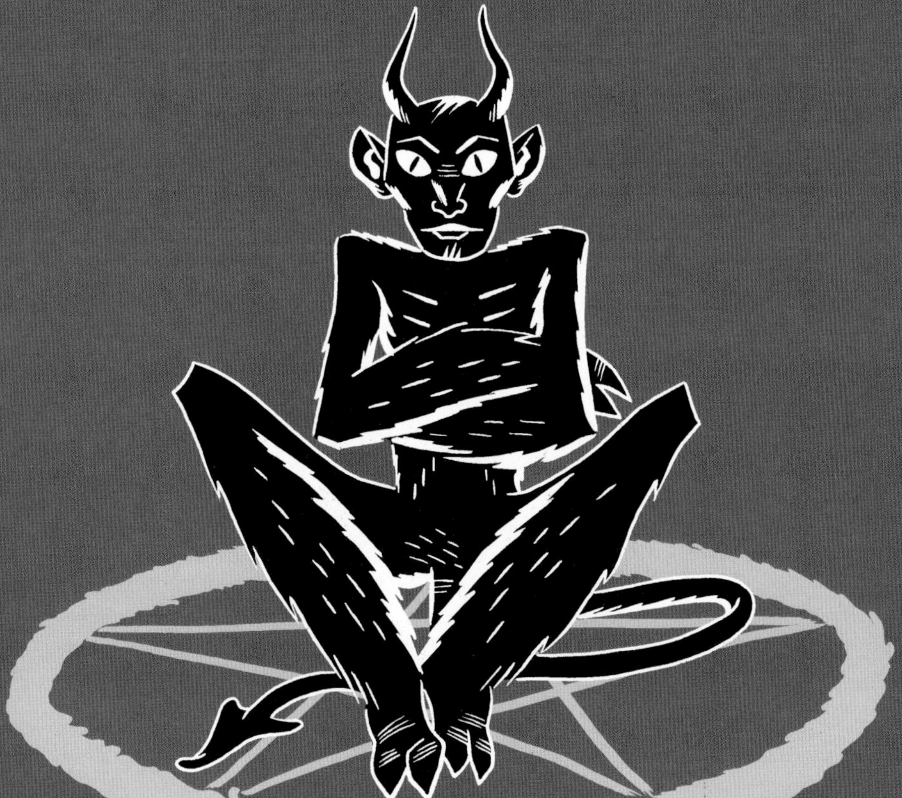

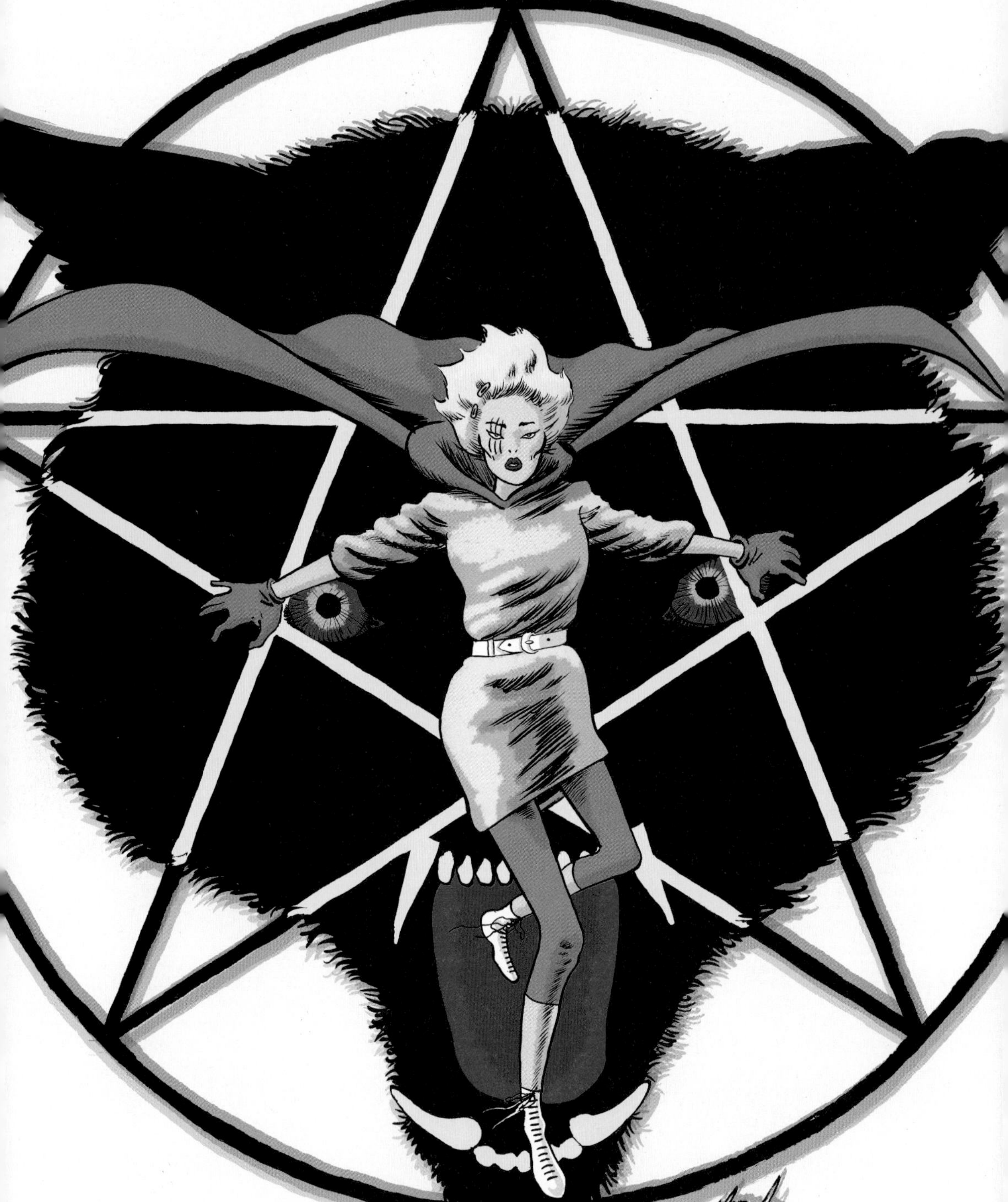

SheWolf

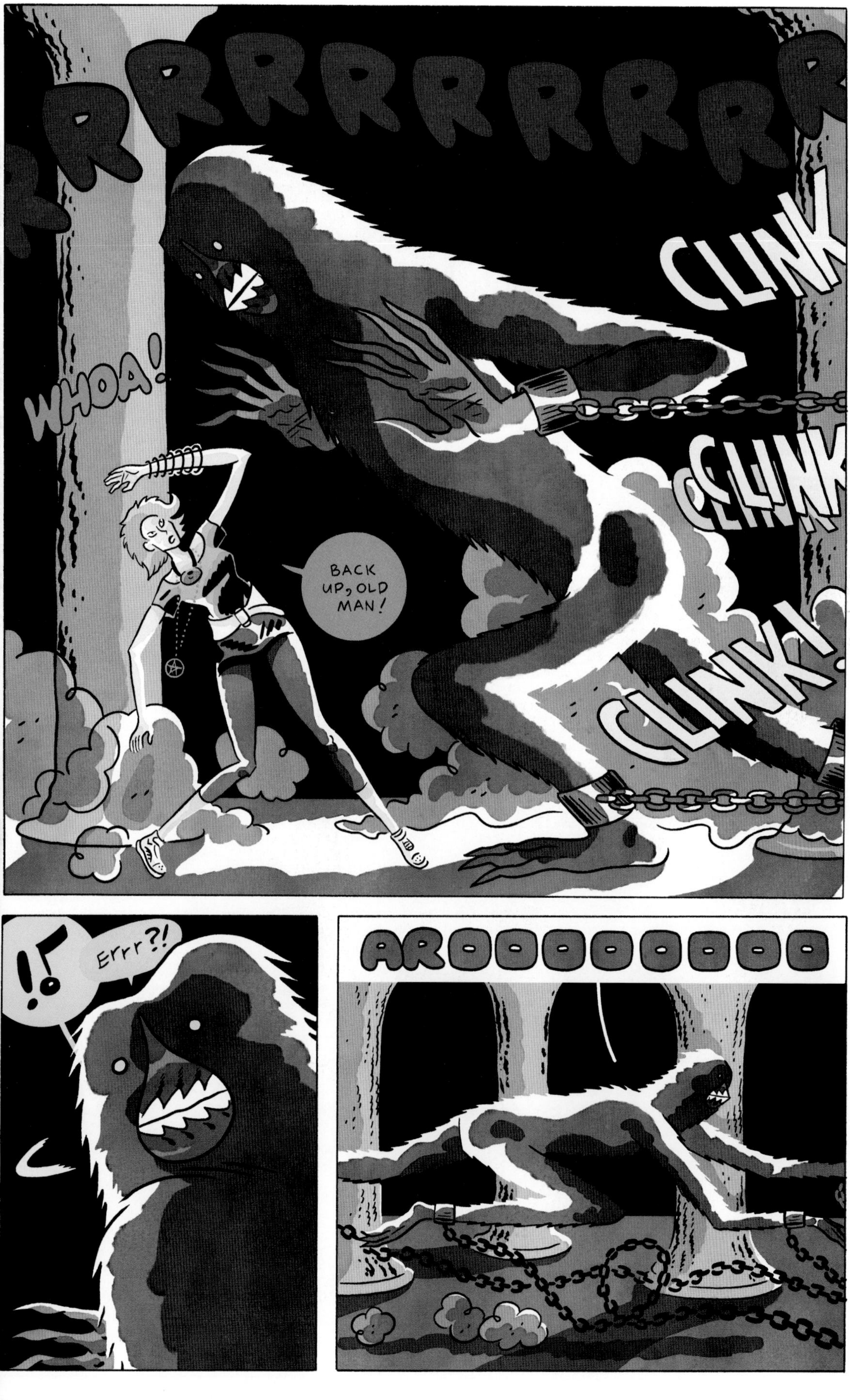
RRRRRRRRRRR
CLINK
WHOA!
CLINK
CLINK
BACK UP, OLD MAN!
CLINK!
!?
Errr?!
AROOOOOOOOO

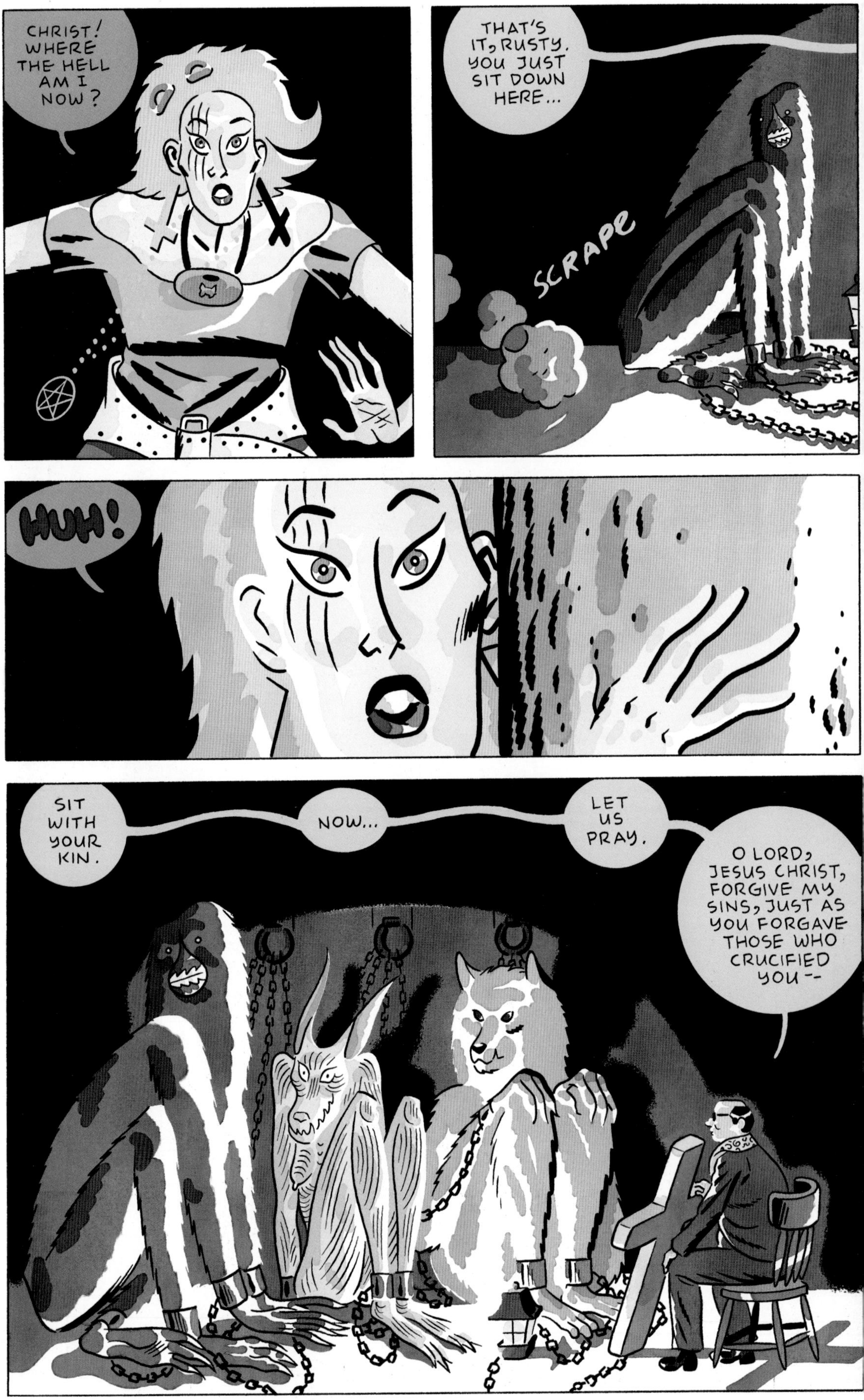

CHRIST! WHERE THE HELL AM I NOW?
THAT'S IT, RUSTY. YOU JUST SIT DOWN HERE...
SCRAPE
HUH!
SIT WITH YOUR KIN.
NOW...
LET US PRAY.
O LORD, JESUS CHRIST, FORGIVE MY SINS, JUST AS YOU FORGAVE THOSE WHO CRUCIFIED YOU--

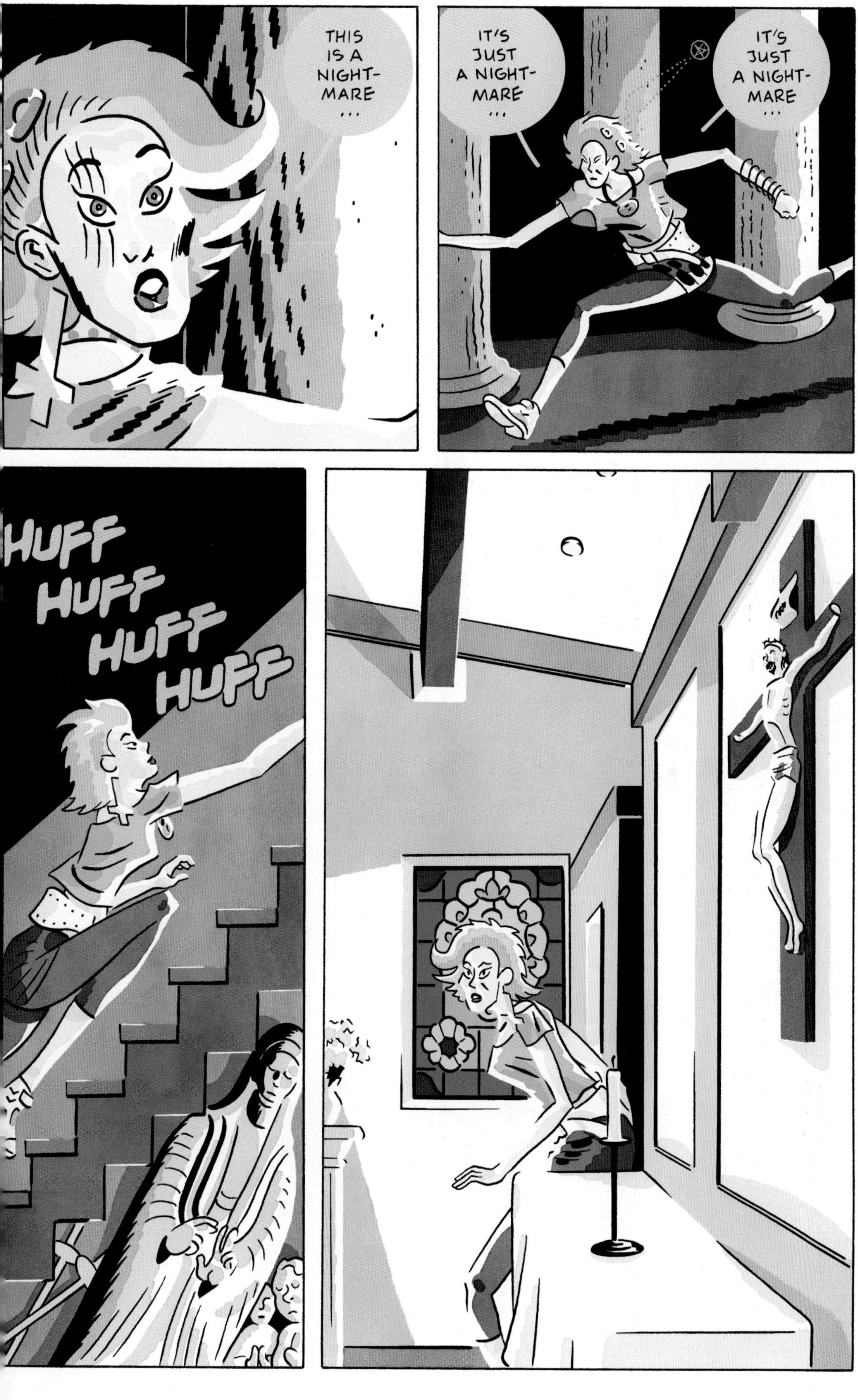
THIS IS A NIGHT-MARE ...
IT'S JUST A NIGHT-MARE ...
IT'S JUST A NIGHT-MARE ...
HUFF HUFF HUFF HUFF

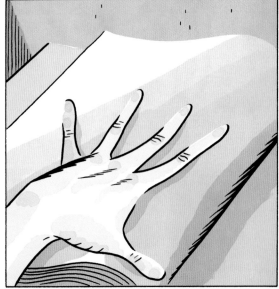

Our Lord Jesus Christ as a young man, concerned over the direction in which the world was turning : towrds pestilence, poverty, and war, visits the Roman poet, Platitonius ...

Jesus asks that he help him write an incanto that would summon The Dark Lord, Satan up from Hell for a discussion. They would need to trap him as well, so as to not have him unleashed unto the human world...

Platitonius worked day and night, for many moons, together with Jesus, until they had constructed a proper cage for the demon. Jesus then summoned up Satan and spoke with him about a great many things ...

life and death, The falling out between Satan and his father, and how much of a hand he had in the troubling ways the world seemed to be moving in as of late...

When there was no more to say, Jesus, with a wave of his hand, cast Satan back into the abyss ...

This entire communion, however, was witnessed first hand, by a Roman citizen named Lycaon ...

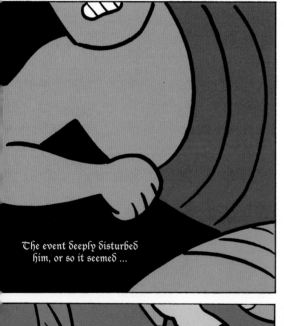

The event deeply disturbed him, or so it seemed ...

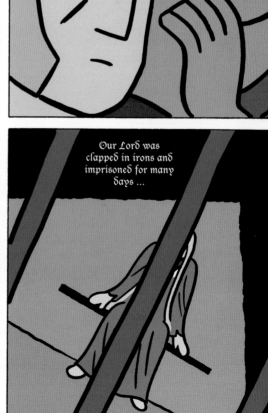

Our Lord was clapped in irons and imprisoned for many days ...

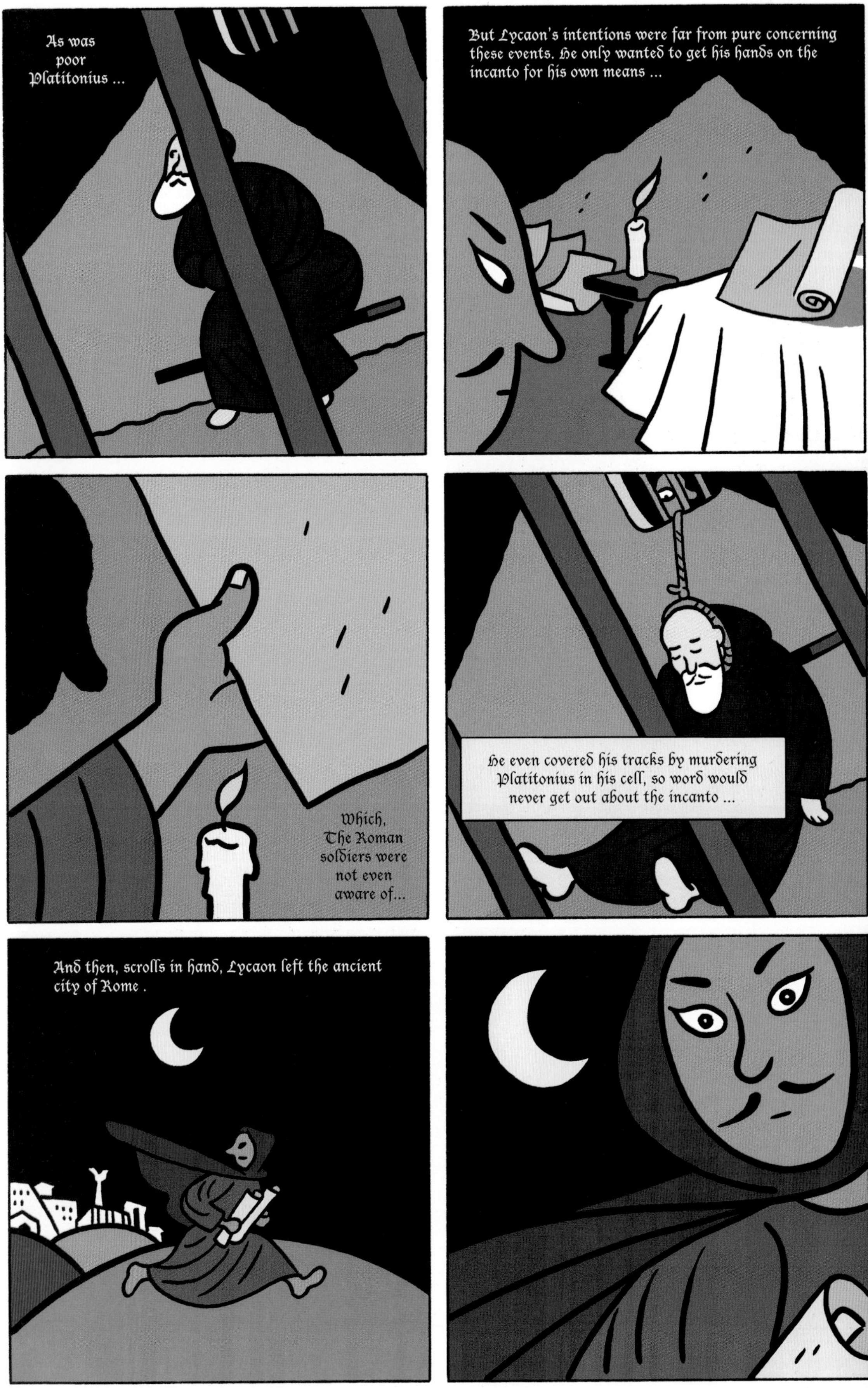
As was poor Platitonius ...
But Lycaon's intentions were far from pure concerning these events. He only wanted to get his hands on the incanto for his own means ...
Which, The Roman soldiers were not even aware of...
He even covered his tracks by murdering Platitonius in his cell, so word would never get out about the incanto ...
And then, scrolls in hand, Lycaon left the ancient city of Rome .

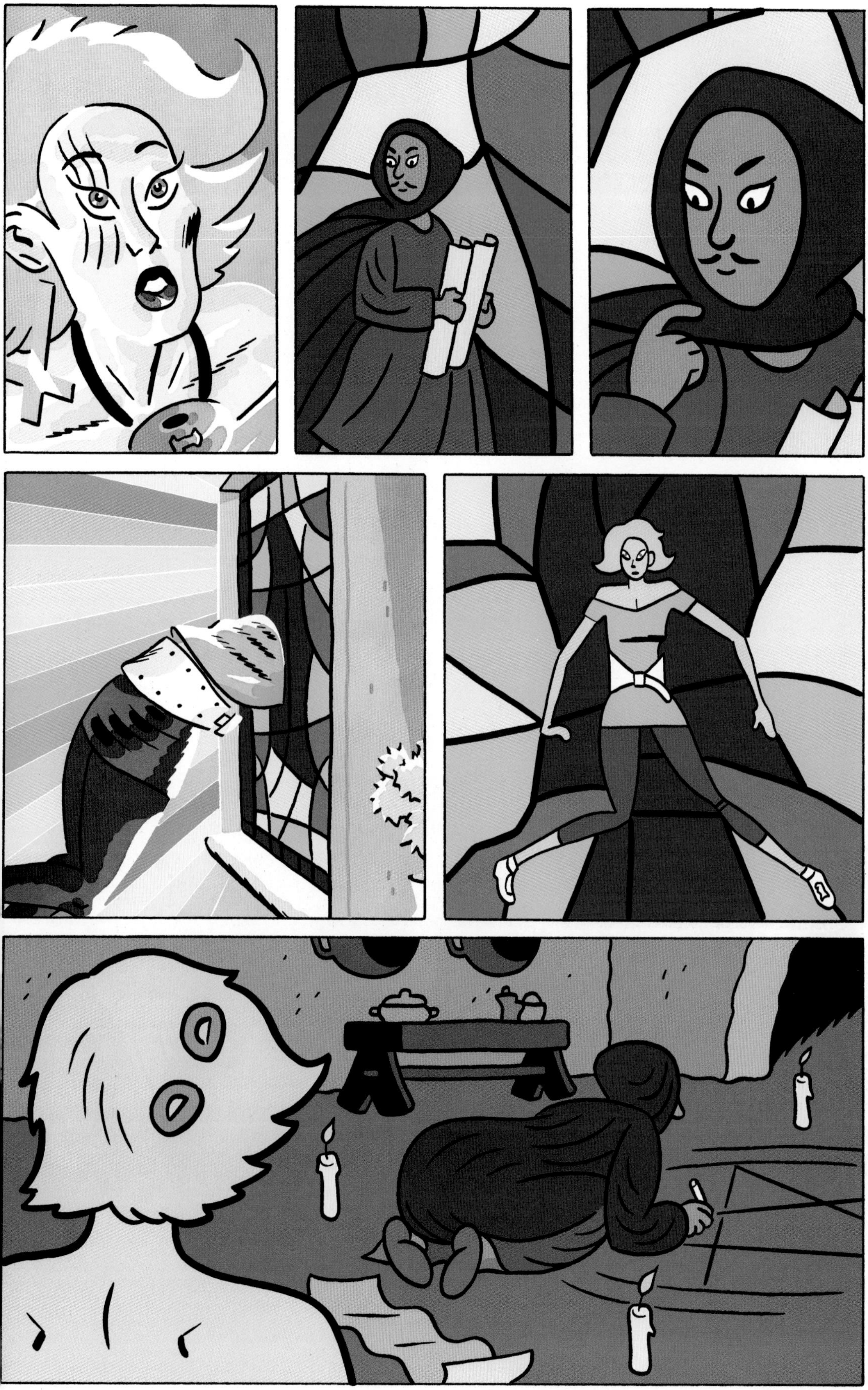

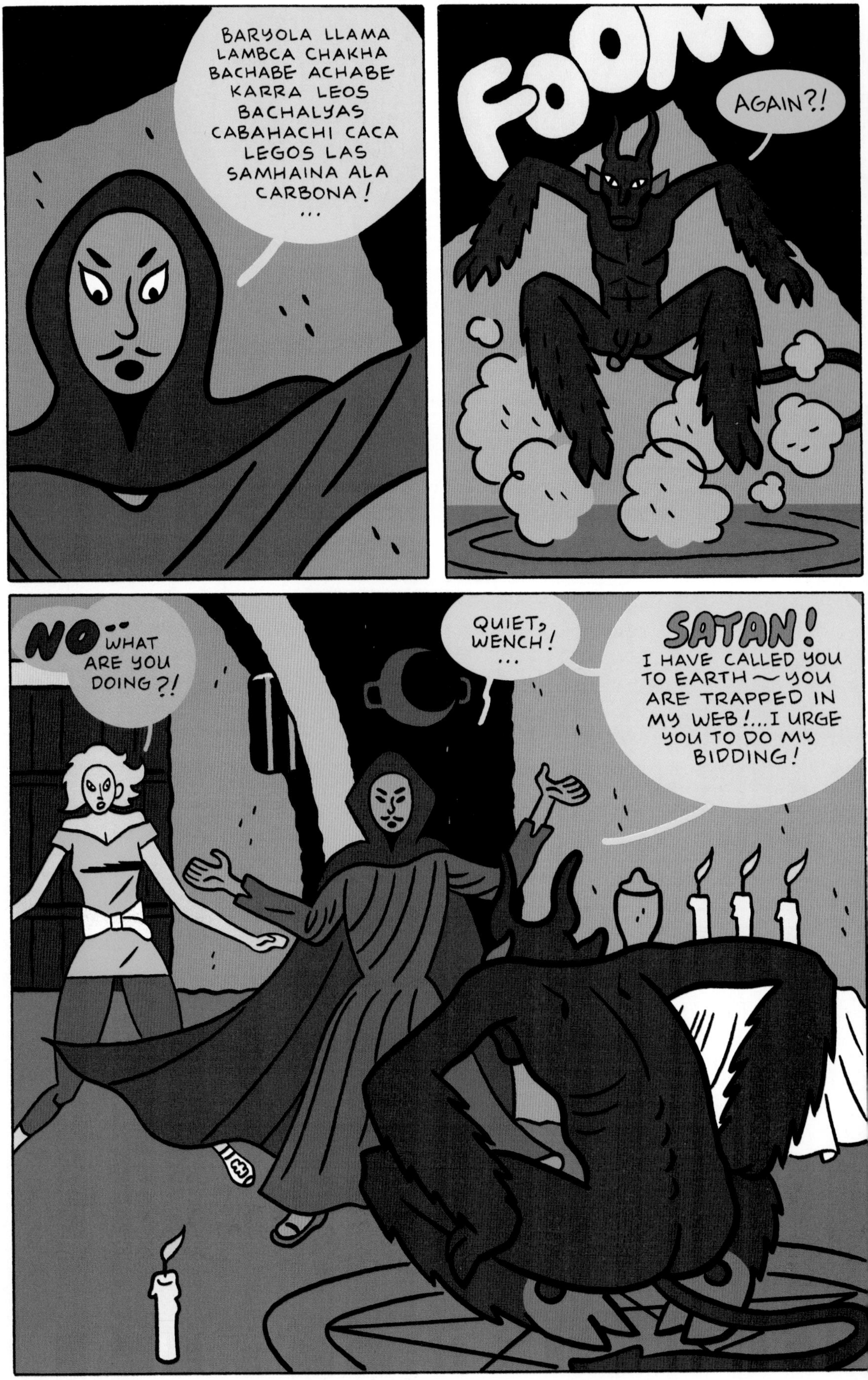

BARYOLA LLAMA LAMBCA CHAKHA BACHABE ACHABE KARRA LEOS BACHALYAS CABAHACHI CACA LEGOS LAS SAMHAINA ALA CARBONA! ...
FOOM
AGAIN?!
NO.. WHAT ARE YOU DOING?!
QUIET, WENCH! ...
SATAN!
I HAVE CALLED YOU TO EARTH ~ YOU ARE TRAPPED IN MY WEB!...I URGE YOU TO DO MY BIDDING!

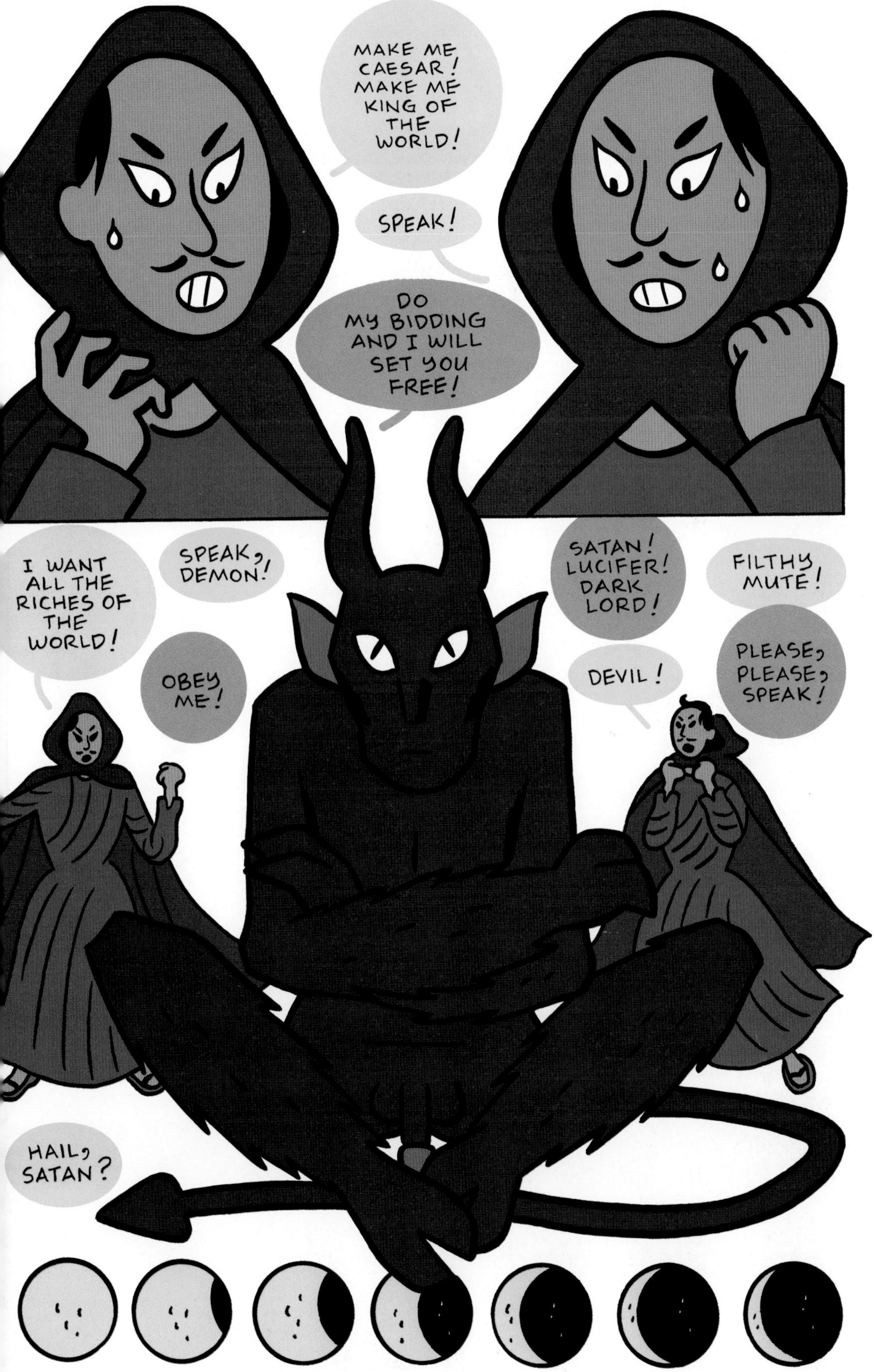
MAKE ME CAESAR! MAKE ME KING OF THE WORLD!
SPEAK!
DO MY BIDDING AND I WILL SET YOU FREE!
I WANT ALL THE RICHES OF THE WORLD!
SPEAK, DEMON!
OBEY ME!
SATAN! LUCIFER! DARK LORD!
FILTHY MUTE!
DEVIL!
PLEASE, PLEASE, SPEAK!
HAIL, SATAN?

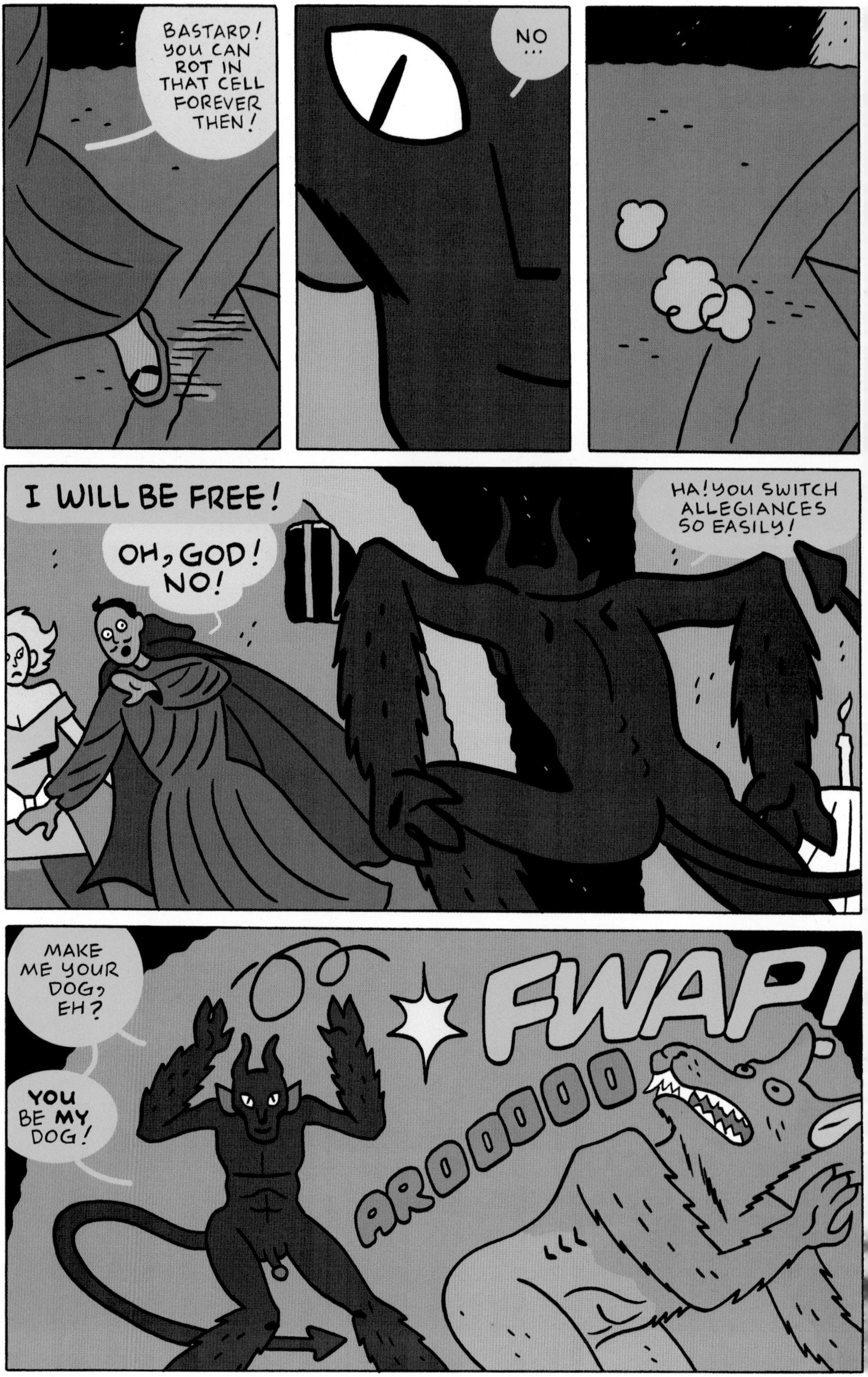
BASTARD! YOU CAN ROT IN THAT CELL FOREVER THEN!
NO ...
I WILL BE FREE!
OH, GOD! NO!
HA! YOU SWITCH ALLEGIANCES SO EASILY!
MAKE ME YOUR DOG, EH?
YOU BE MY DOG!
FWAP!
AROOOOOO

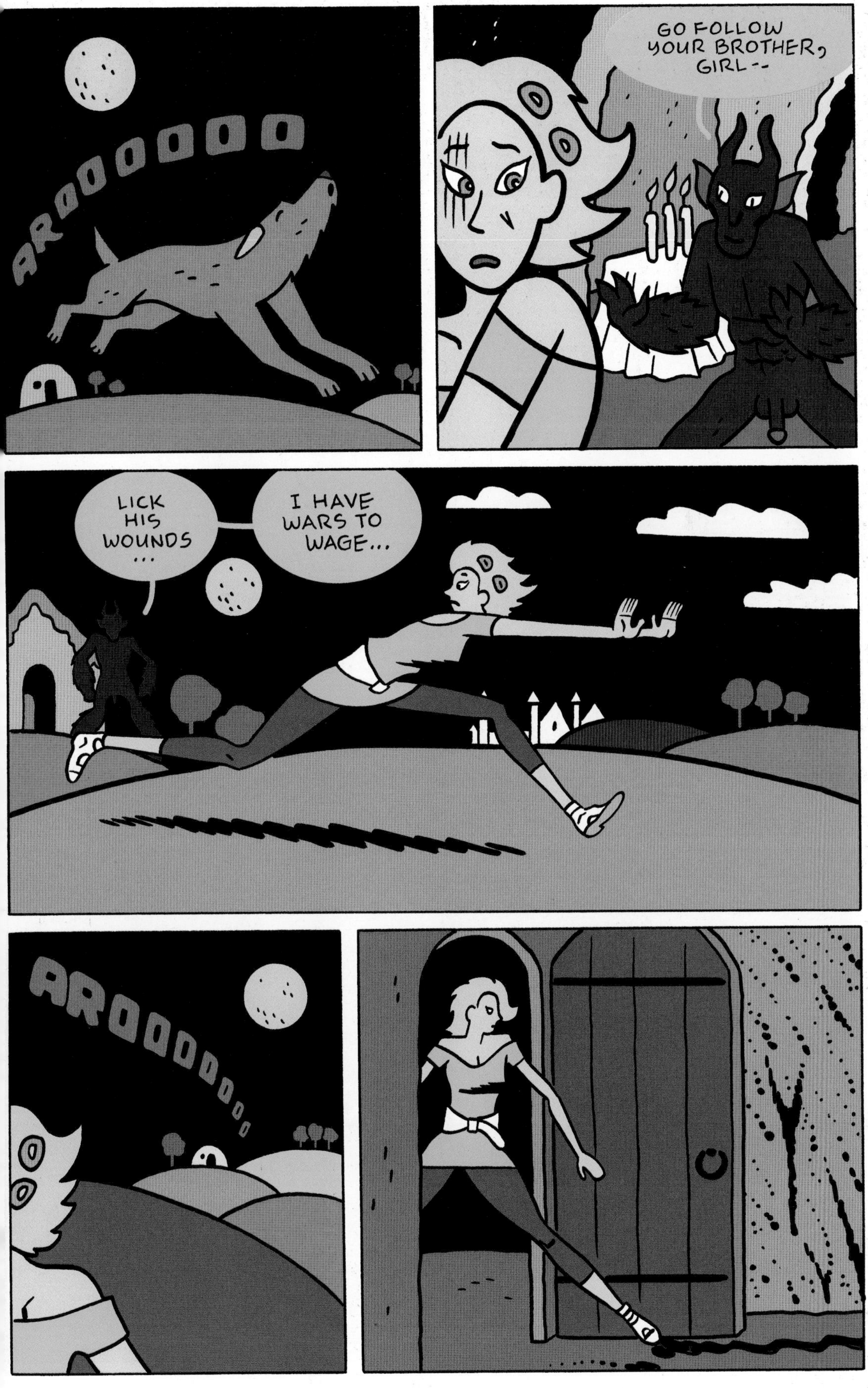
AROOOOOOO
GO FOLLOW YOUR BROTHER, GIRL--
LICK HIS WOUNDS ...
I HAVE WARS TO WAGE...
AROOOooo

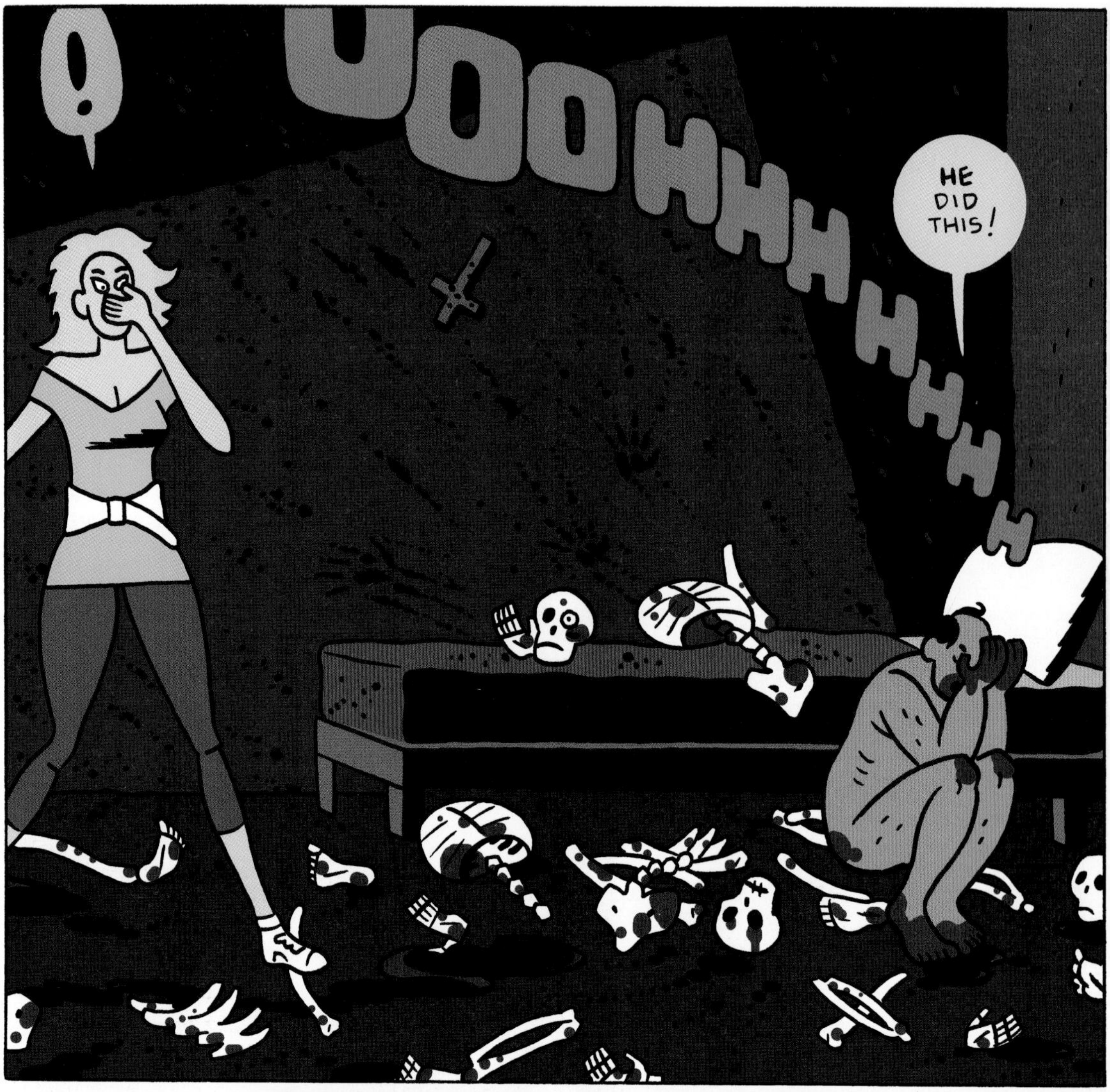
!
UOOHHHHHHHHH
HE DID THIS!

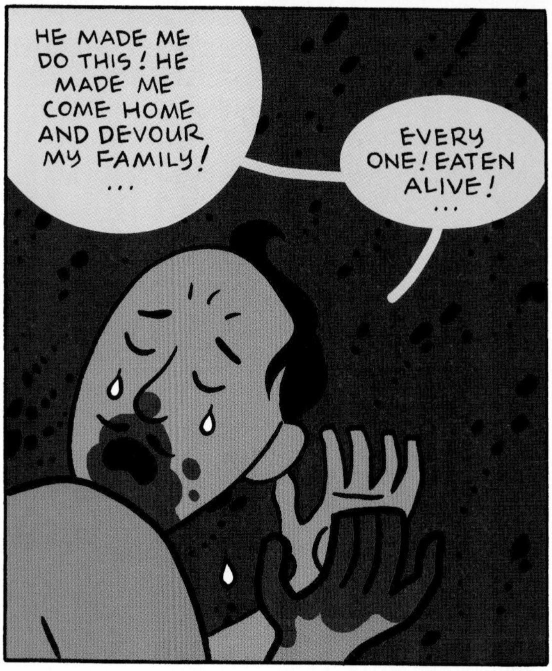
HE MADE ME DO THIS! HE MADE ME COME HOME AND DEVOUR MY FAMILY! ...
EVERY ONE! EATEN ALIVE! ...

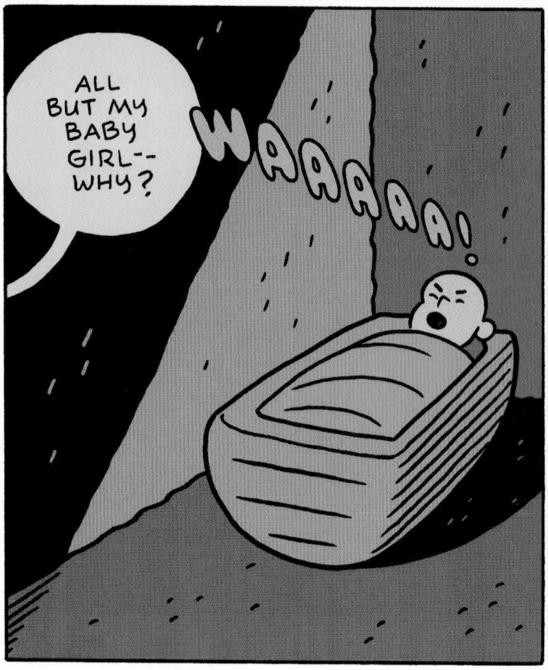
ALL BUT MY BABY GIRL-- WHY?
WAAAAAA!

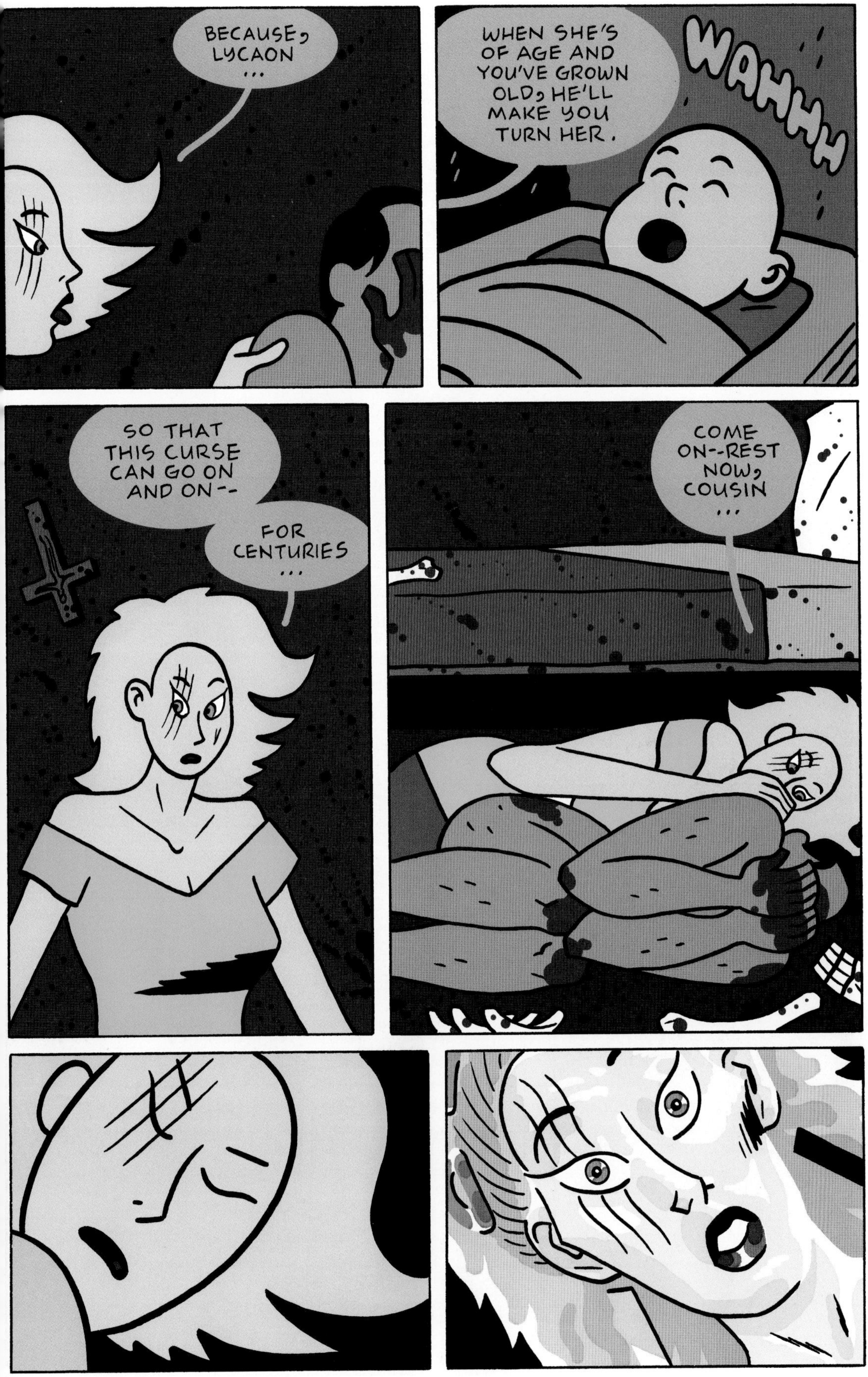
BECAUSE, LYCAON ...
WHEN SHE'S OF AGE AND YOU'VE GROWN OLD, HE'LL MAKE YOU TURN HER.
WAHHH
SO THAT THIS CURSE CAN GO ON AND ON--
FOR CENTURIES ...
COME ON--REST NOW, COUSIN ...

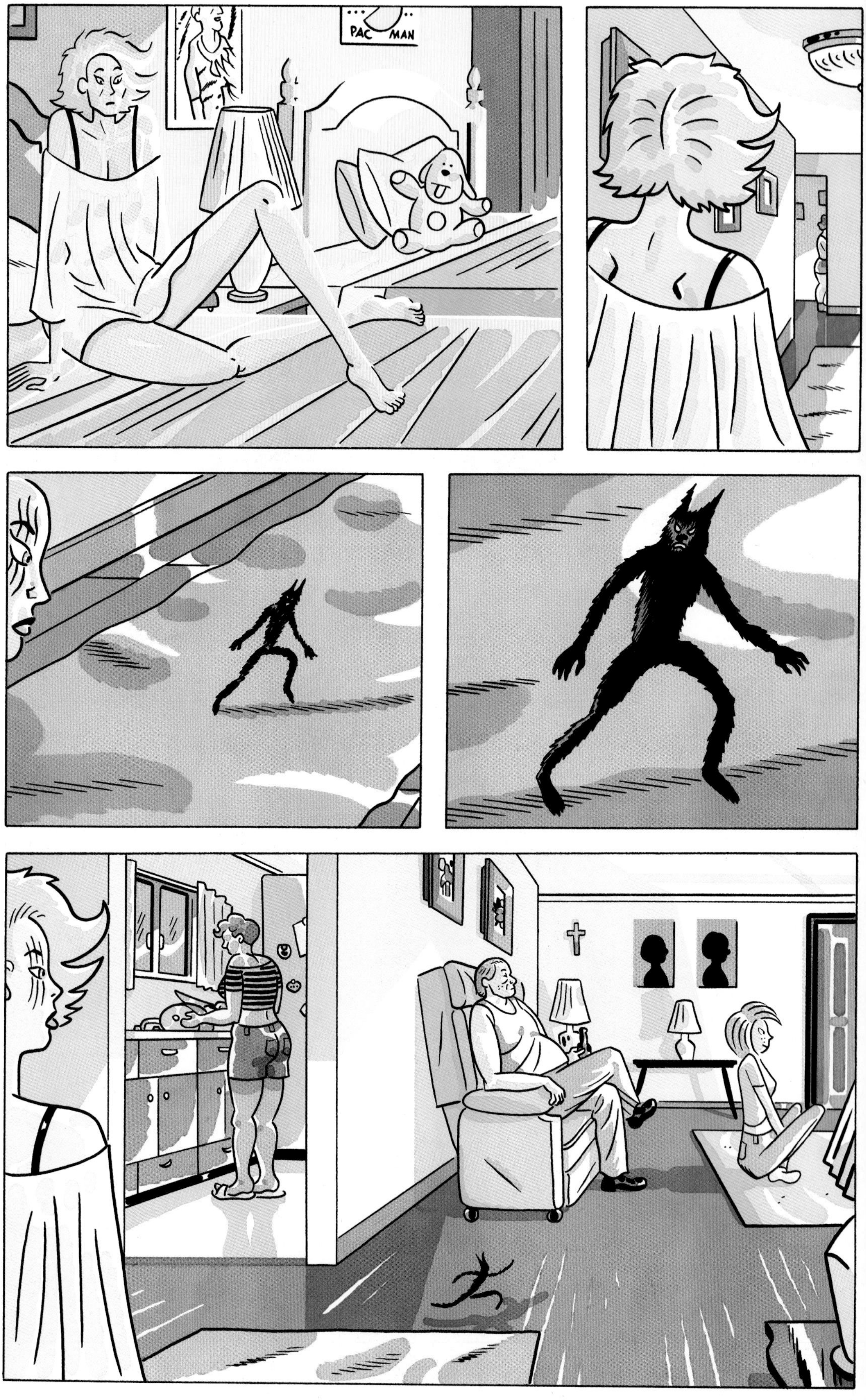
PAC MAN

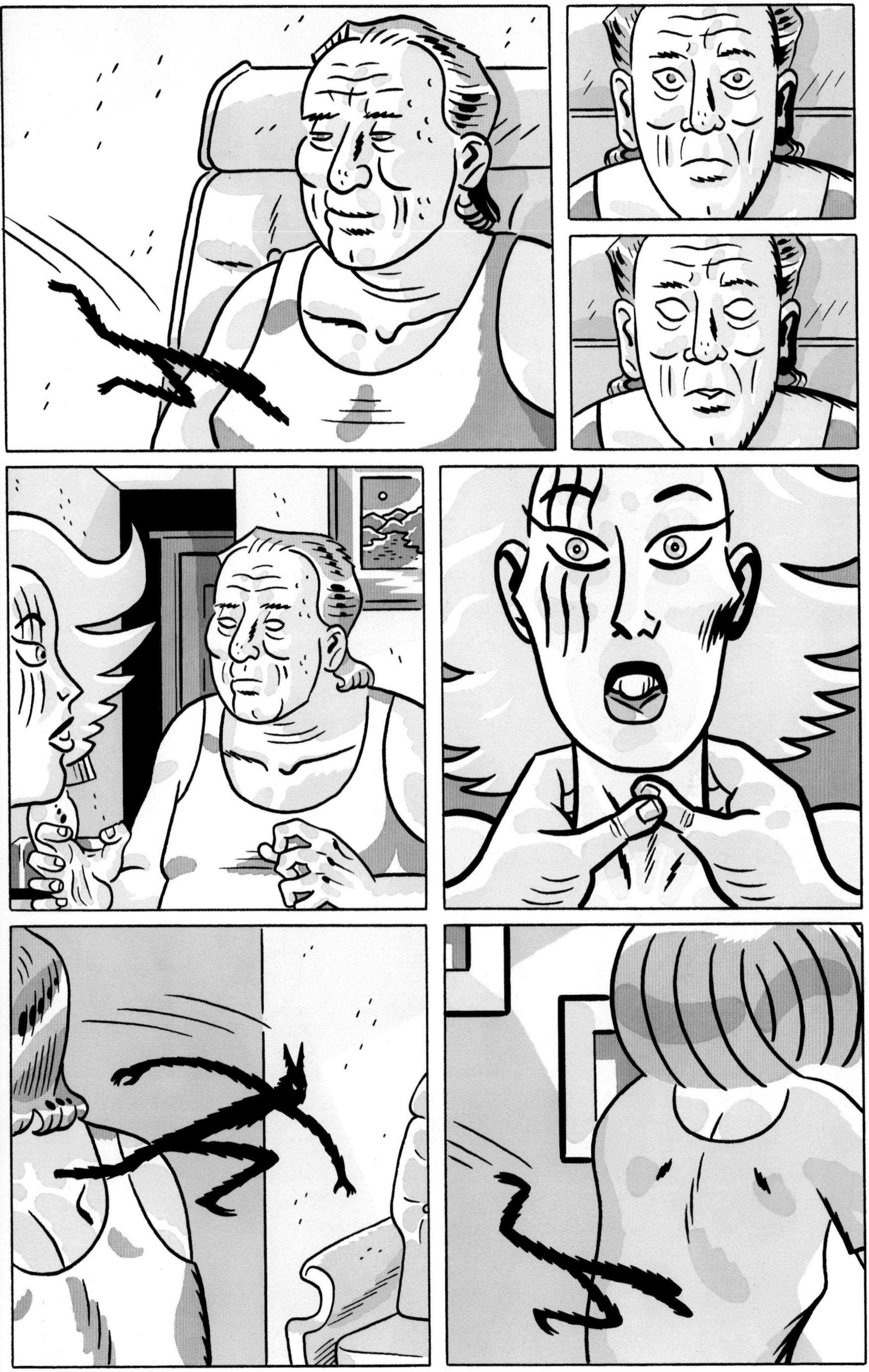

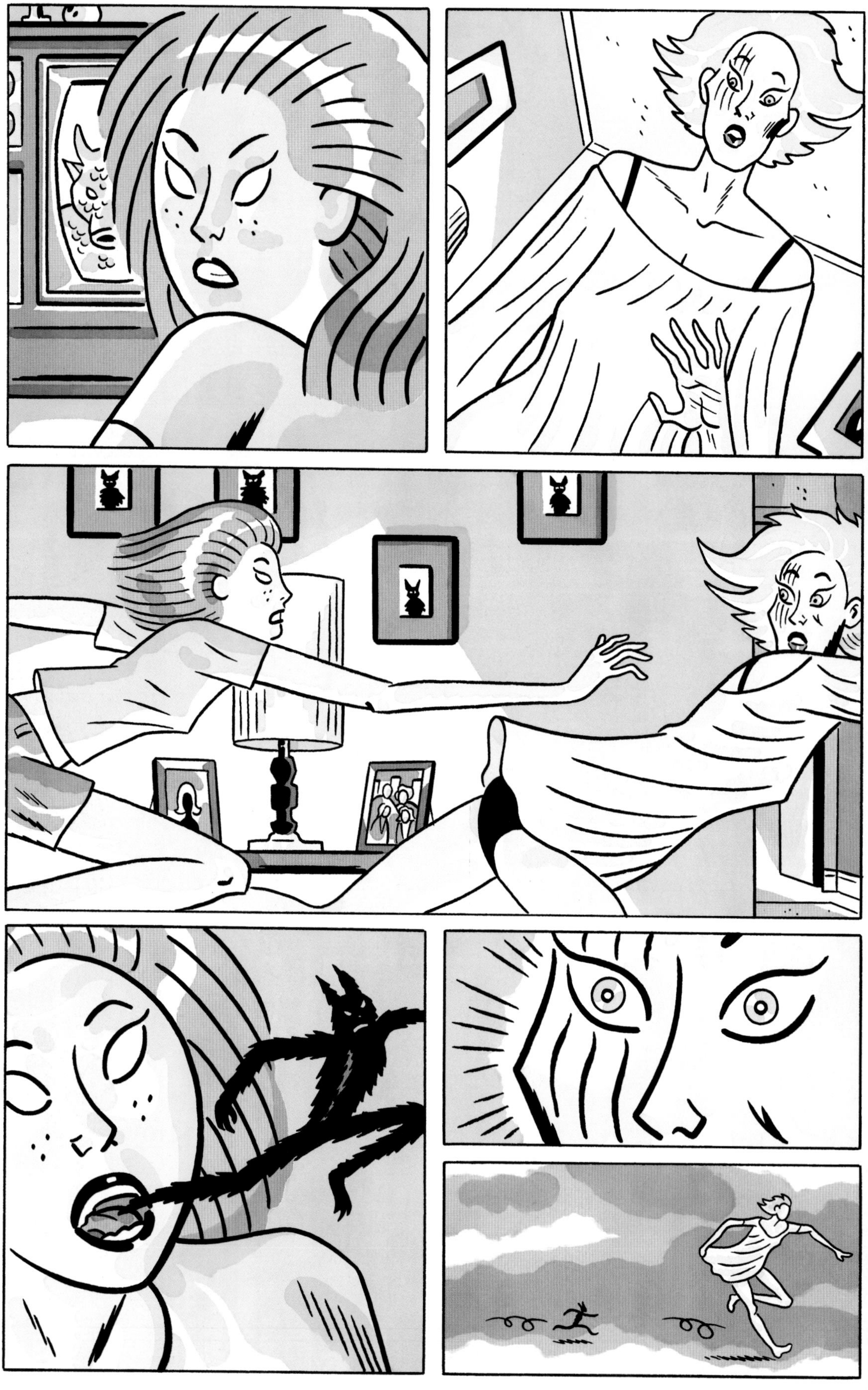

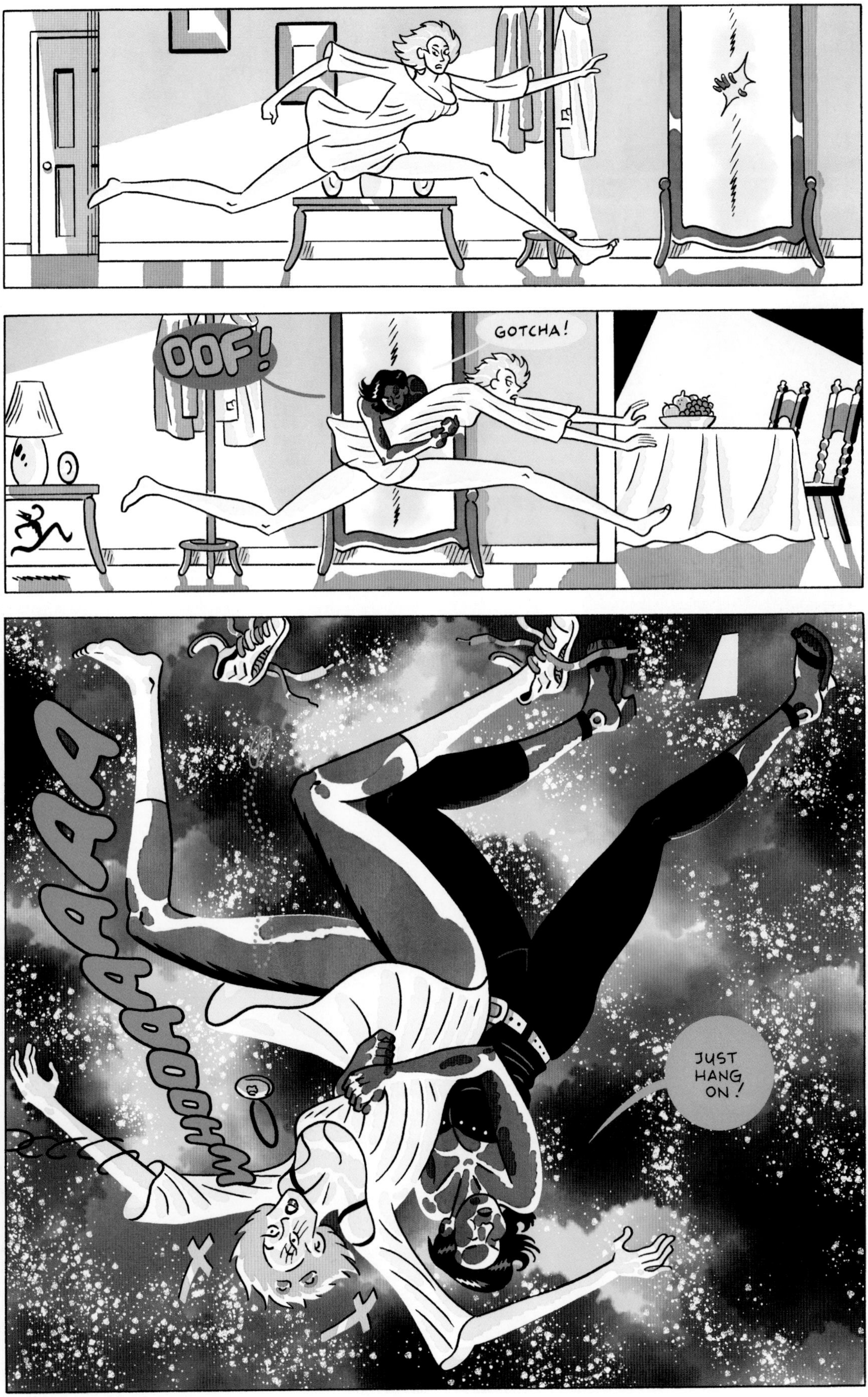
OOF!
GOTCHA!
WHOOOAAAAA
JUST HANG ON!

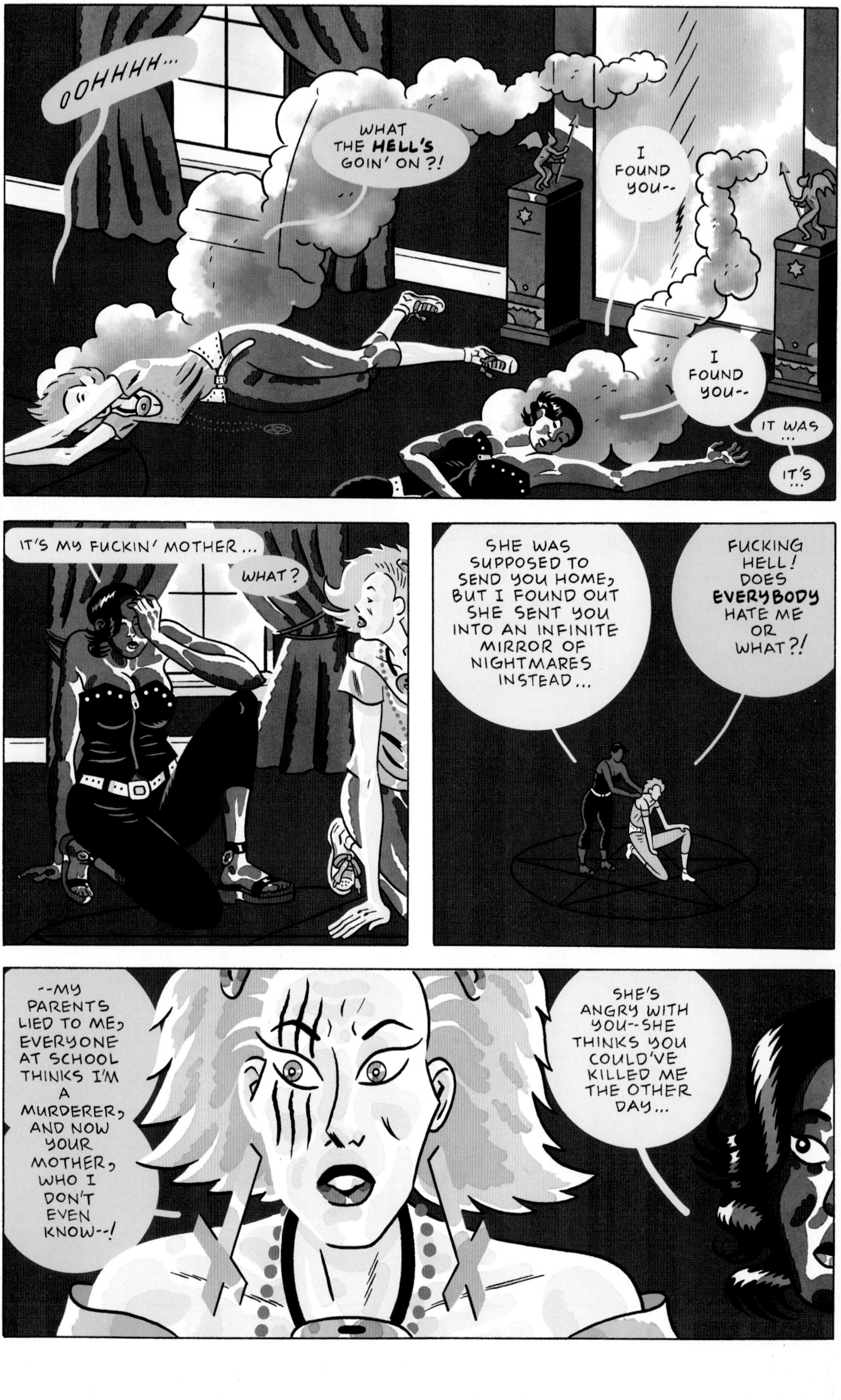

oOHHHH...
WHAT THE **HELL'S** GOIN' ON?!
I FOUND YOU--
I FOUND YOU--
IT WAS ...
IT'S ...
IT'S MY FUCKIN' MOTHER...
WHAT?
SHE WAS SUPPOSED TO SEND YOU HOME, BUT I FOUND OUT SHE SENT YOU INTO AN INFINITE MIRROR OF NIGHTMARES INSTEAD...
FUCKING HELL! DOES **EVERYBODY** HATE ME OR WHAT?!
--MY PARENTS LIED TO ME, EVERYONE AT SCHOOL THINKS I'M A MURDERER, AND NOW YOUR MOTHER, WHO I DON'T EVEN KNOW--!
SHE'S ANGRY WITH YOU--SHE THINKS YOU COULD'VE KILLED ME THE OTHER DAY...

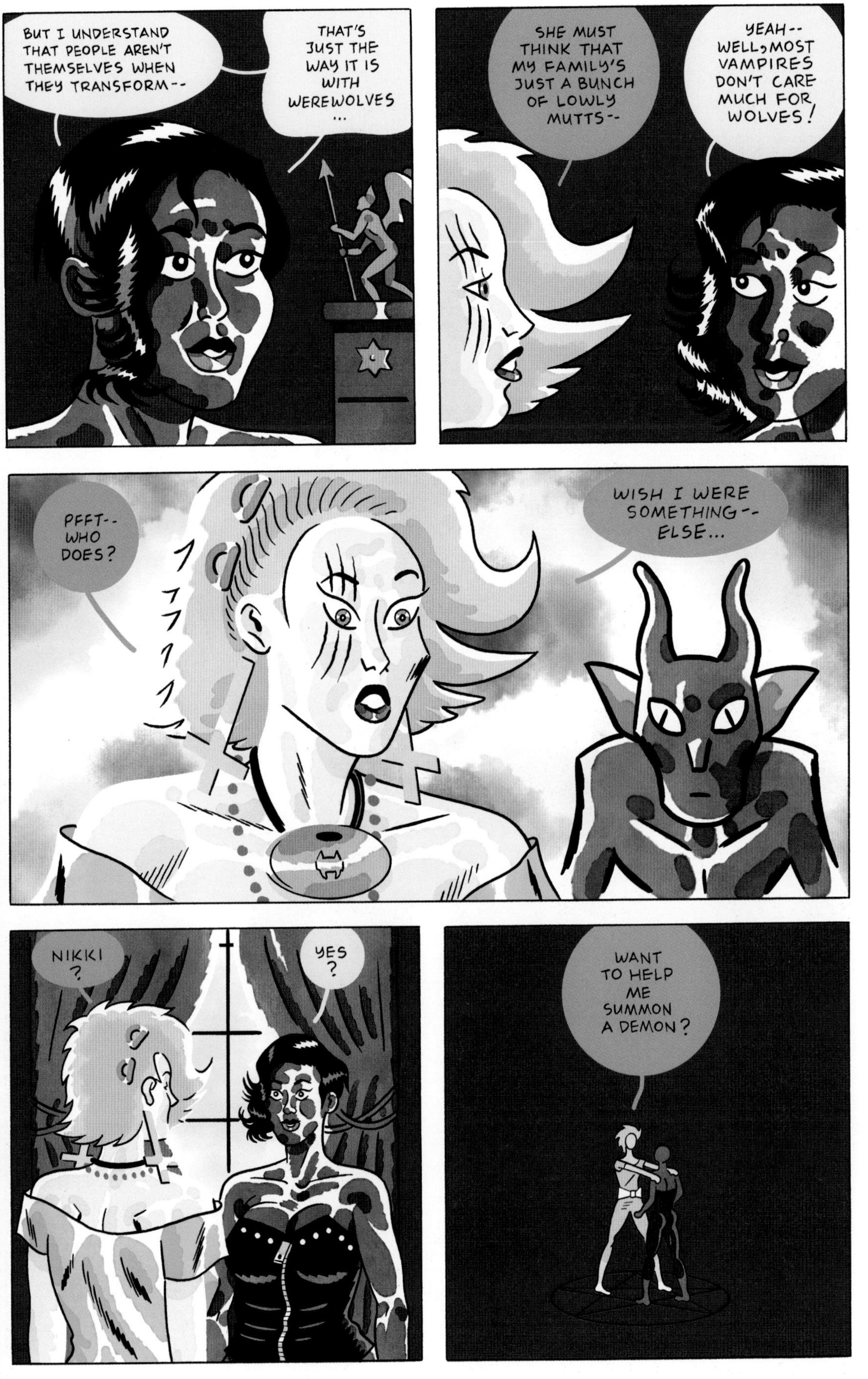

BUT I UNDERSTAND THAT PEOPLE AREN'T THEMSELVES WHEN THEY TRANSFORM--
THAT'S JUST THE WAY IT IS WITH WEREWOLVES ...
SHE MUST THINK THAT MY FAMILY'S JUST A BUNCH OF LOWLY MUTTS--
YEAH-- WELL, MOST VAMPIRES DON'T CARE MUCH FOR WOLVES!
PFFT-- WHO DOES?
WISH I WERE SOMETHING-- ELSE...
NIKKI ?
YES ?
WANT TO HELP ME SUMMON A DEMON?

Spell Number

4

Demon Trapping

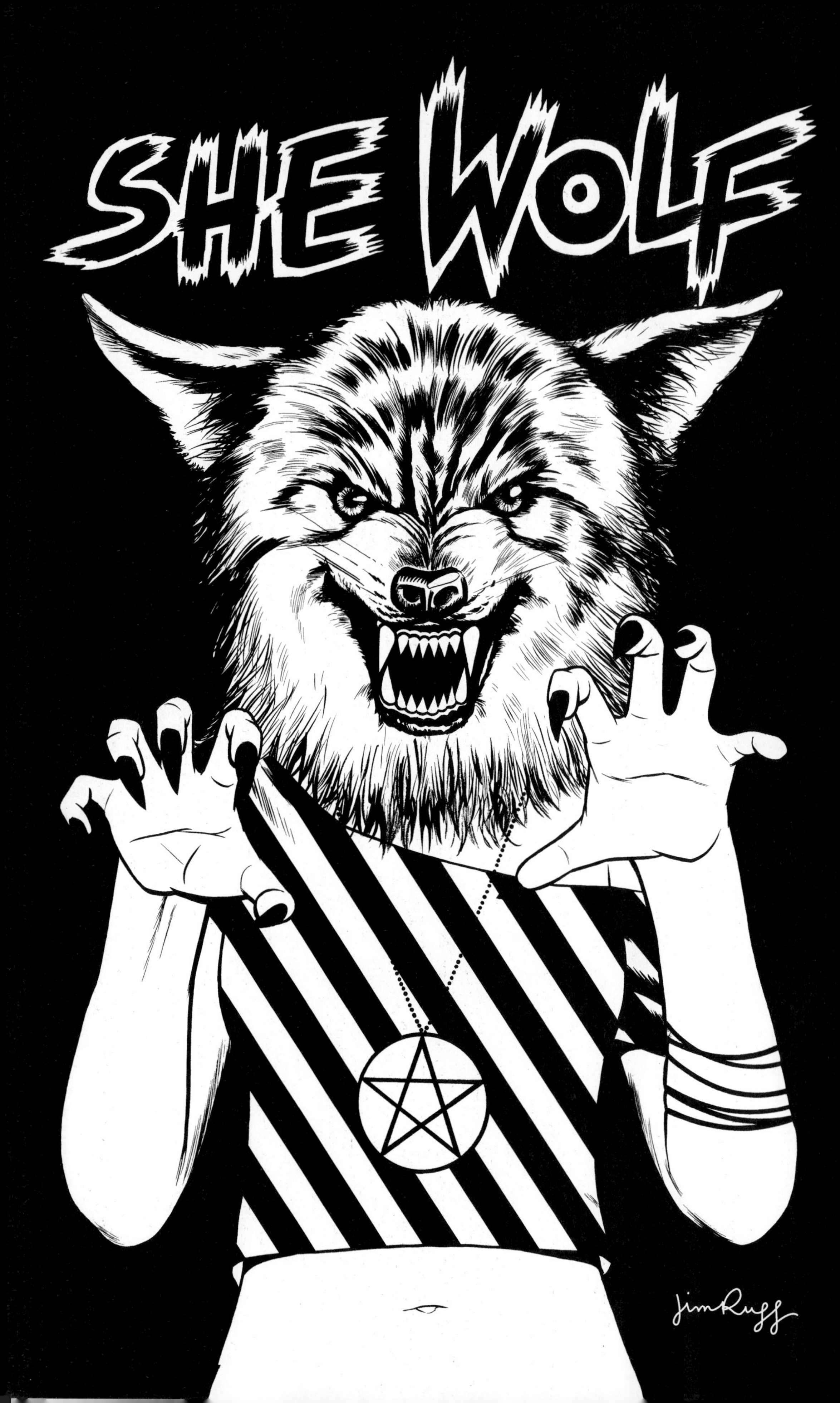
SHE WOLF
Jim Rugg

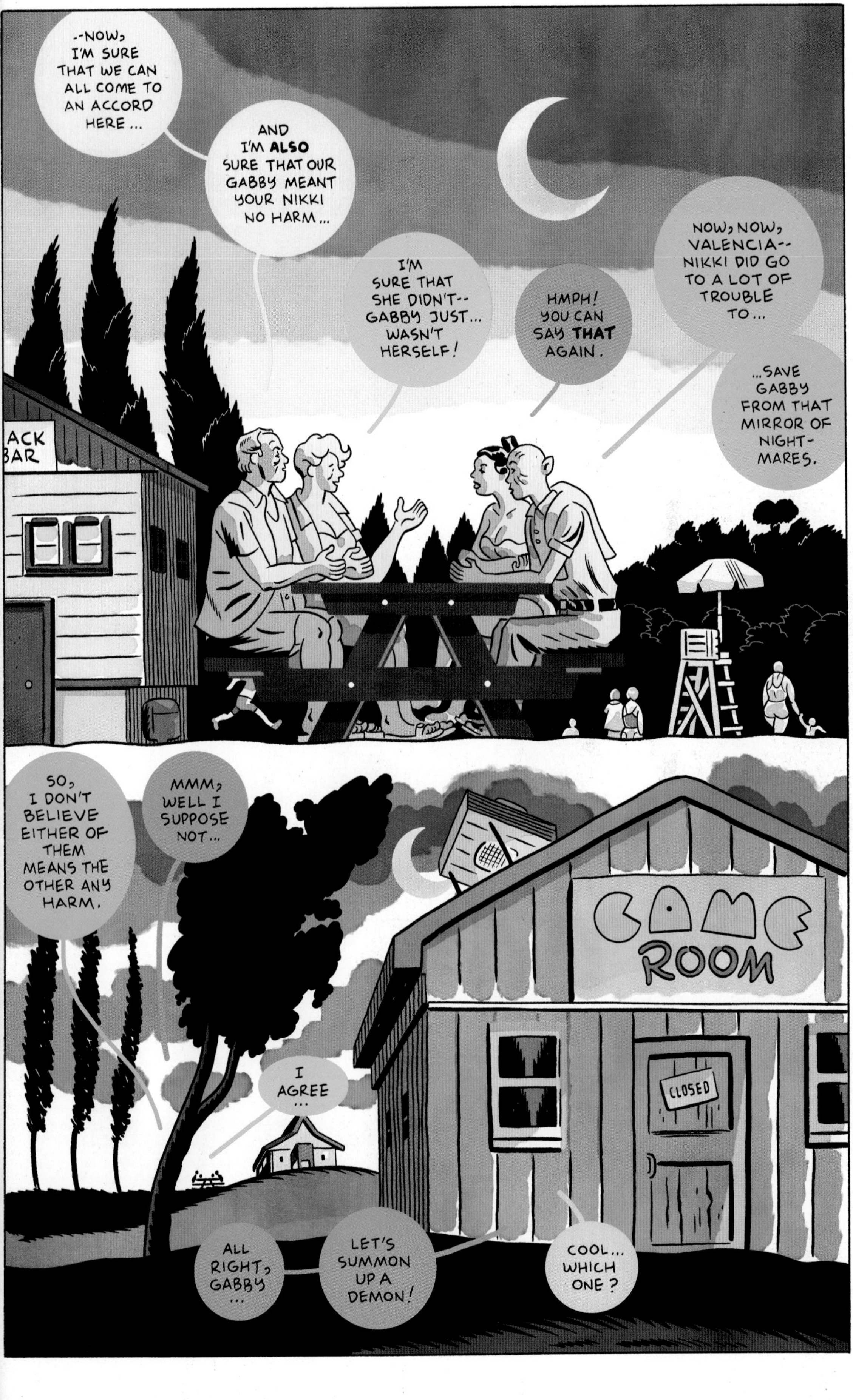

--NOW, I'M SURE THAT WE CAN ALL COME TO AN ACCORD HERE...
AND I'M **ALSO** SURE THAT OUR GABBY MEANT YOUR NIKKI NO HARM...
I'M SURE THAT SHE DIDN'T--GABBY JUST... WASN'T HERSELF!
HMPH! YOU CAN SAY **THAT** AGAIN.
NOW, NOW, VALENCIA--NIKKI DID GO TO A LOT OF TROUBLE TO...
...SAVE GABBY FROM THAT MIRROR OF NIGHT-MARES.
ACK
BAR
SO, I DON'T BELIEVE EITHER OF THEM MEANS THE OTHER ANY HARM.
MMM, WELL I SUPPOSE NOT...
GAME ROOM
CLOSED
I AGREE...
ALL RIGHT, GABBY...
LET'S SUMMON UP A DEMON!
COOL... WHICH ONE?

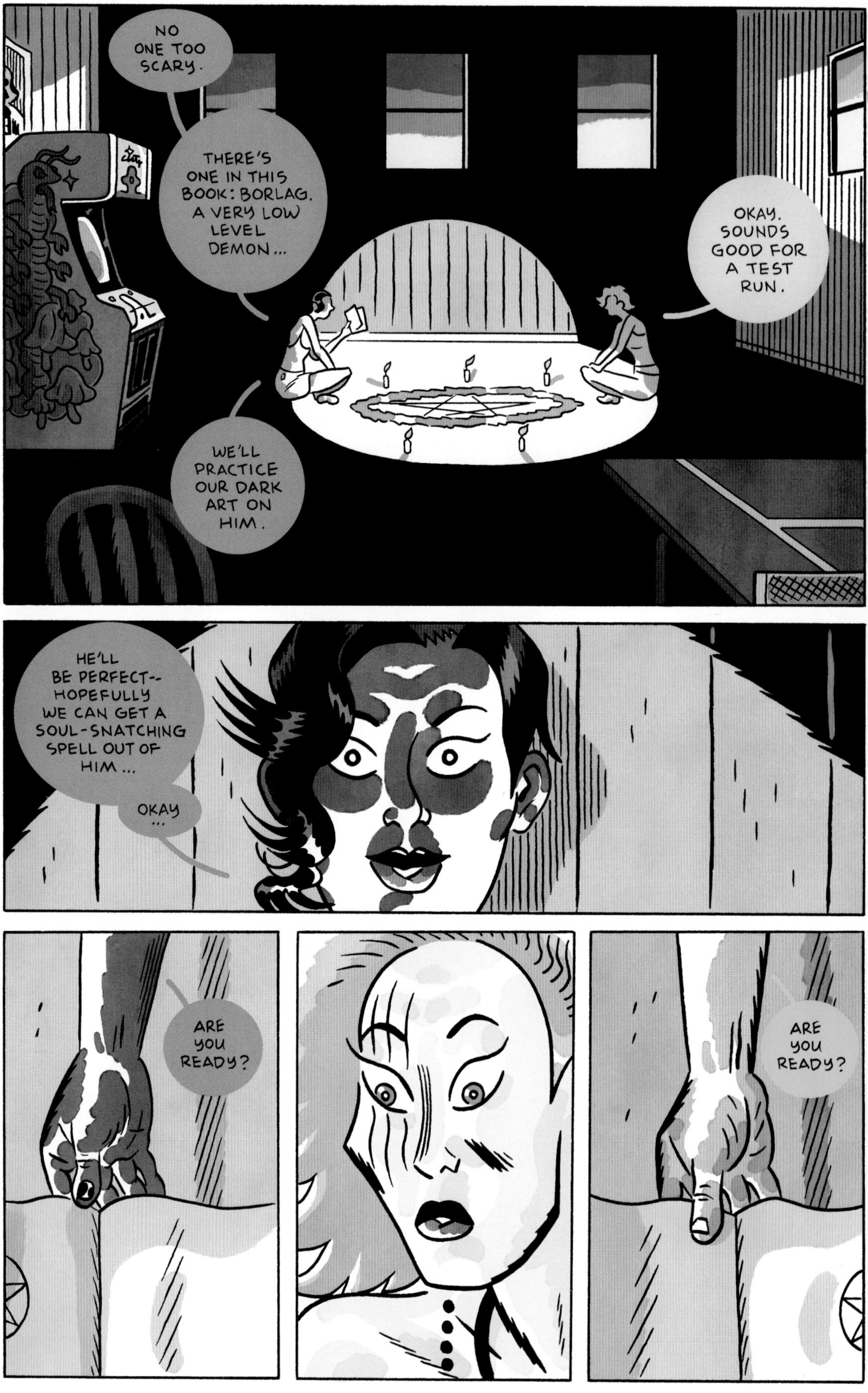
NO ONE TOO SCARY.
THERE'S ONE IN THIS BOOK: BORLAG. A VERY LOW LEVEL DEMON...
WE'LL PRACTICE OUR DARK ART ON HIM.
OKAY. SOUNDS GOOD FOR A TEST RUN.
HE'LL BE PERFECT-- HOPEFULLY WE CAN GET A SOUL-SNATCHING SPELL OUT OF HIM...
OKAY ...
ARE YOU READY?
ARE YOU READY?

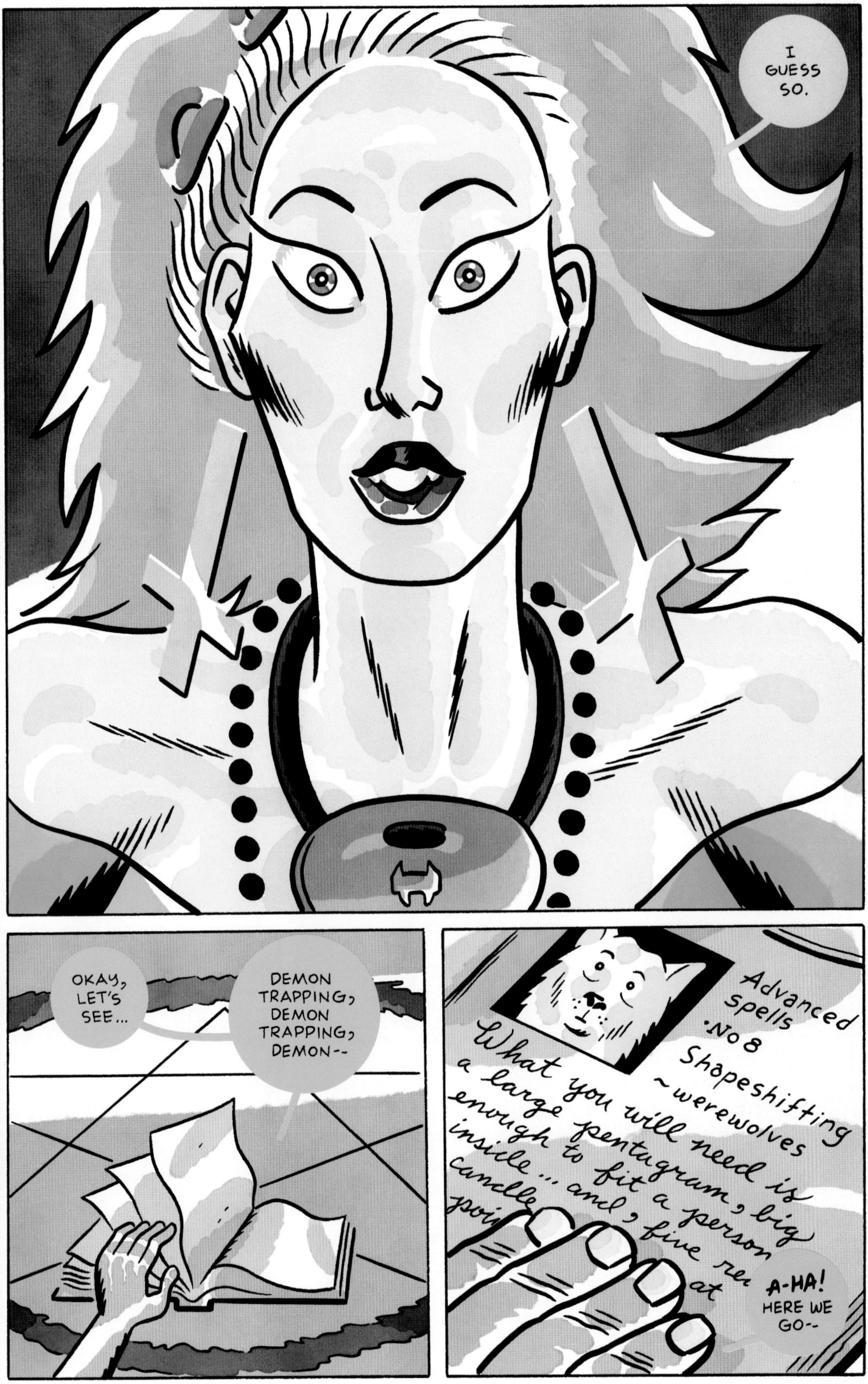

I GUESS SO.
OKAY, LET'S SEE...
DEMON TRAPPING, DEMON TRAPPING, DEMON--
Advanced spells
•No 8
Shapeshifting
~werewolves
What you will need is a large pentagram, big enough to fit a person inside... and, five
A-HA! HERE WE GO--

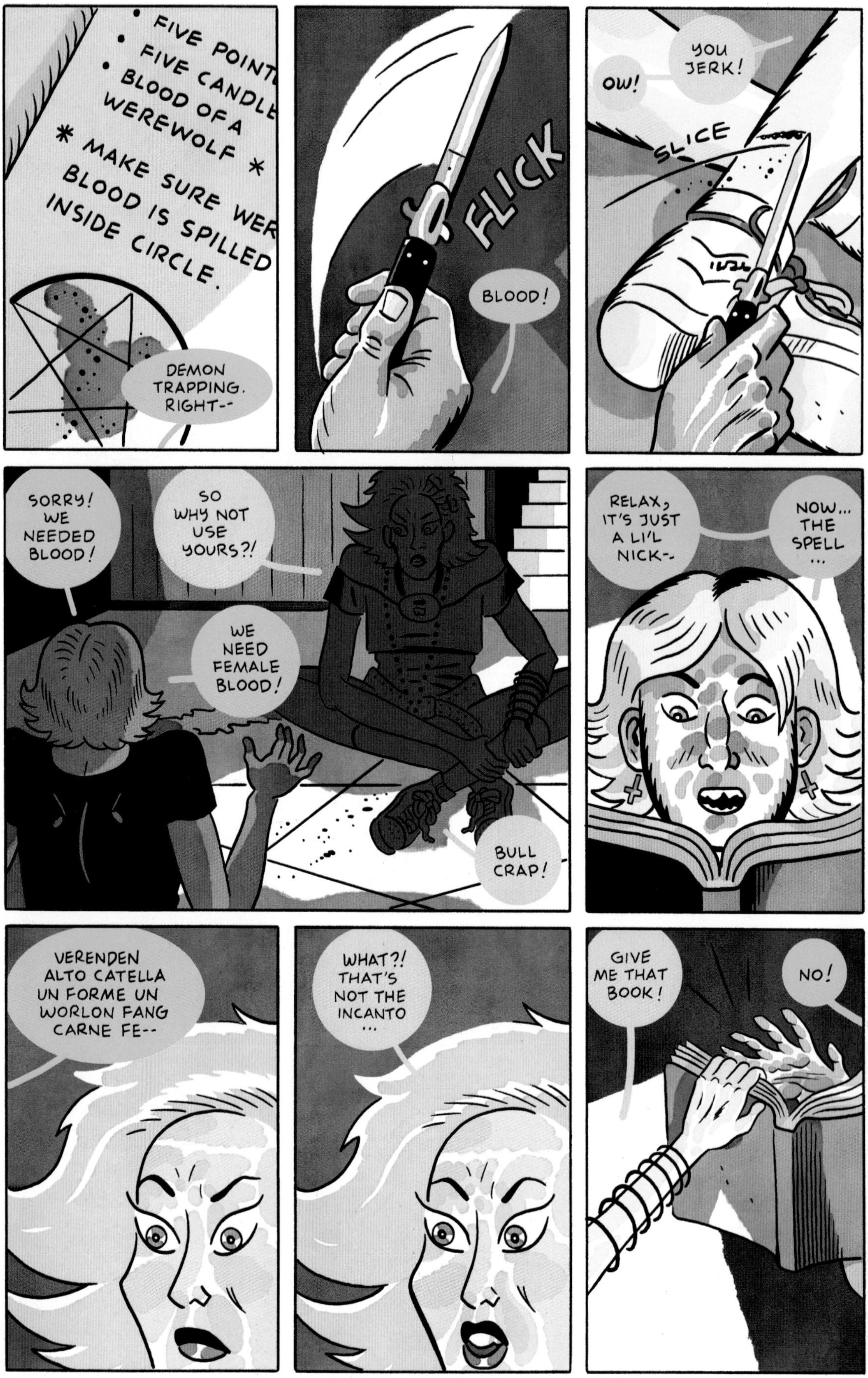
• FIVE POINT
• FIVE CANDLE
• BLOOD OF A WEREWOLF
* MAKE SURE WER BLOOD IS SPILLED INSIDE CIRCLE. *
DEMON TRAPPING. RIGHT--
FLICK
BLOOD!
YOU JERK!
OW!
SLICE
SORRY! WE NEEDED BLOOD!
SO WHY NOT USE YOURS?!
WE NEED FEMALE BLOOD!
BULL CRAP!
RELAX, IT'S JUST A LI'L NICK--
NOW... THE SPELL ...
VERENDEN ALTO CATELLA UN FORME UN WORLON FANG CARNE FE--
WHAT?! THAT'S NOT THE INCANTO ...
GIVE ME THAT BOOK!
NO!

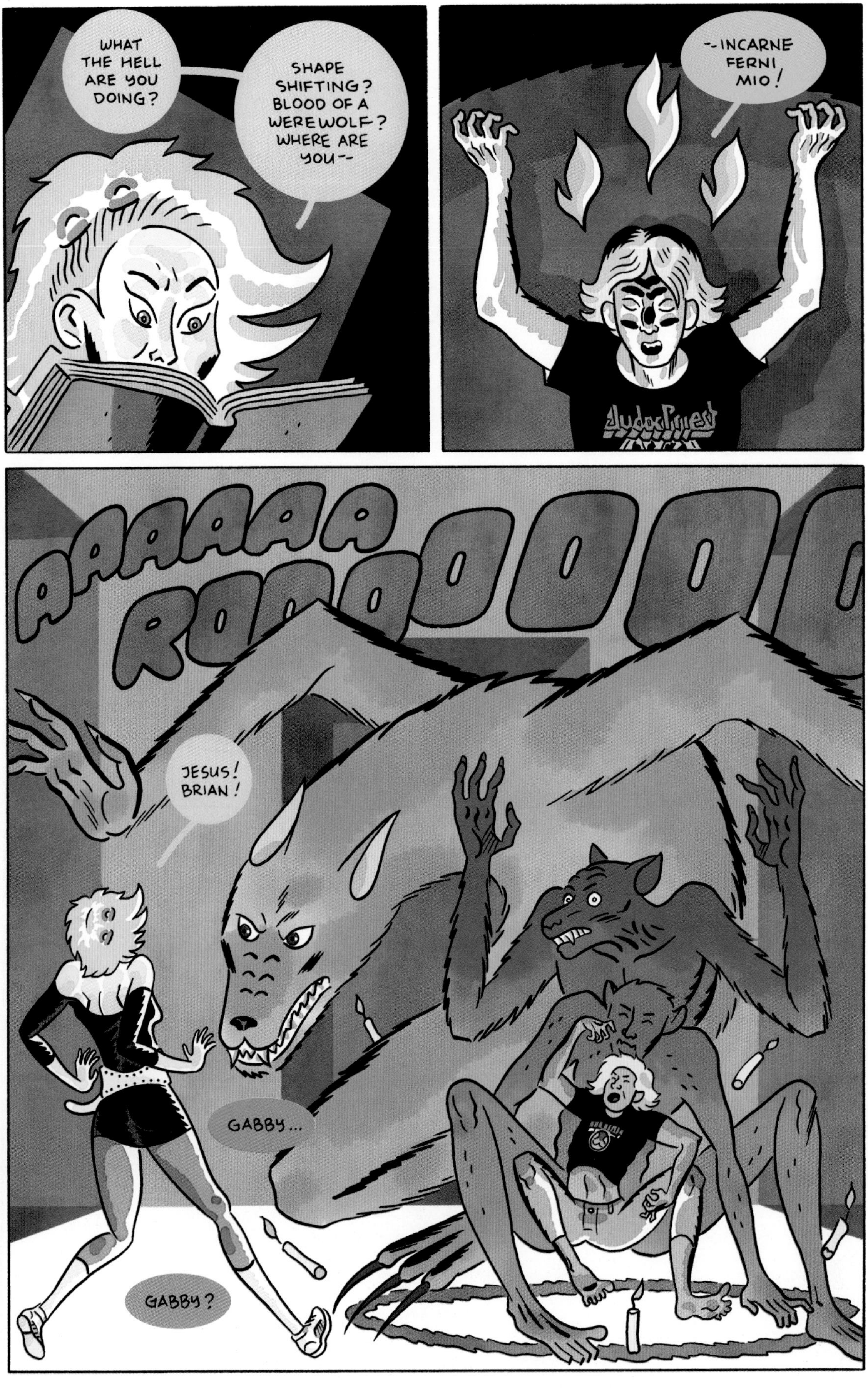

WHAT THE HELL ARE YOU DOING?
SHAPE SHIFTING? BLOOD OF A WEREWOLF? WHERE ARE YOU--
--INCARNE FERNI MIO!
AAAAAA ROOOOOO
JESUS! BRIAN!
GABBY...
GABBY?

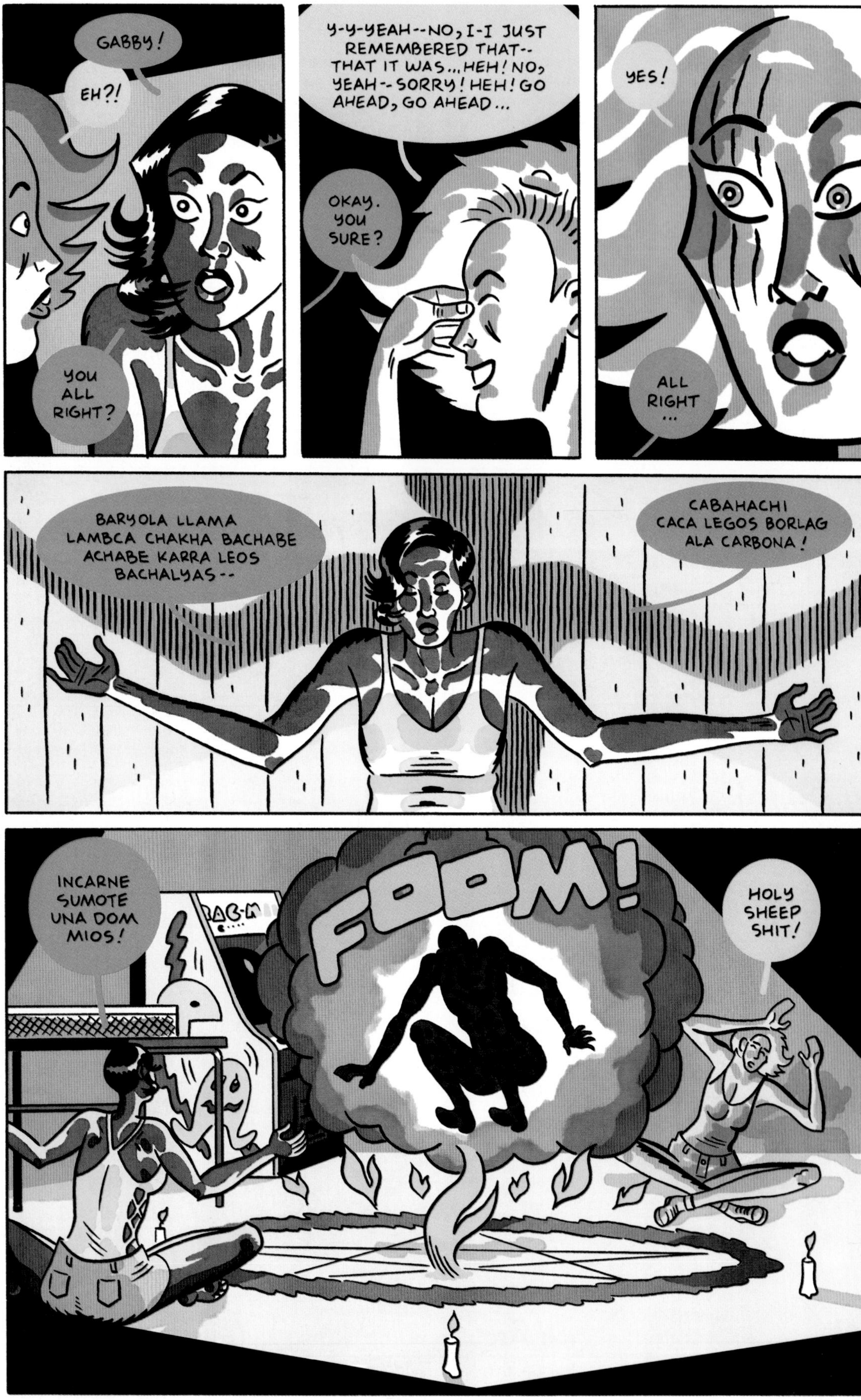
GABBY!
EH?!
YOU ALL RIGHT?
Y-Y-YEAH--NO, I-I JUST REMEMBERED THAT--THAT IT WAS... HEH! NO, YEAH--SORRY! HEH! GO AHEAD, GO AHEAD...
OKAY. YOU SURE?
YES!
ALL RIGHT...
BARYOLA LLAMA LAMBCA CHAKHA BACHABE ACHABE KARRA LEOS BACHALYAS--
CABAHACHI CACA LEGOS BORLAG ALA CARBONA!
INCARNE SUMOTE UNA DOM MIOS!
FOOM!
HOLY SHEEP SHIT!

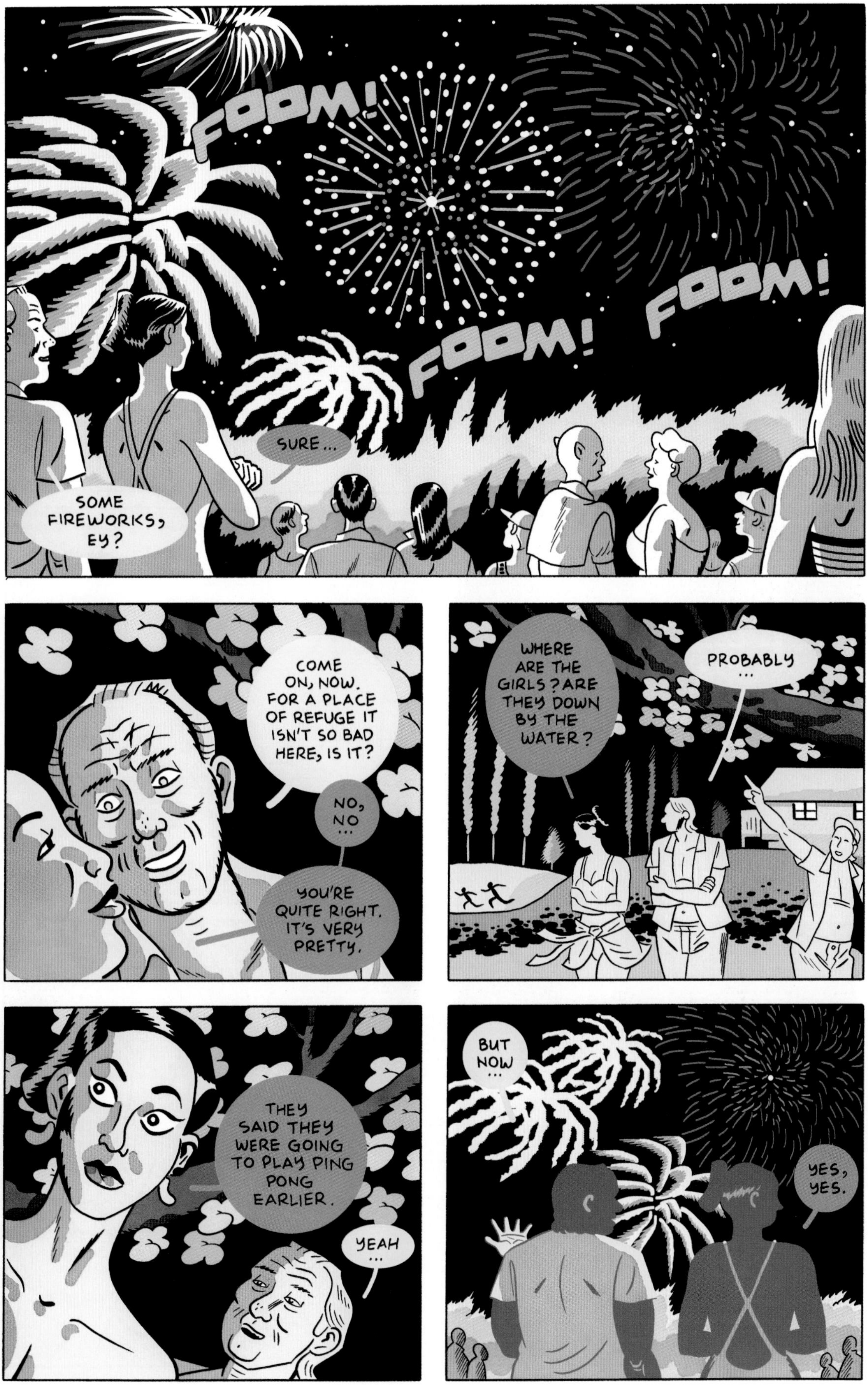
FOOM!
FOOM! FOOM!
SURE...
SOME FIREWORKS, EY?
COME ON, NOW. FOR A PLACE OF REFUGE IT ISN'T SO BAD HERE, IS IT?
NO, NO ...
YOU'RE QUITE RIGHT. IT'S VERY PRETTY.
WHERE ARE THE GIRLS? ARE THEY DOWN BY THE WATER?
PROBABLY ...
THEY SAID THEY WERE GOING TO PLAY PING PONG EARLIER.
YEAH ...
BUT NOW ...
YES, YES.

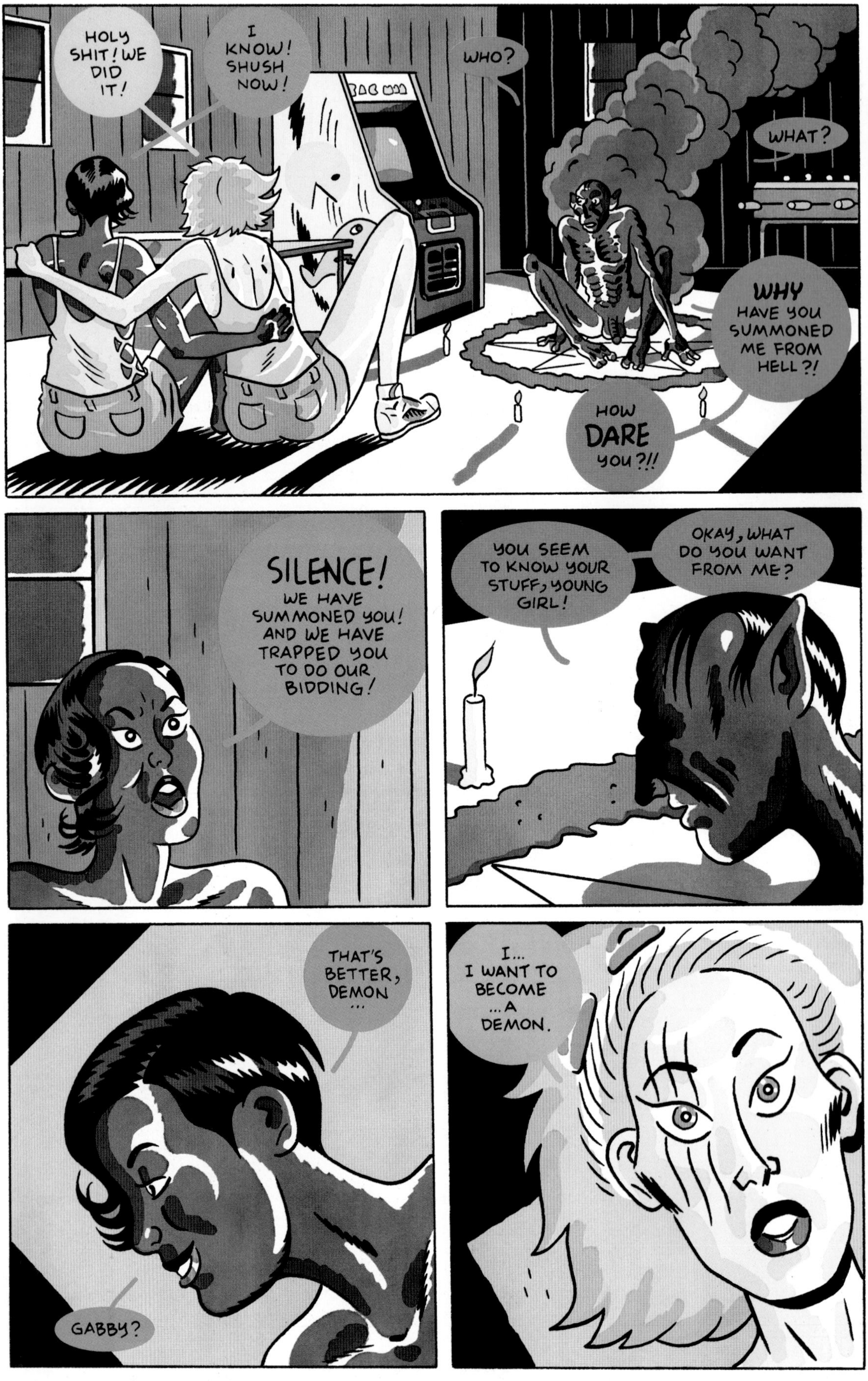
HOLY SHIT! WE DID IT!
I KNOW! SHUSH NOW!
WHO?
WHAT?
WHY HAVE YOU SUMMONED ME FROM HELL?!
HOW DARE YOU?!!
SILENCE! WE HAVE SUMMONED YOU! AND WE HAVE TRAPPED YOU TO DO OUR BIDDING!
YOU SEEM TO KNOW YOUR STUFF, YOUNG GIRL!
OKAY, WHAT DO YOU WANT FROM ME?
THAT'S BETTER, DEMON ...
GABBY?
I... I WANT TO BECOME ...A DEMON.

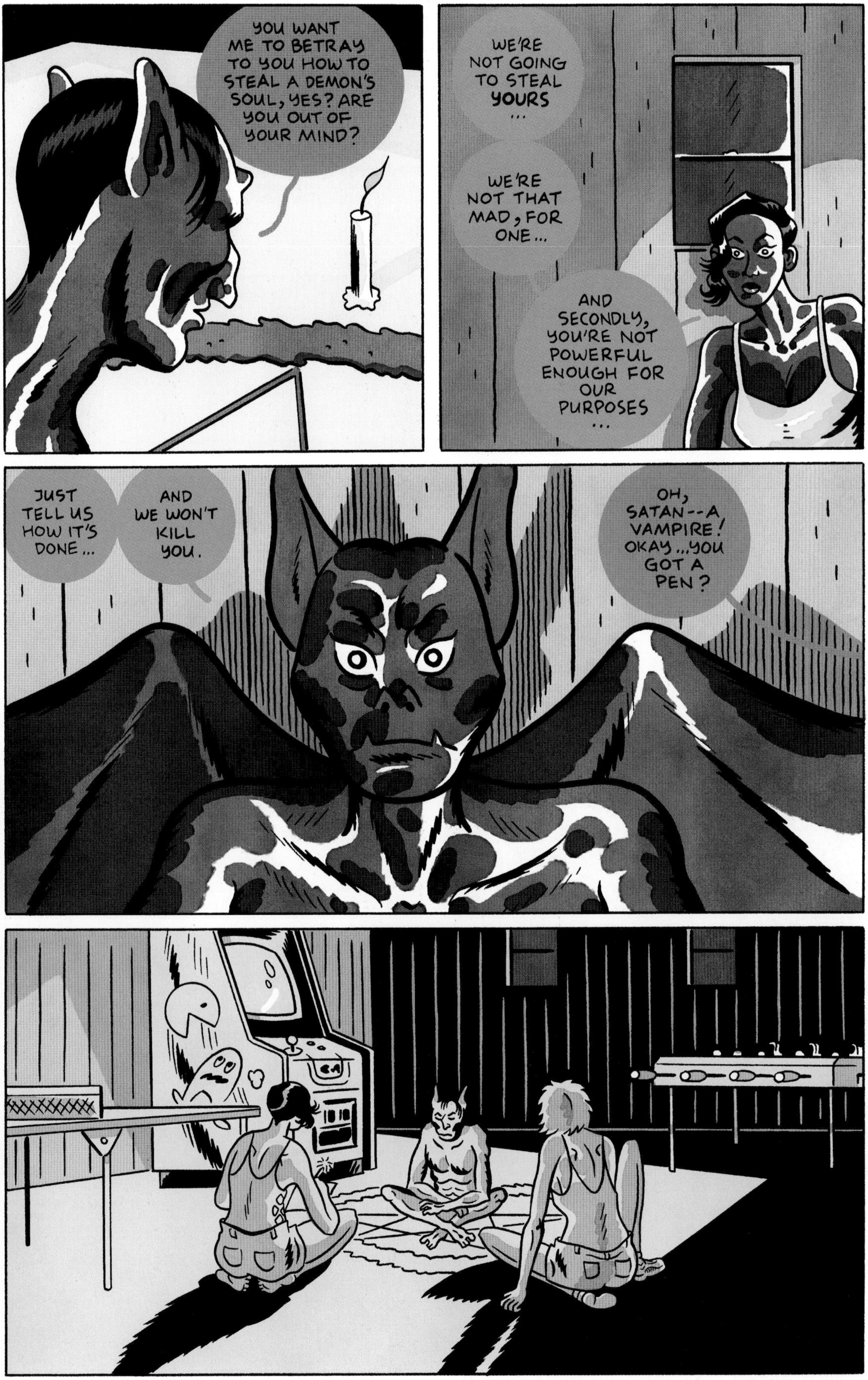
YOU WANT ME TO BETRAY TO YOU HOW TO STEAL A DEMON'S SOUL, YES? ARE YOU OUT OF YOUR MIND?
WE'RE NOT GOING TO STEAL **YOURS** ...
WE'RE NOT THAT MAD, FOR ONE...
AND SECONDLY, YOU'RE NOT POWERFUL ENOUGH FOR OUR PURPOSES ...
JUST TELL US HOW IT'S DONE...
AND WE WON'T KILL YOU.
OH, SATAN--A VAMPIRE! OKAY ...YOU GOT A PEN?

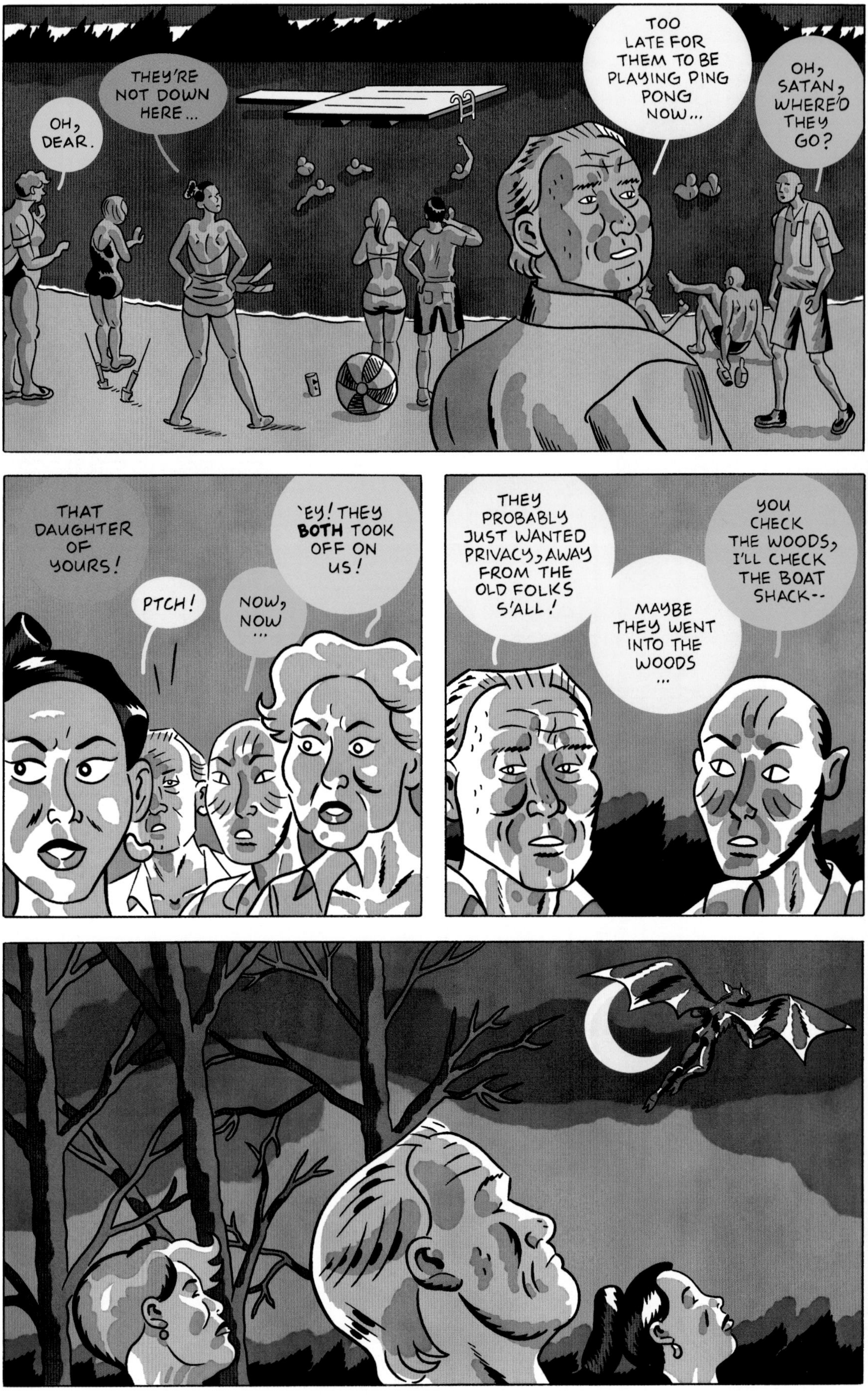
OH, DEAR.
THEY'RE NOT DOWN HERE...
TOO LATE FOR THEM TO BE PLAYING PING PONG NOW...
OH, SATAN, WHERE'D THEY GO?
THAT DAUGHTER OF YOURS!
PTCH!
NOW, NOW ...
`EY! THEY **BOTH** TOOK OFF ON US!
THEY PROBABLY JUST WANTED PRIVACY, AWAY FROM THE OLD FOLKS S'ALL!
MAYBE THEY WENT INTO THE WOODS ...
YOU CHECK THE WOODS, I'LL CHECK THE BOAT SHACK--

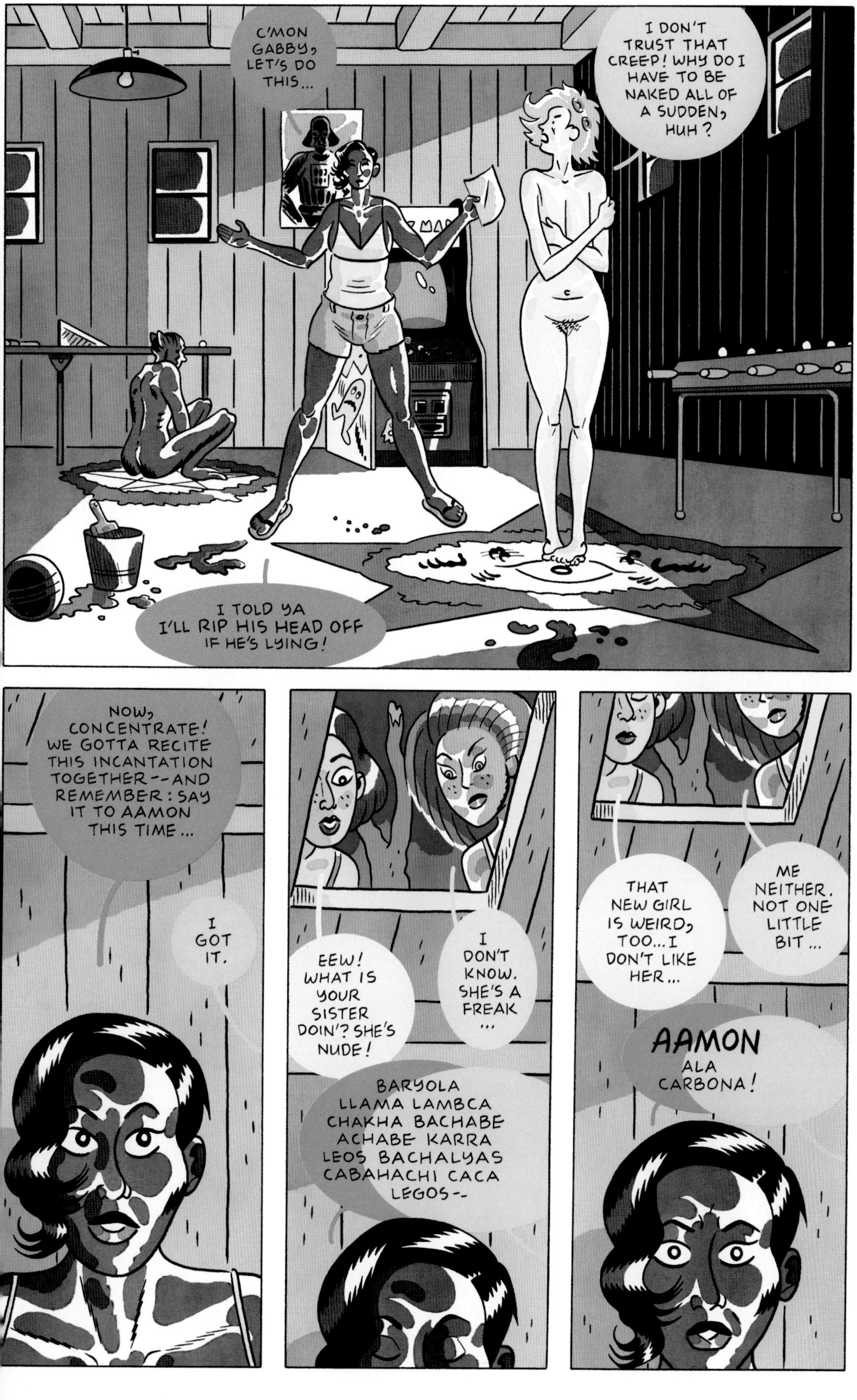
C'MON GABBY, LET'S DO THIS...
I DON'T TRUST THAT CREEP! WHY DO I HAVE TO BE NAKED ALL OF A SUDDEN, HUH?
I TOLD YA I'LL RIP HIS HEAD OFF IF HE'S LYING!
NOW, CONCENTRATE! WE GOTTA RECITE THIS INCANTATION TOGETHER--AND REMEMBER: SAY IT TO AAMON THIS TIME...
I GOT IT.
EEW! WHAT IS YOUR SISTER DOIN'? SHE'S NUDE!
I DON'T KNOW. SHE'S A FREAK...
BARYOLA LLAMA LAMBCA CHAKHA BACHABE ACHABE KARRA LEOS BACHALYAS CABAHACHI CACA LEGOS--
THAT NEW GIRL IS WEIRD, TOO... I DON'T LIKE HER...
ME NEITHER. NOT ONE LITTLE BIT...
AAMON ALA CARBONA!

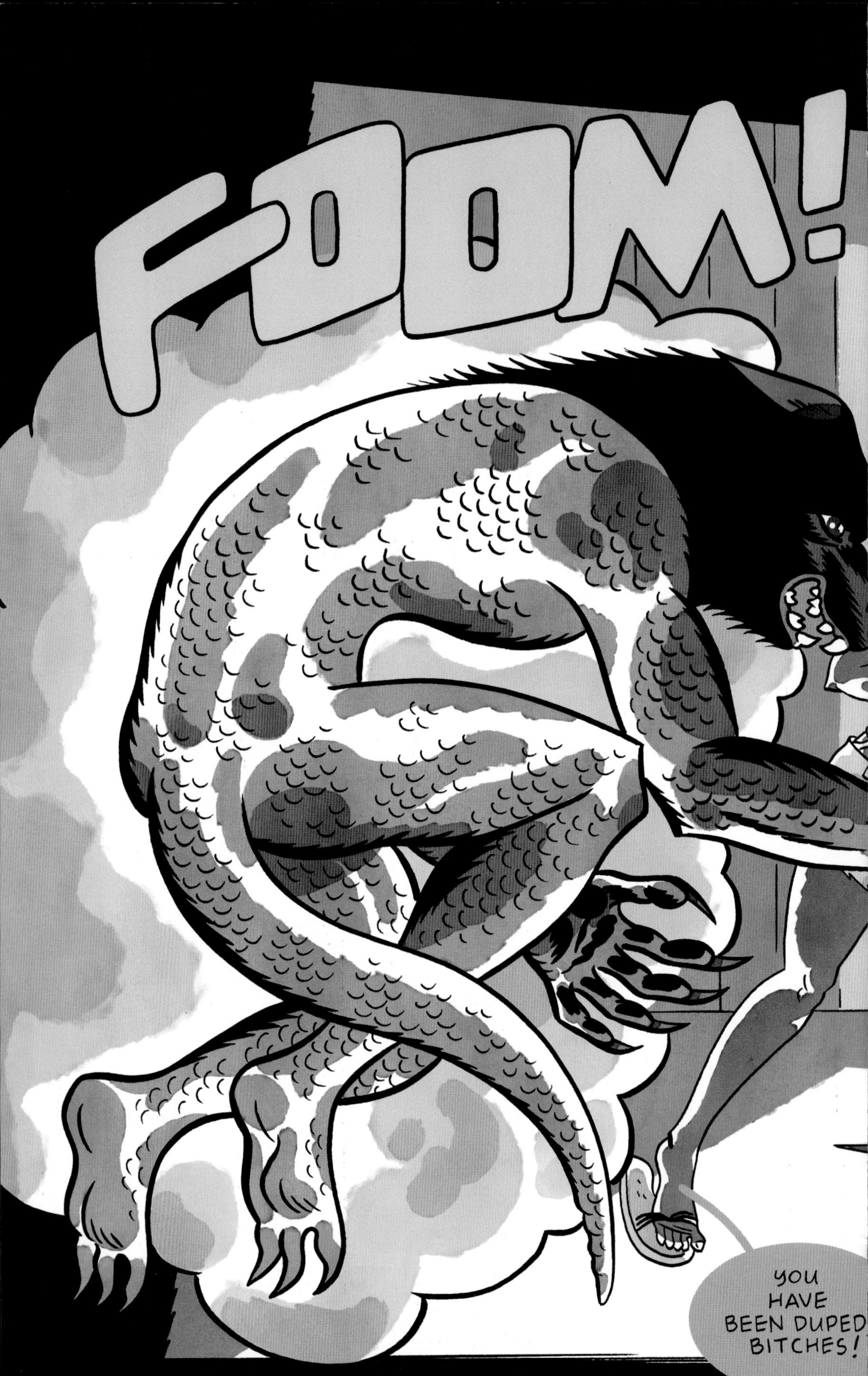
FOOM!
YOU HAVE BEEN DUPED BITCHES!

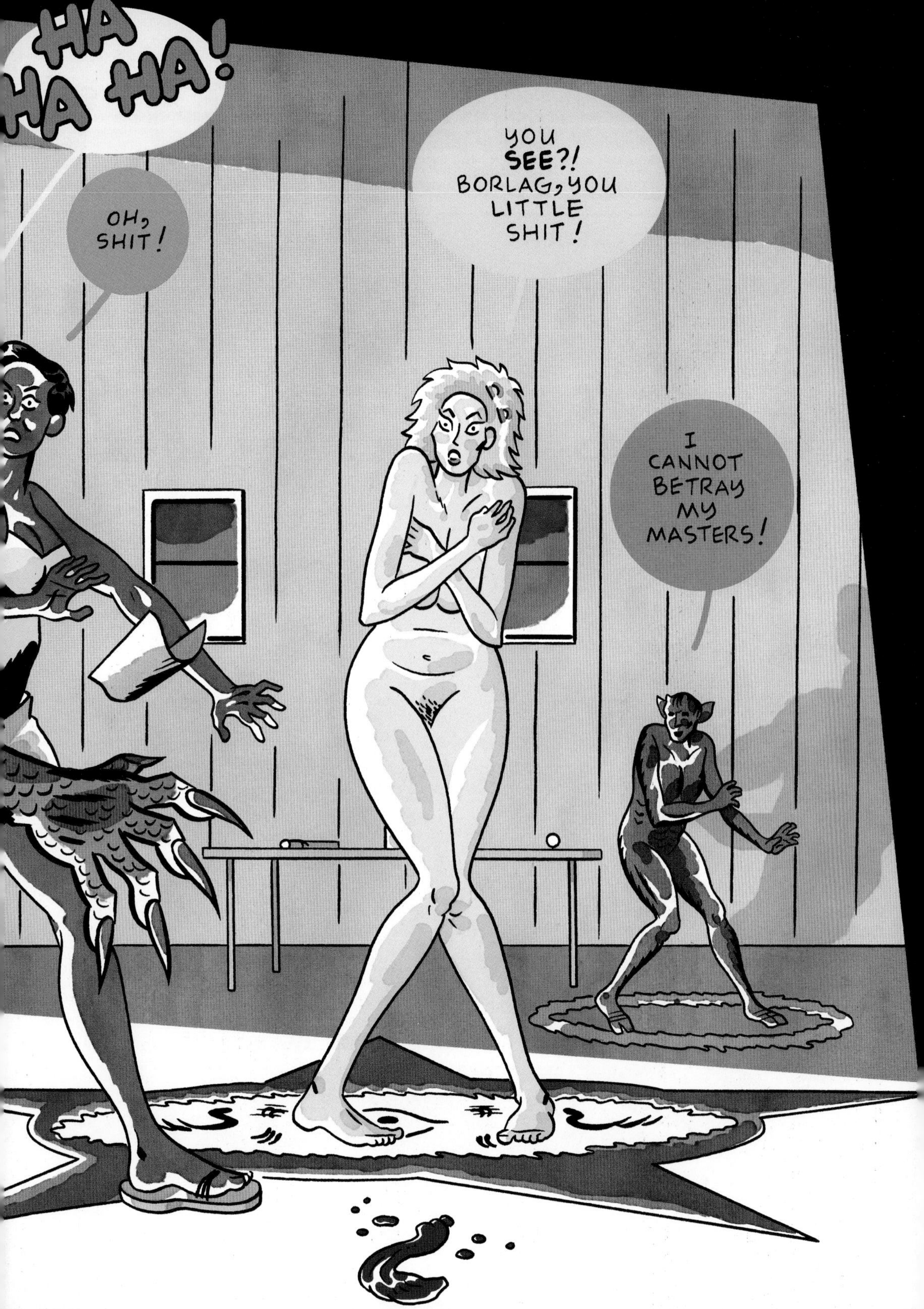
HA HA HA!
OH, SHIT!
YOU SEE?! BORLAG, YOU LITTLE SHIT!
I CANNOT BETRAY MY MASTERS!

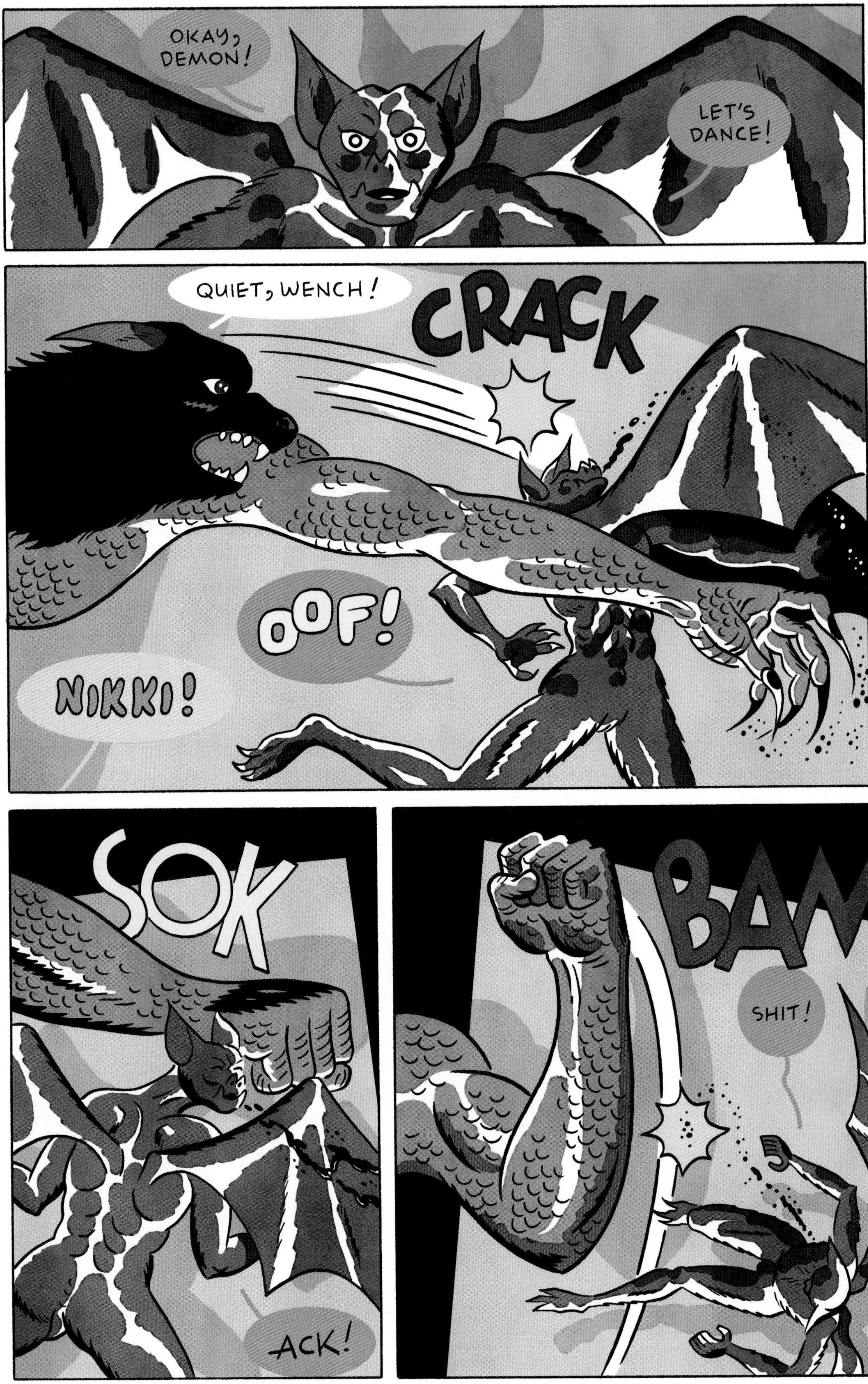
OKAY, DEMON!
LET'S DANCE!
QUIET, WENCH!
CRACK
OOF!
NIKKI!
SOK
ACK!
BAM
SHIT!

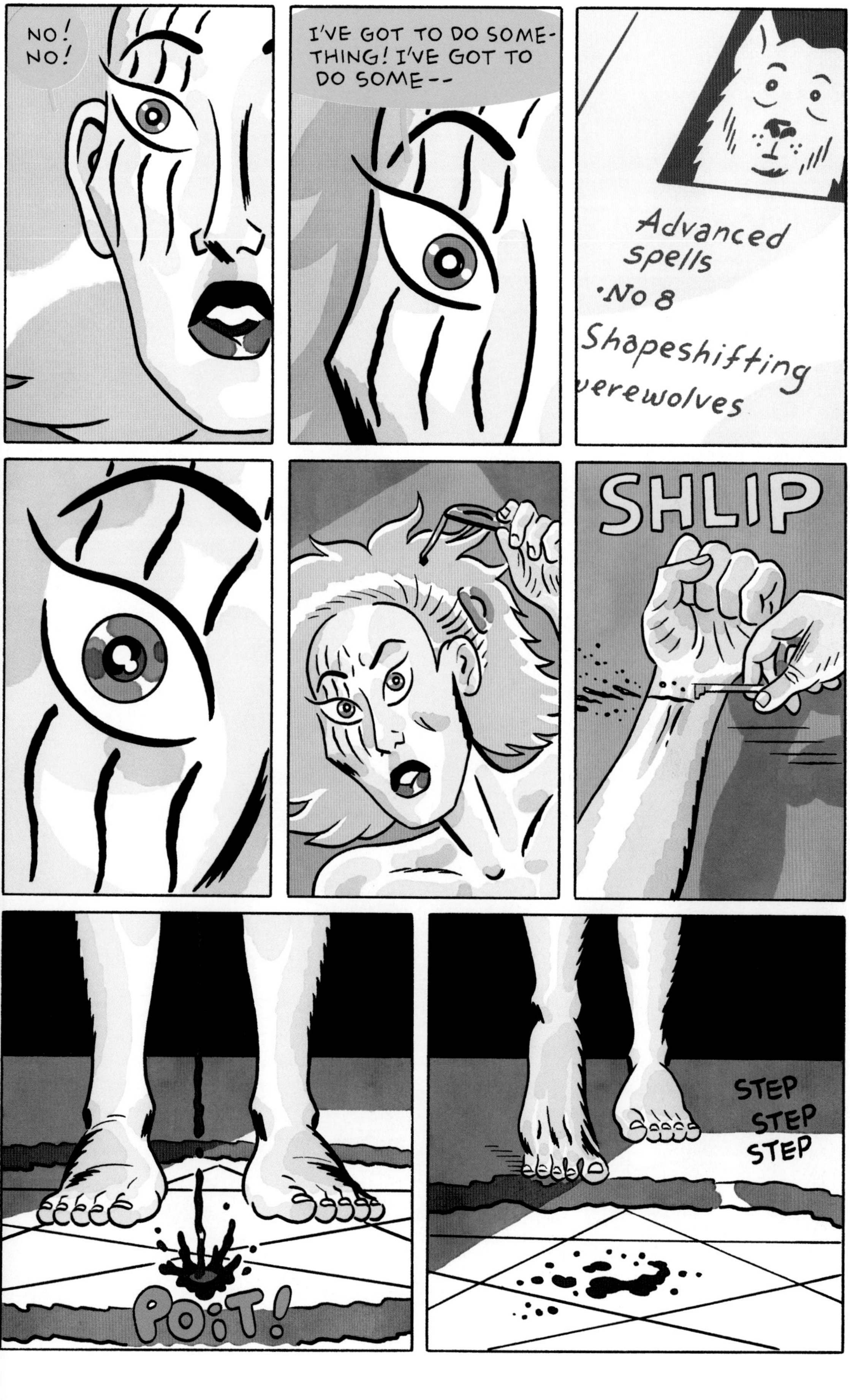
NO! NO!
I'VE GOT TO DO SOMETHING! I'VE GOT TO DO SOME--
Advanced Spells
•No 8
Shapeshifting
werewolves
SHLIP
POiT!
STEP STEP STEP

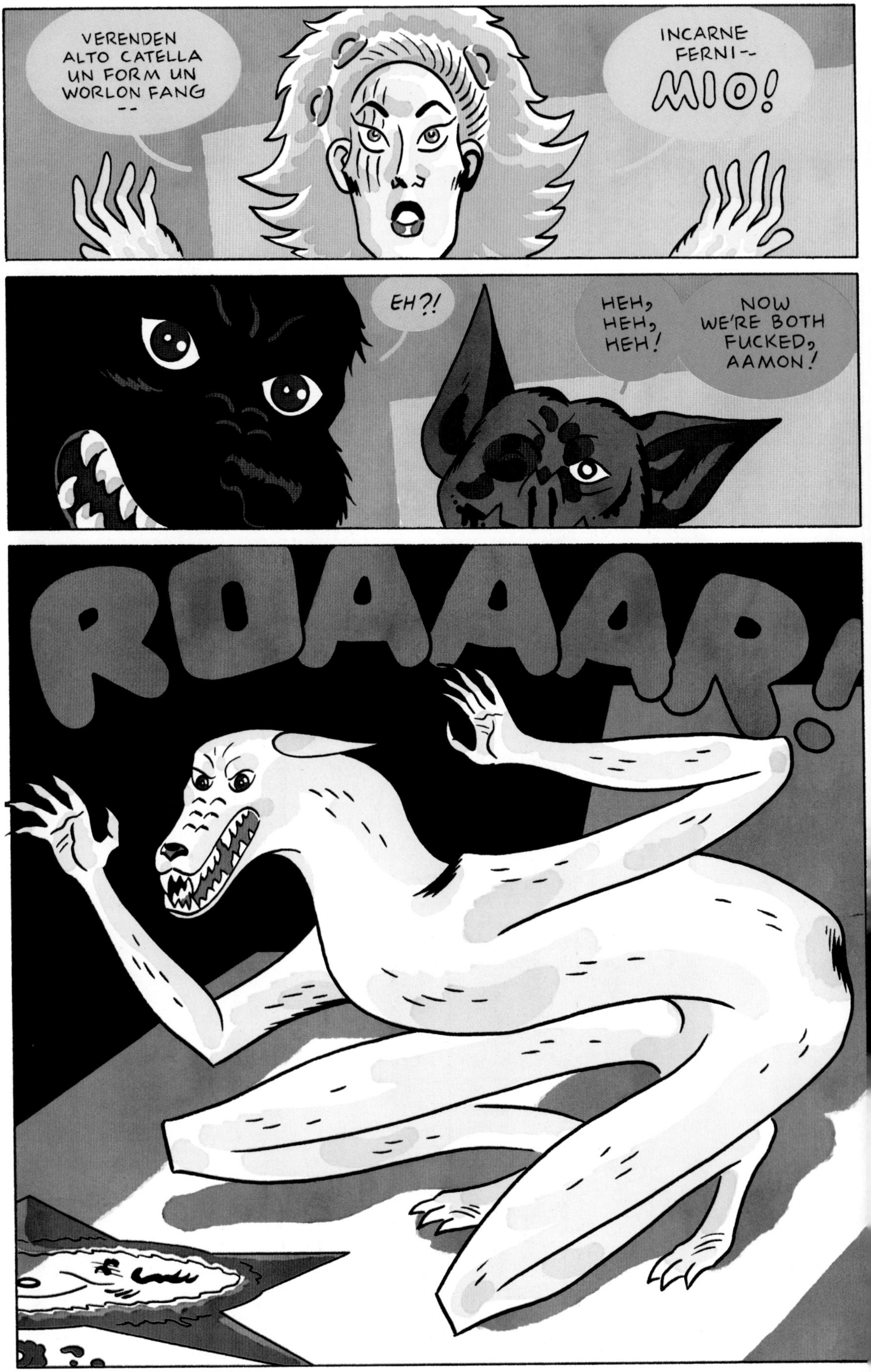
VERENDEN ALTO CATELLA UN FORM UN WORLON FANG --
INCARNE FERNI-- MIO!
EH?!
HEH, HEH, HEH!
NOW WE'RE BOTH FUCKED, AAMON!
ROAAAR!

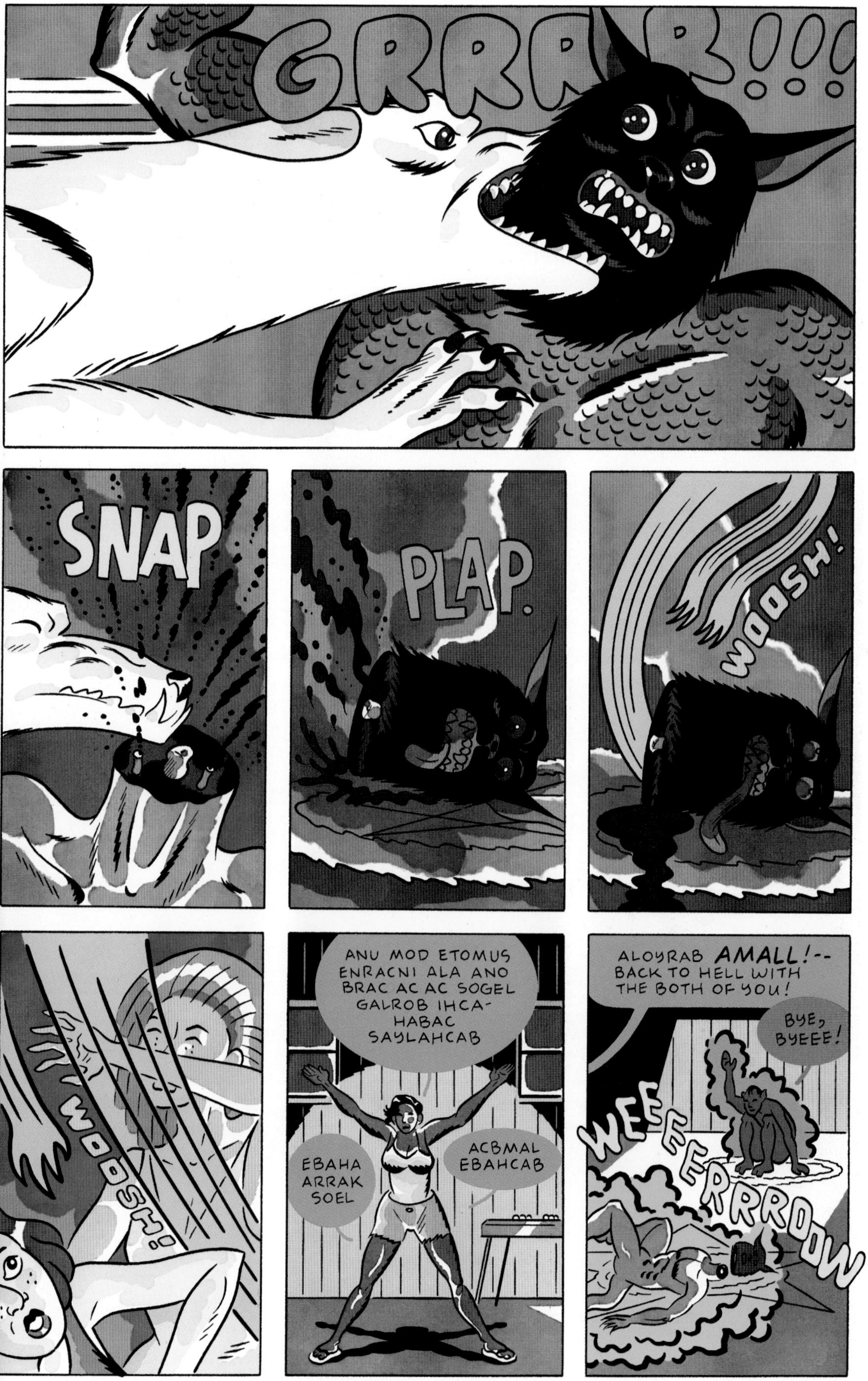
GRRAR!!!
SNAP
PLAP.
WOOSH!
WOOSH!
ANU MOD ETOMUS ENRACNI ALA ANO BRAC AC AC SOGEL GALROB IHCA-HABAC SAYLAHCAB
EBAHA ARRAK SOEL
ACBMAL EBAHCAB
ALOYRAB AMALL!-- BACK TO HELL WITH THE BOTH OF YOU!
BYE, BYEEE!
WEEERRRROOW

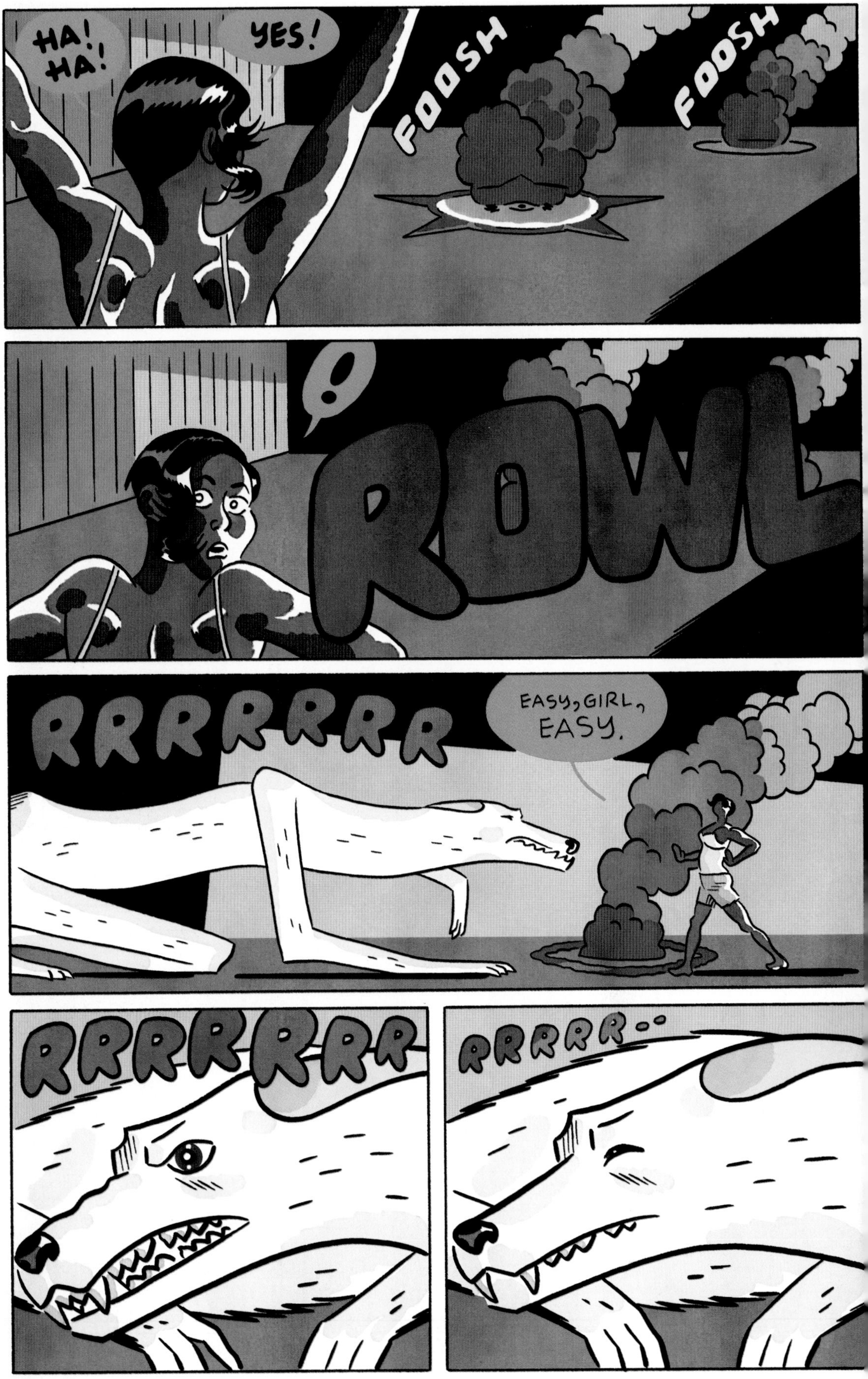
HA! HA!
YES!
FOOSH
FOOSH
!
ROWL
RRRRRRRR
EASY, GIRL, EASY.
RRRRRRRR
RRRRR..

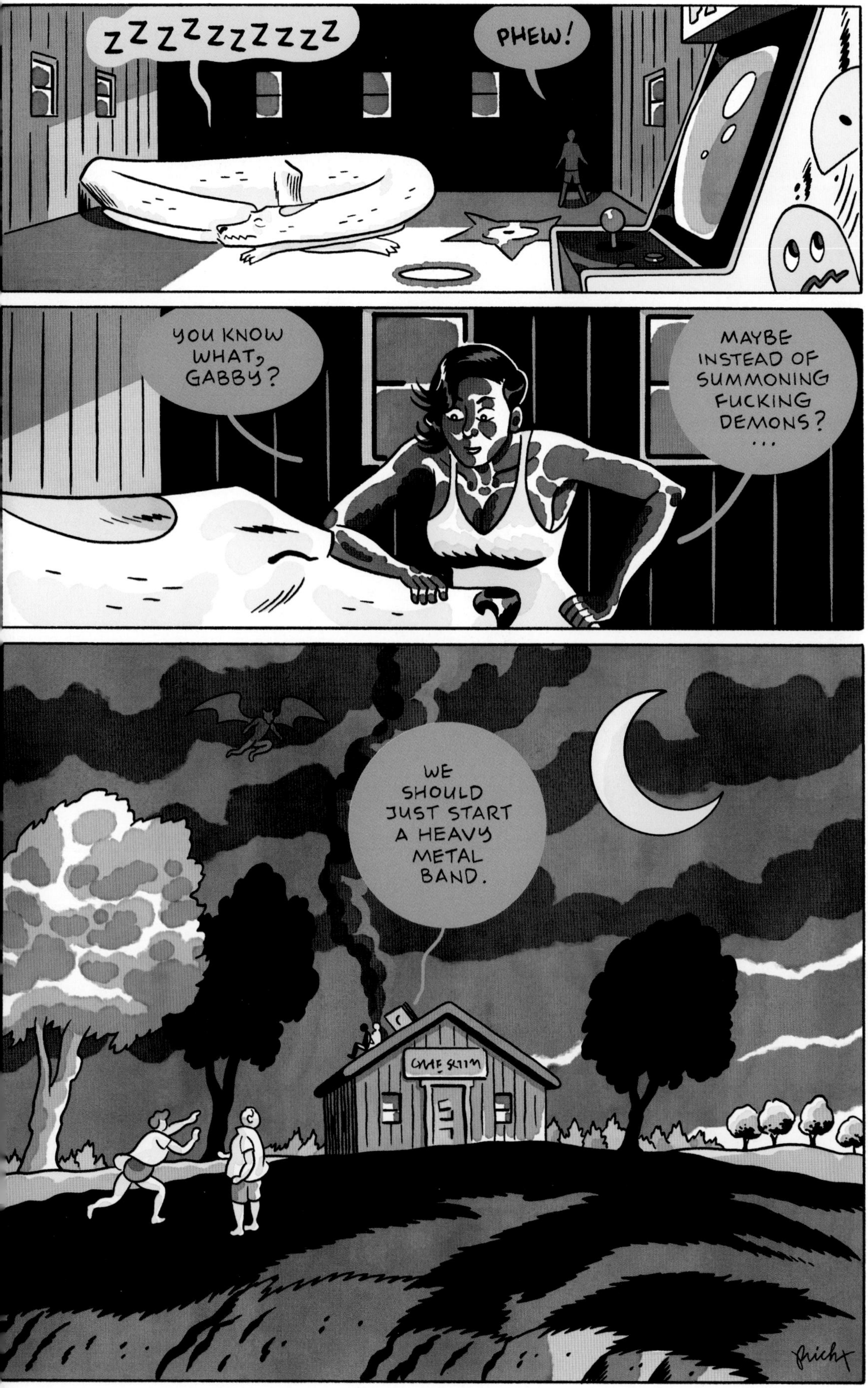
ZZZZZZZZZZZ
PHEW!
YOU KNOW WHAT, GABBY?
MAYBE INSTEAD OF SUMMONING FUCKING DEMONS? ...
WE SHOULD JUST START A HEAVY METAL BAND.

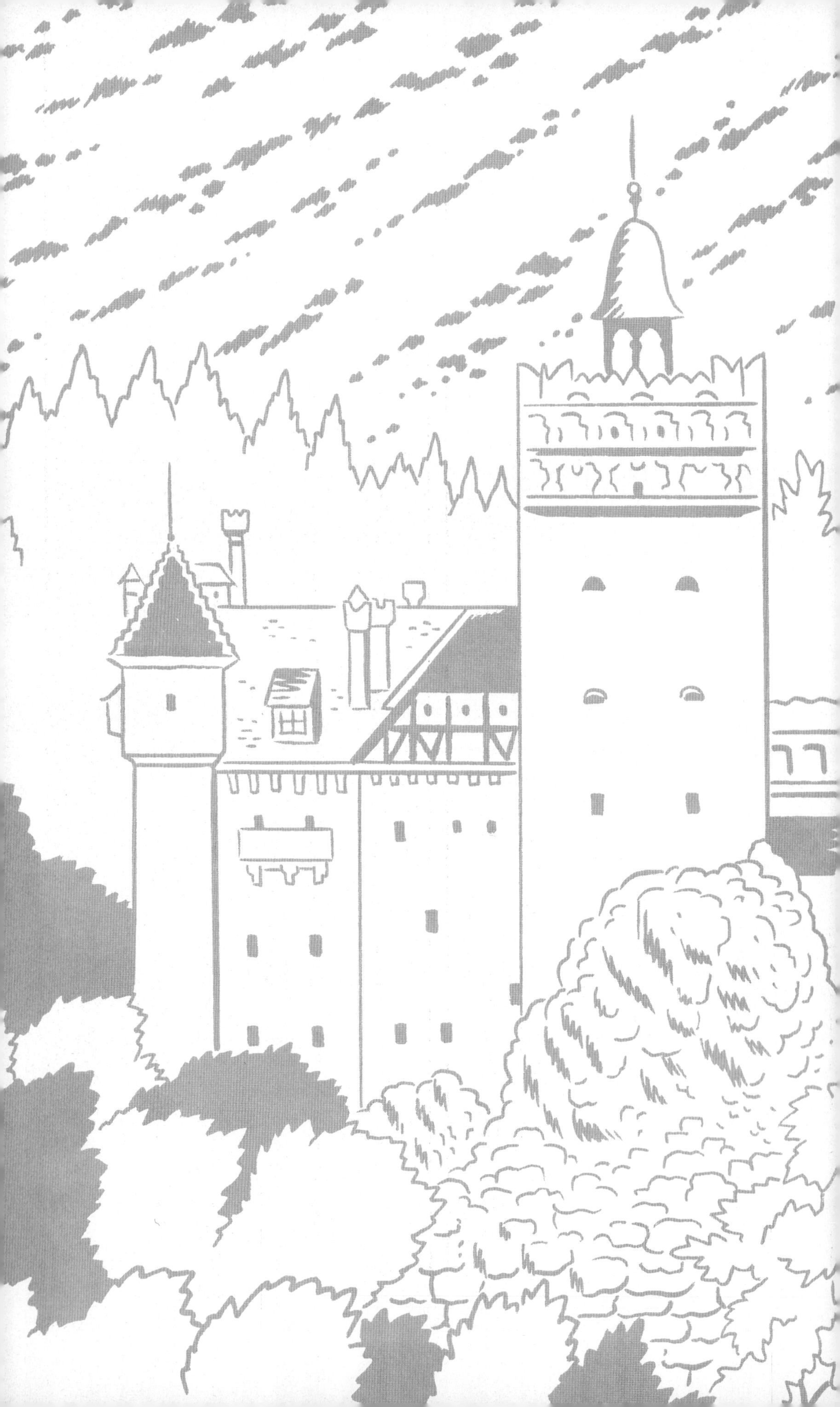

Extra Bonus Comic

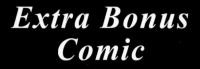

KING BLOOD

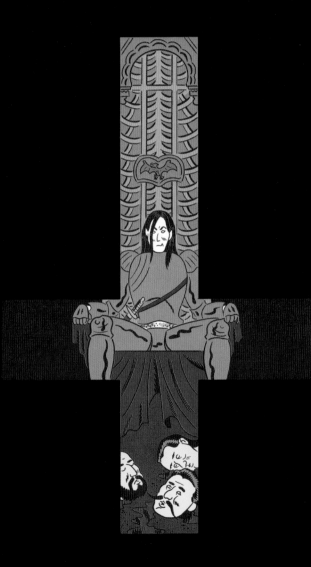

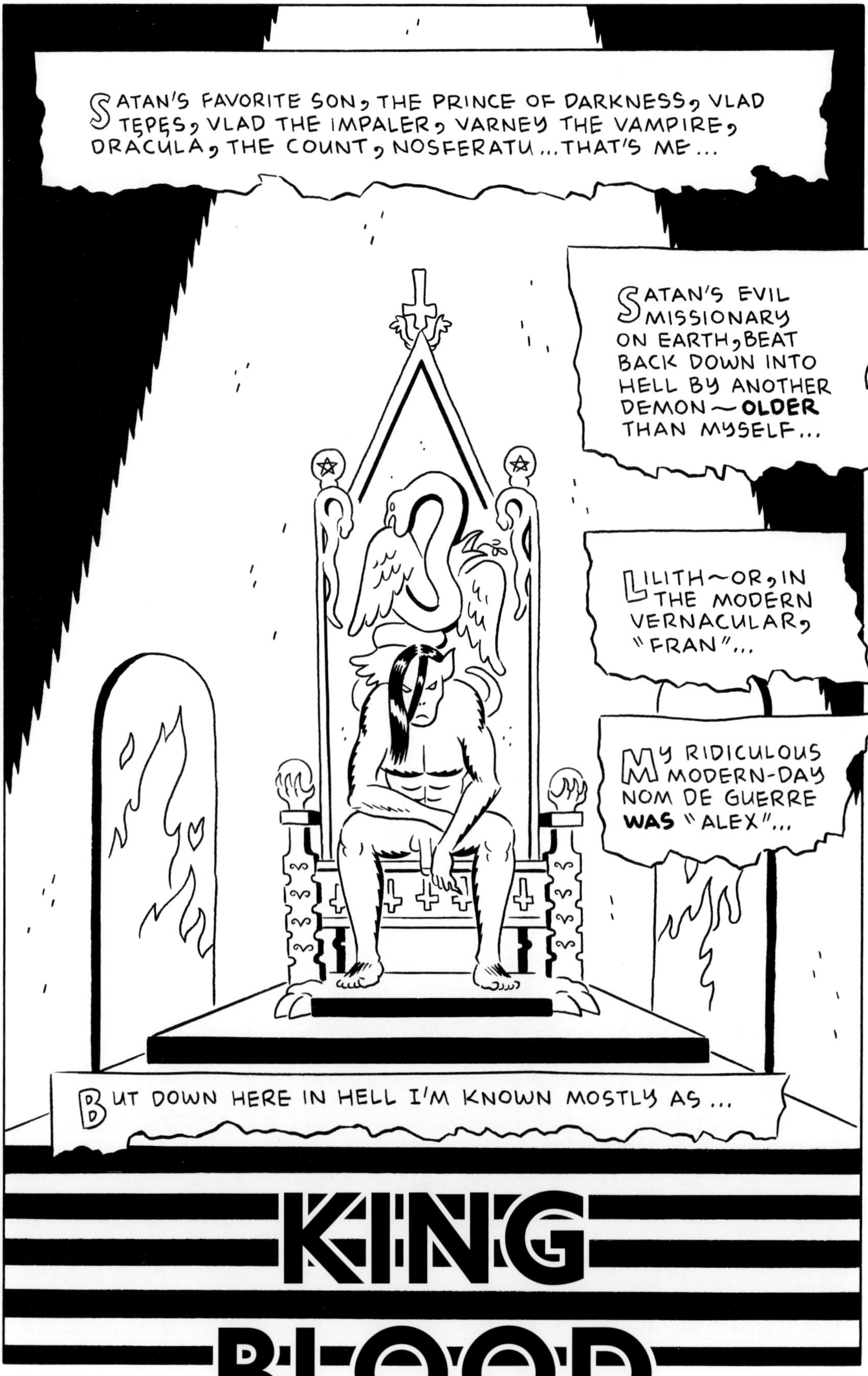
SATAN'S FAVORITE SON, THE PRINCE OF DARKNESS, VLAD TEPES, VLAD THE IMPALER, VARNEY THE VAMPIRE, DRACULA, THE COUNT, NOSFERATU...THAT'S ME...
SATAN'S EVIL MISSIONARY ON EARTH, BEAT BACK DOWN INTO HELL BY ANOTHER DEMON~**OLDER** THAN MYSELF...
LILITH~OR, IN THE MODERN VERNACULAR, "FRAN"...
MY RIDICULOUS MODERN-DAY NOM DE GUERRE **WAS** "ALEX"...
BUT DOWN HERE IN HELL I'M KNOWN MOSTLY AS...
KING
BLOOD

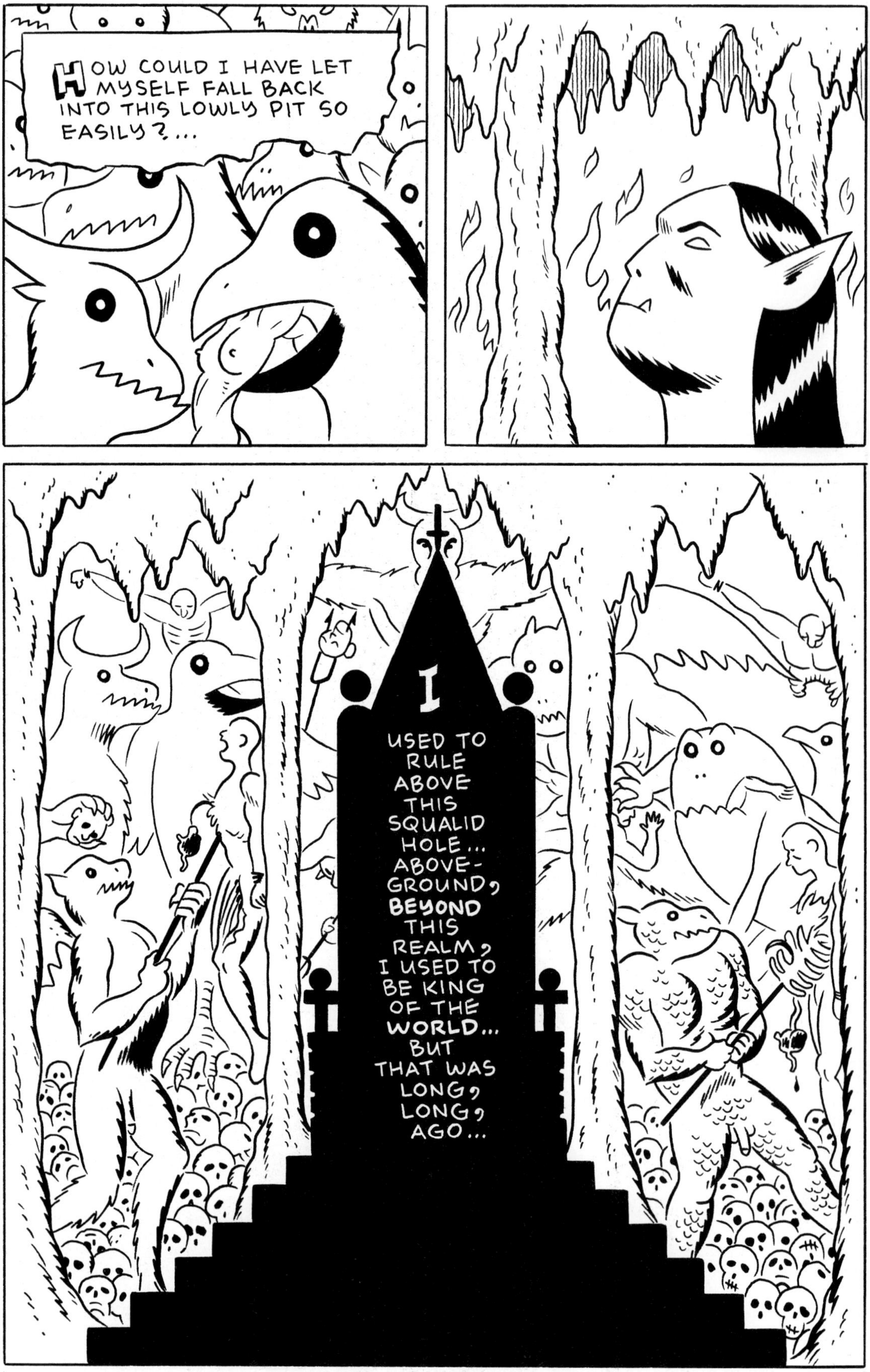
HOW COULD I HAVE LET MYSELF FALL BACK INTO THIS LOWLY PIT SO EASILY?...
I USED TO RULE ABOVE THIS SQUALID HOLE... ABOVE-GROUND, **BEYOND** THIS REALM, I USED TO BE KING OF THE **WORLD**... BUT THAT WAS LONG, LONG, AGO...

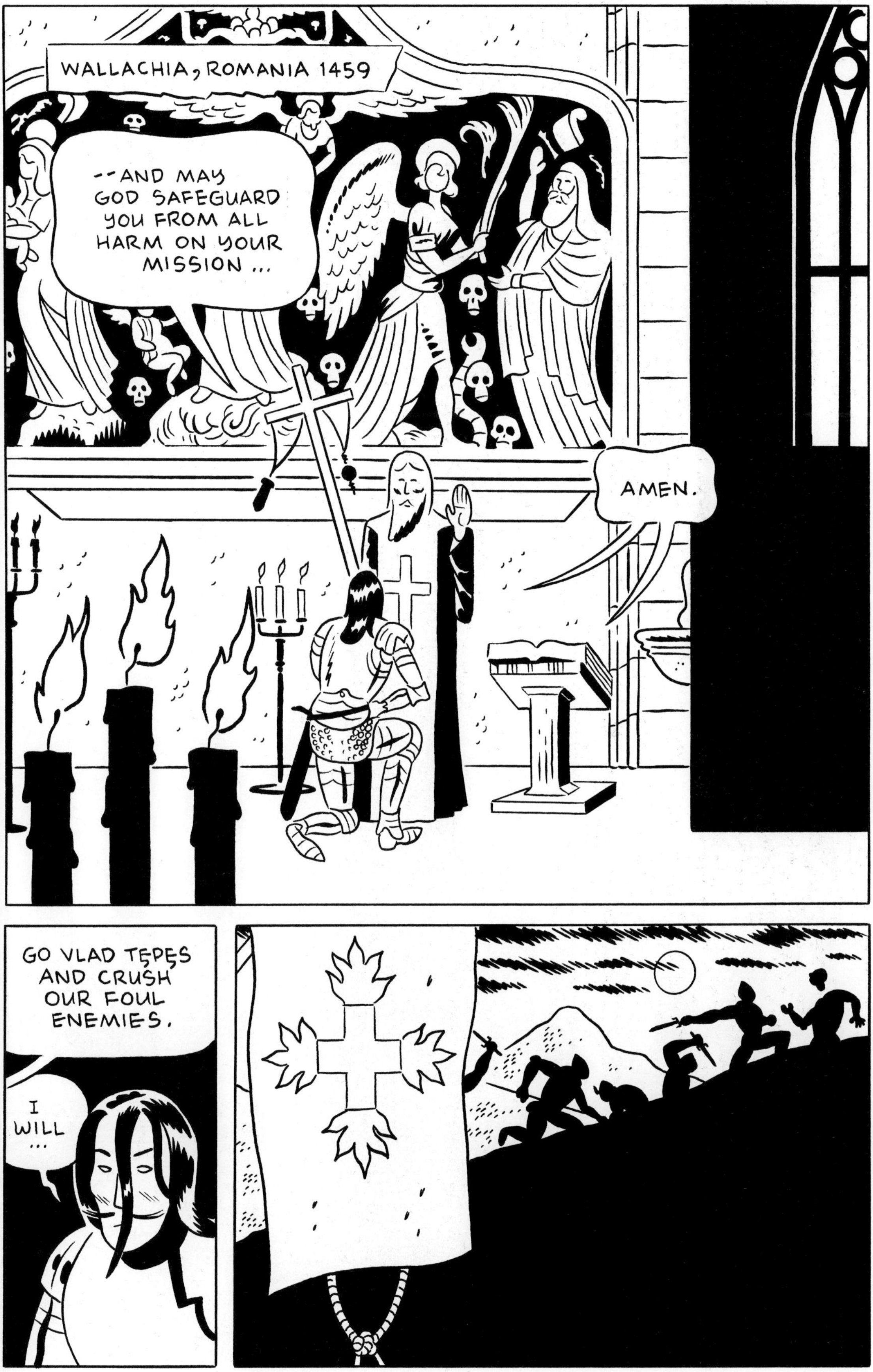
WALLACHIA, ROMANIA 1459
--AND MAY GOD SAFEGUARD YOU FROM ALL HARM ON YOUR MISSION ...
AMEN.
GO VLAD ŢEPEŞ AND CRUSH OUR FOUL ENEMIES.
I WILL ...

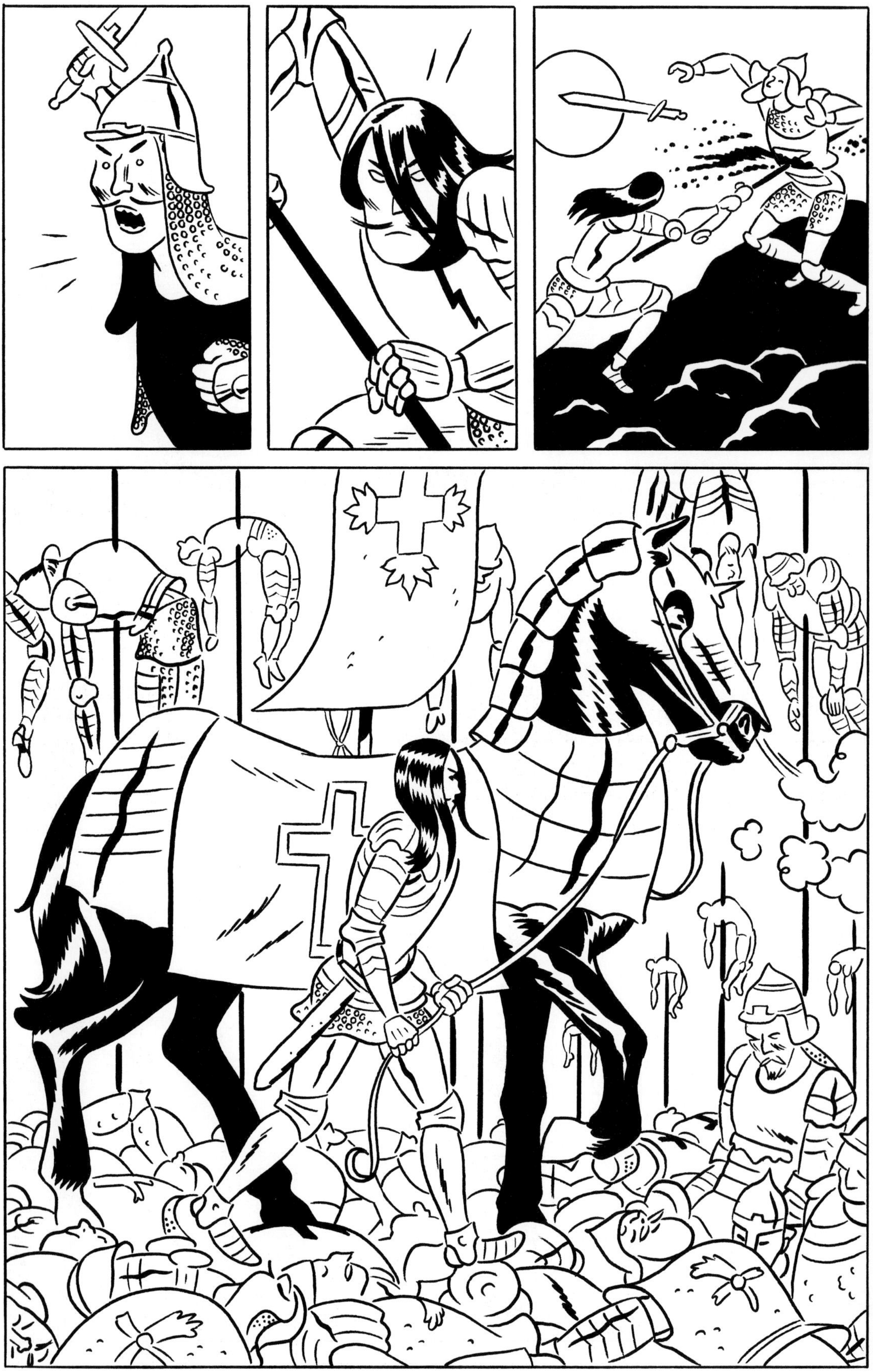

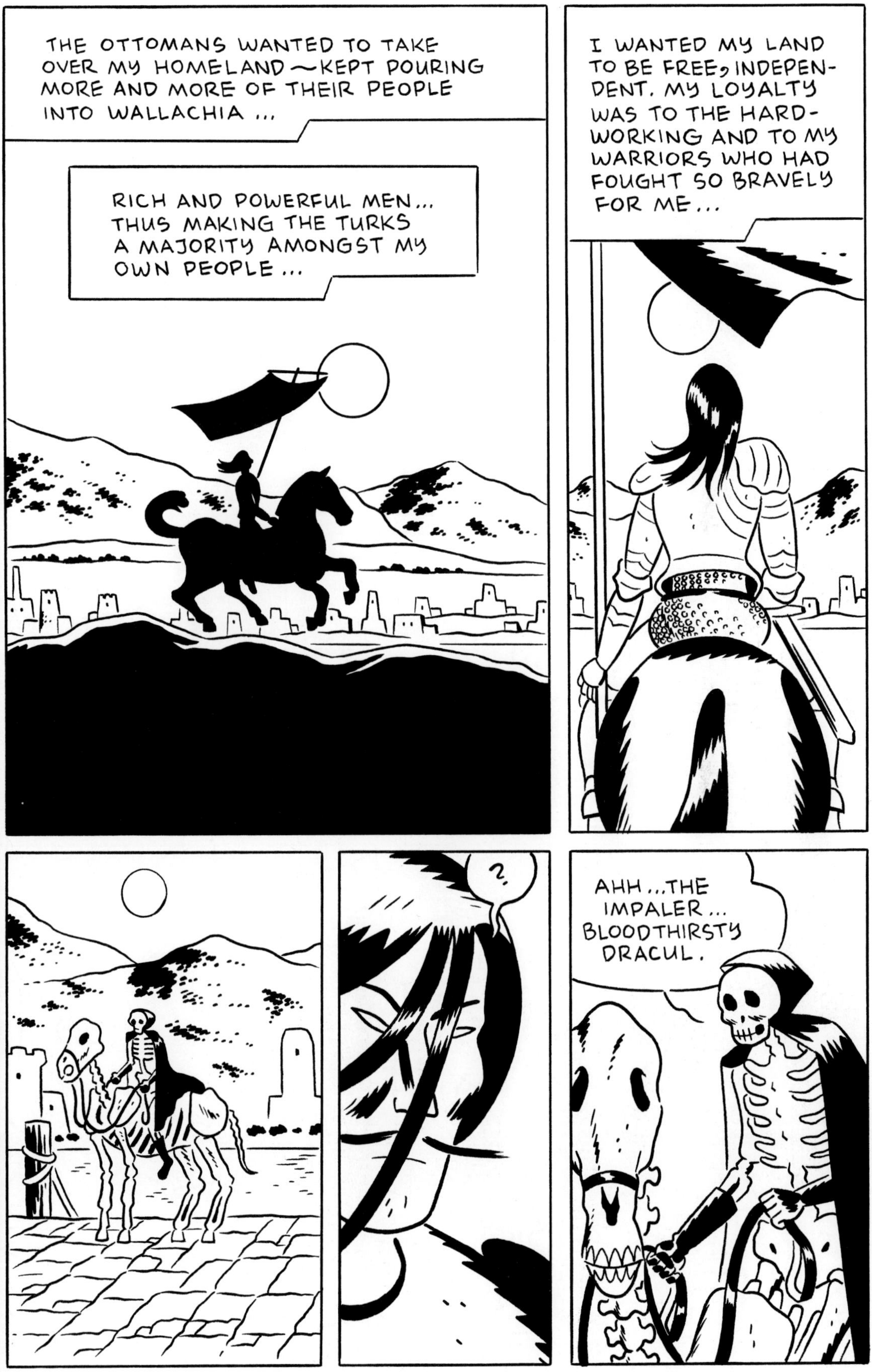
THE OTTOMANS WANTED TO TAKE OVER MY HOMELAND~KEPT POURING MORE AND MORE OF THEIR PEOPLE INTO WALLACHIA ...
RICH AND POWERFUL MEN... THUS MAKING THE TURKS A MAJORITY AMONGST MY OWN PEOPLE...
I WANTED MY LAND TO BE FREE, INDEPENDENT. MY LOYALTY WAS TO THE HARD-WORKING AND TO MY WARRIORS WHO HAD FOUGHT SO BRAVELY FOR ME...
?
AHH...THE IMPALER... BLOODTHIRSTY DRACUL.

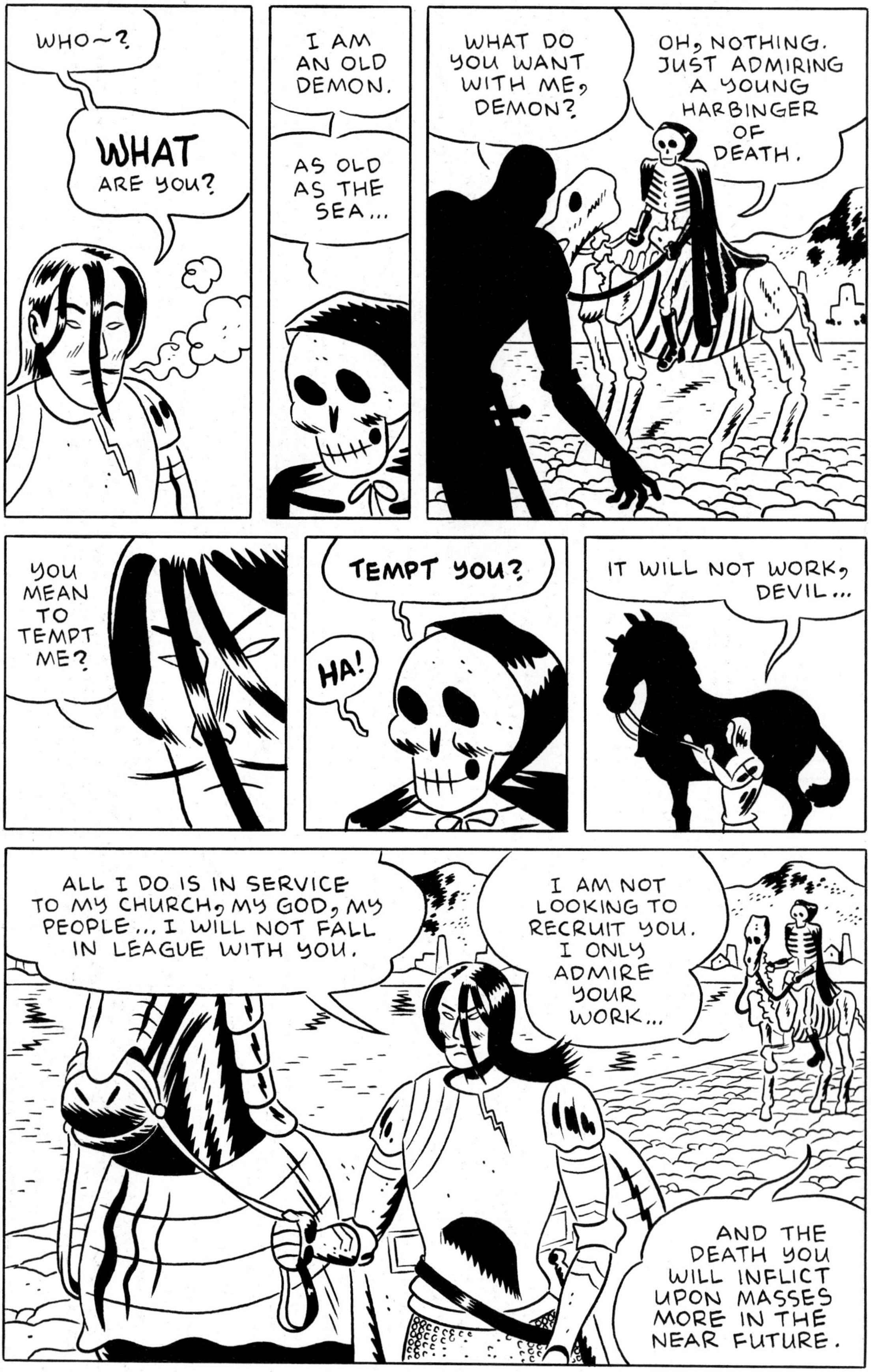
WHO~?
WHAT ARE YOU?
I AM AN OLD DEMON.
AS OLD AS THE SEA...
WHAT DO YOU WANT WITH ME, DEMON?
OH, NOTHING. JUST ADMIRING A YOUNG HARBINGER OF DEATH.
YOU MEAN TO TEMPT ME?
HA!
TEMPT YOU?
IT WILL NOT WORK, DEVIL...
ALL I DO IS IN SERVICE TO MY CHURCH, MY GOD, MY PEOPLE... I WILL NOT FALL IN LEAGUE WITH YOU.
I AM NOT LOOKING TO RECRUIT YOU. I ONLY ADMIRE YOUR WORK...
AND THE DEATH YOU WILL INFLICT UPON MASSES MORE IN THE NEAR FUTURE.

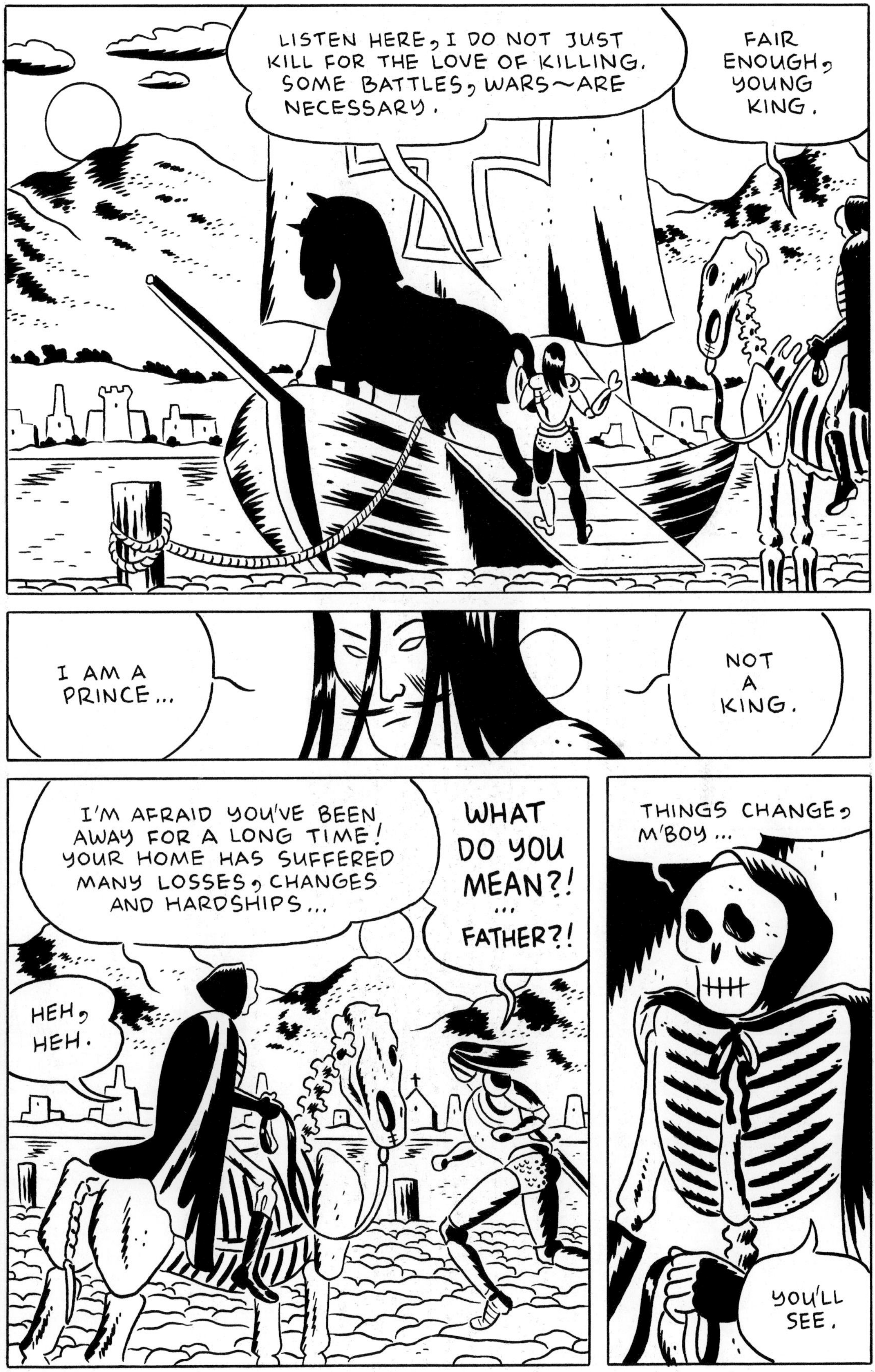

LISTEN HERE, I DO NOT JUST KILL FOR THE LOVE OF KILLING. SOME BATTLES, WARS~ARE NECESSARY.
FAIR ENOUGH, YOUNG KING.
I AM A PRINCE...
NOT A KING.
I'M AFRAID YOU'VE BEEN AWAY FOR A LONG TIME! YOUR HOME HAS SUFFERED MANY LOSSES, CHANGES AND HARDSHIPS...
WHAT DO YOU MEAN?! ... FATHER?!
HEH, HEH.
THINGS CHANGE, M'BOY...
YOU'LL SEE.

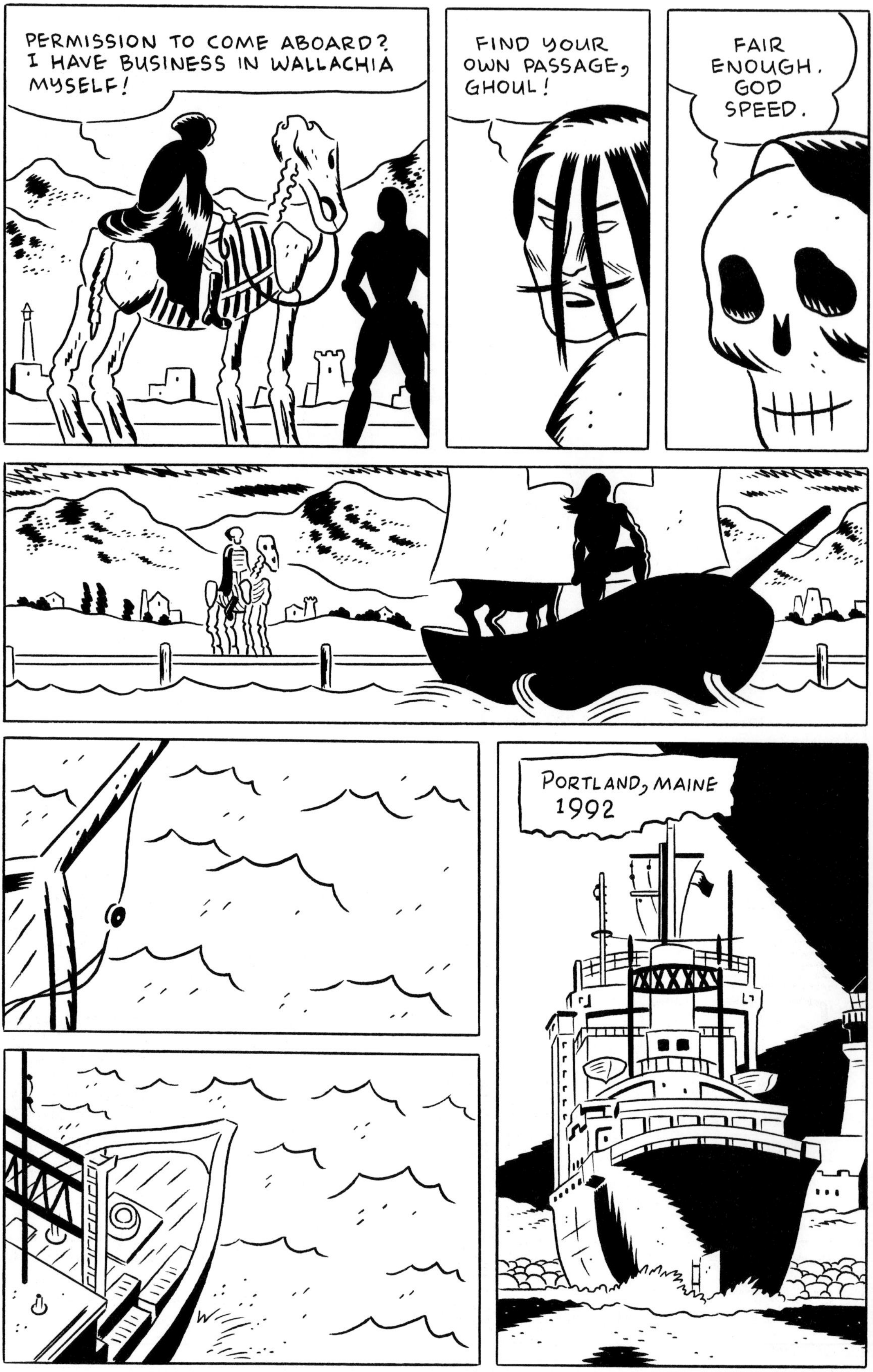
PERMISSION TO COME ABOARD? I HAVE BUSINESS IN WALLACHIA MYSELF!
FIND YOUR OWN PASSAGE, GHOUL!
FAIR ENOUGH. GOD SPEED.
PORTLAND, MAINE 1992

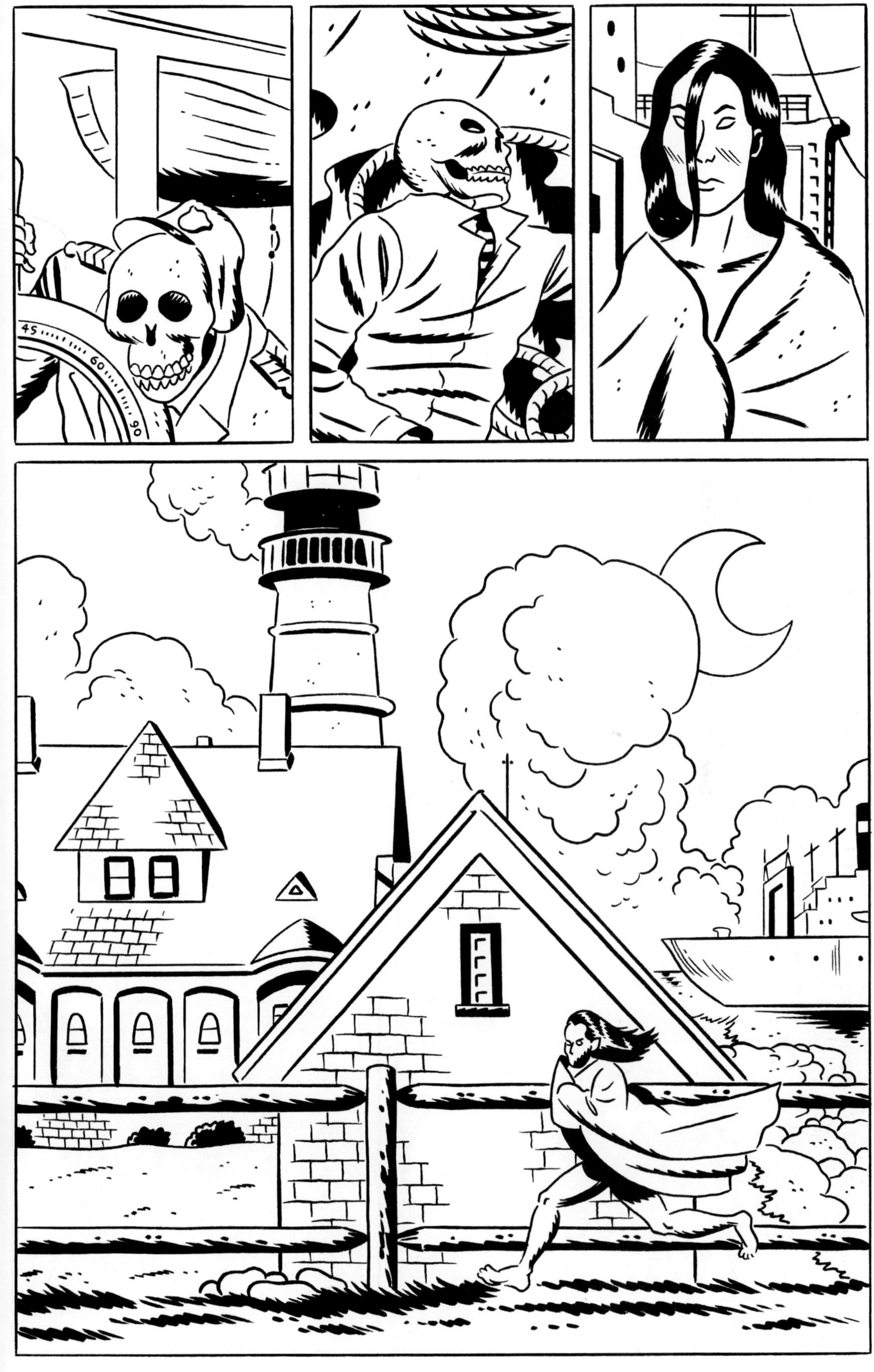
45
60
90

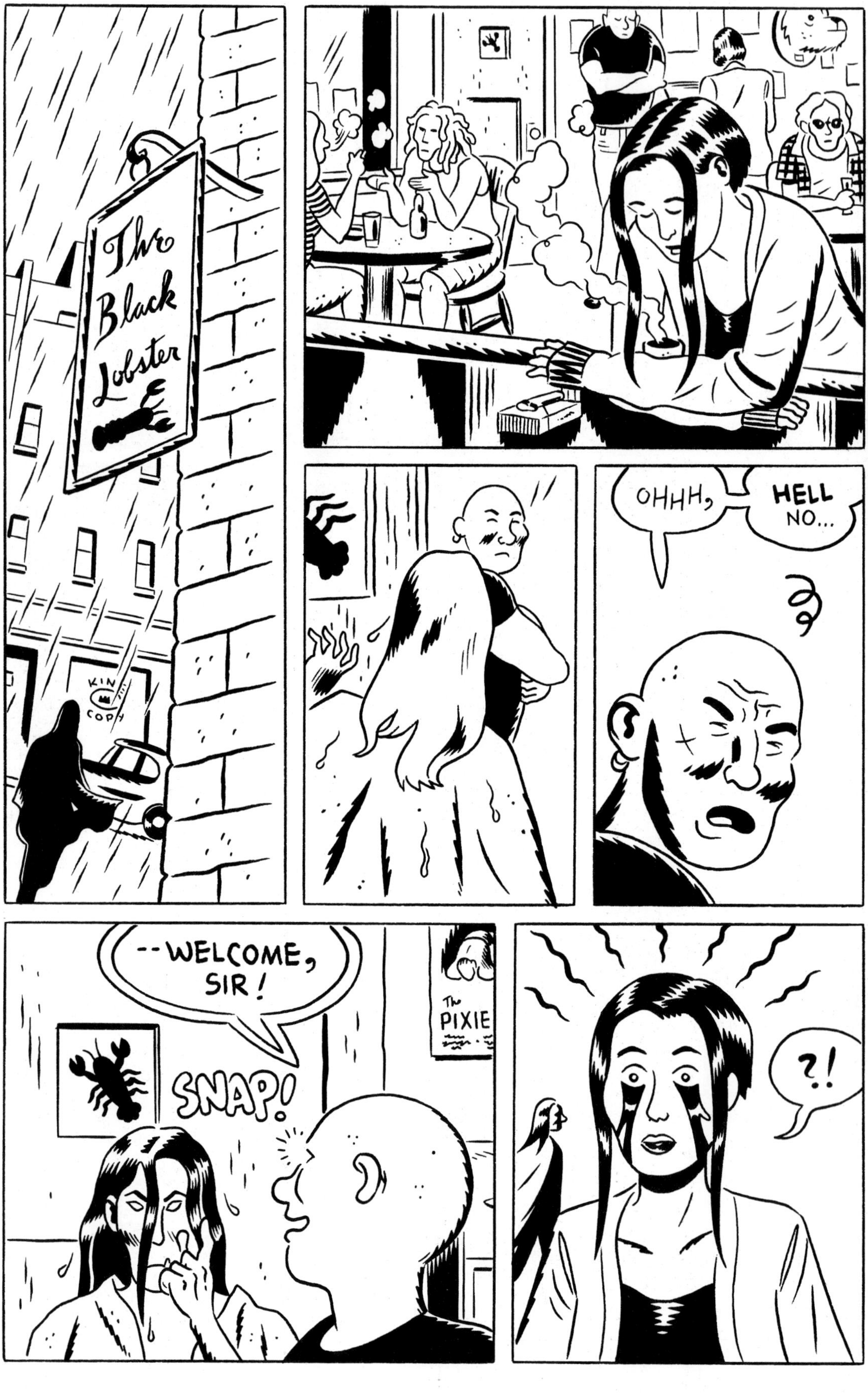
The Black Lobster
KIN COPY
OHHH,
HELL NO...
--WELCOME, SIR!
SNAP!
The PIXIE
?!

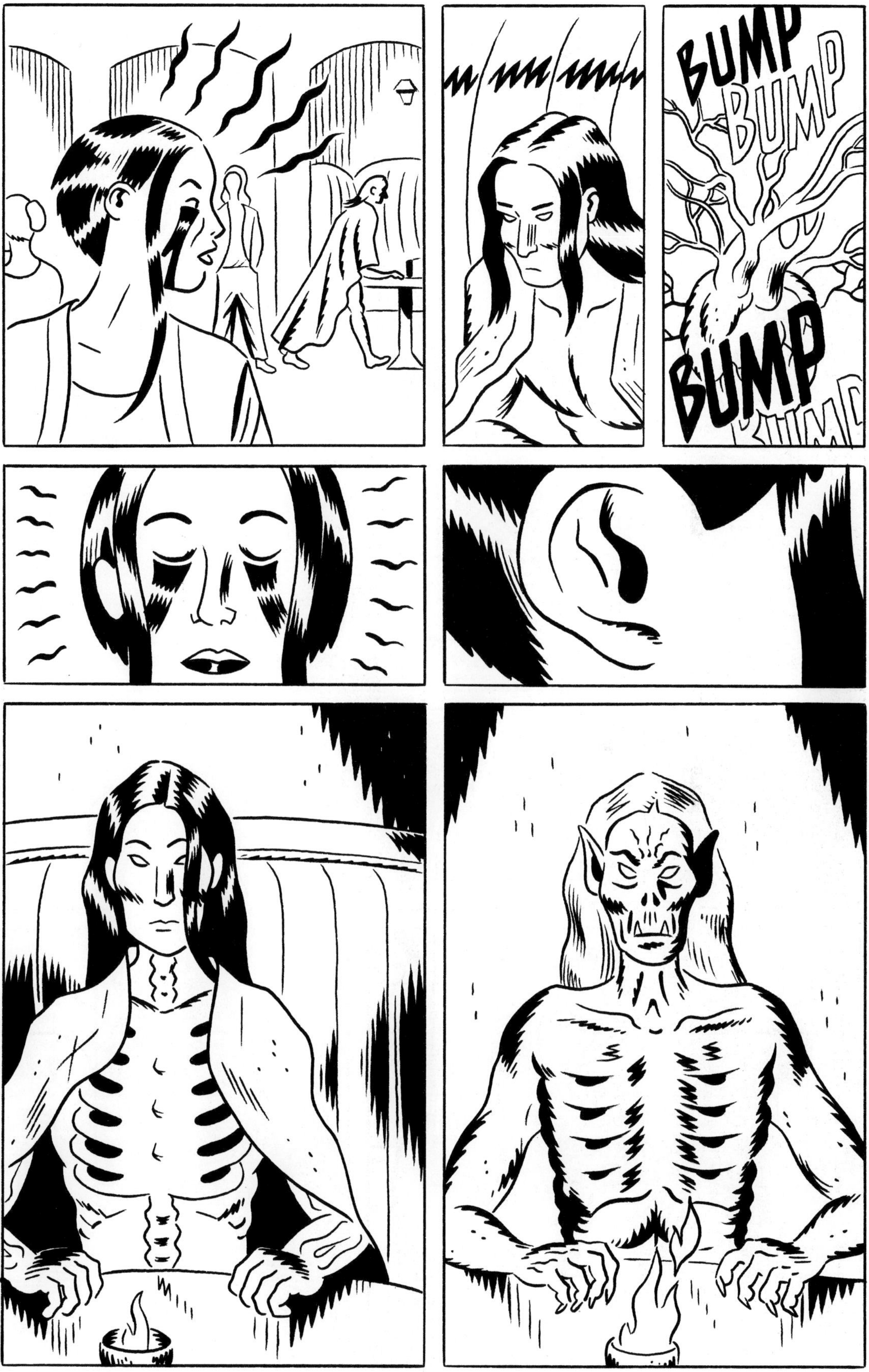
BUMP
BUMP
BUMP

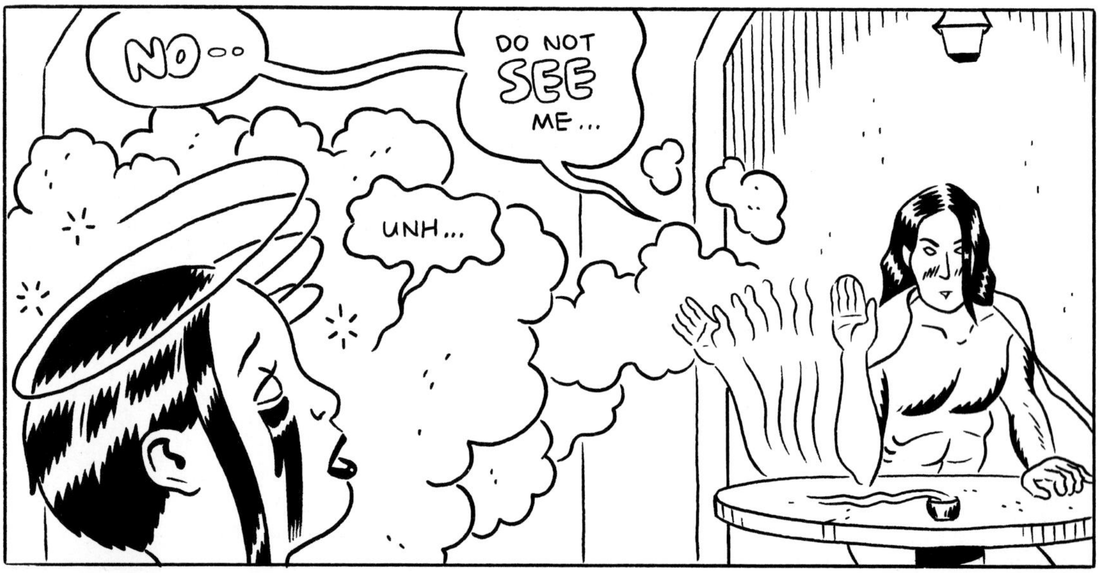
NO..
DO NOT SEE ME...
UNH...

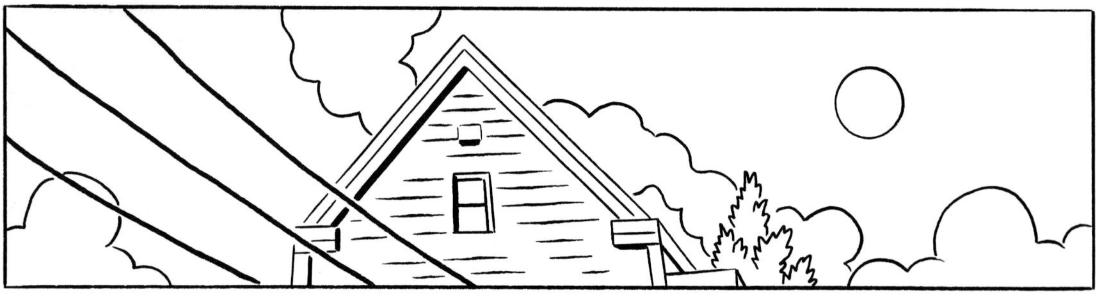

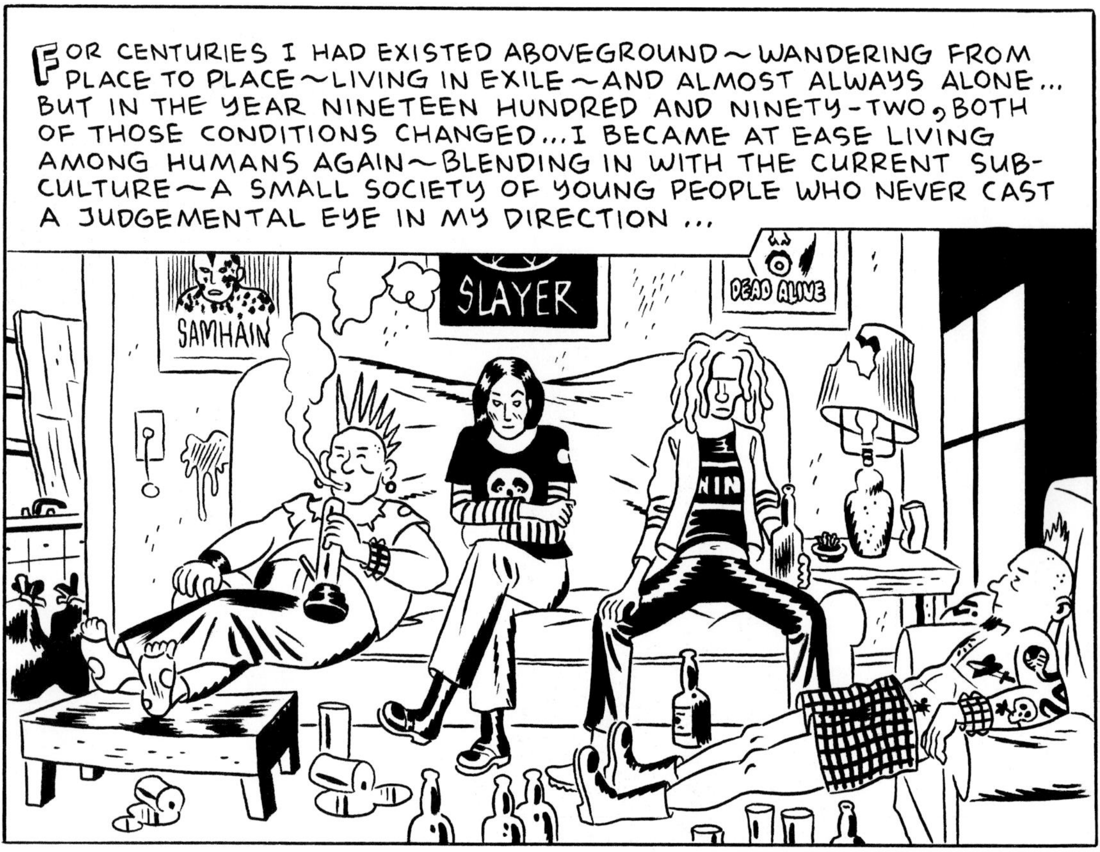
FOR CENTURIES I HAD EXISTED ABOVEGROUND~WANDERING FROM PLACE TO PLACE~LIVING IN EXILE~AND ALMOST ALWAYS ALONE... BUT IN THE YEAR NINETEEN HUNDRED AND NINETY-TWO, BOTH OF THOSE CONDITIONS CHANGED...I BECAME AT EASE LIVING AMONG HUMANS AGAIN~BLENDING IN WITH THE CURRENT SUB-CULTURE~A SMALL SOCIETY OF YOUNG PEOPLE WHO NEVER CAST A JUDGEMENTAL EYE IN MY DIRECTION...
SAMHAIN
SLAYER
DEAD ALIVE
NIN

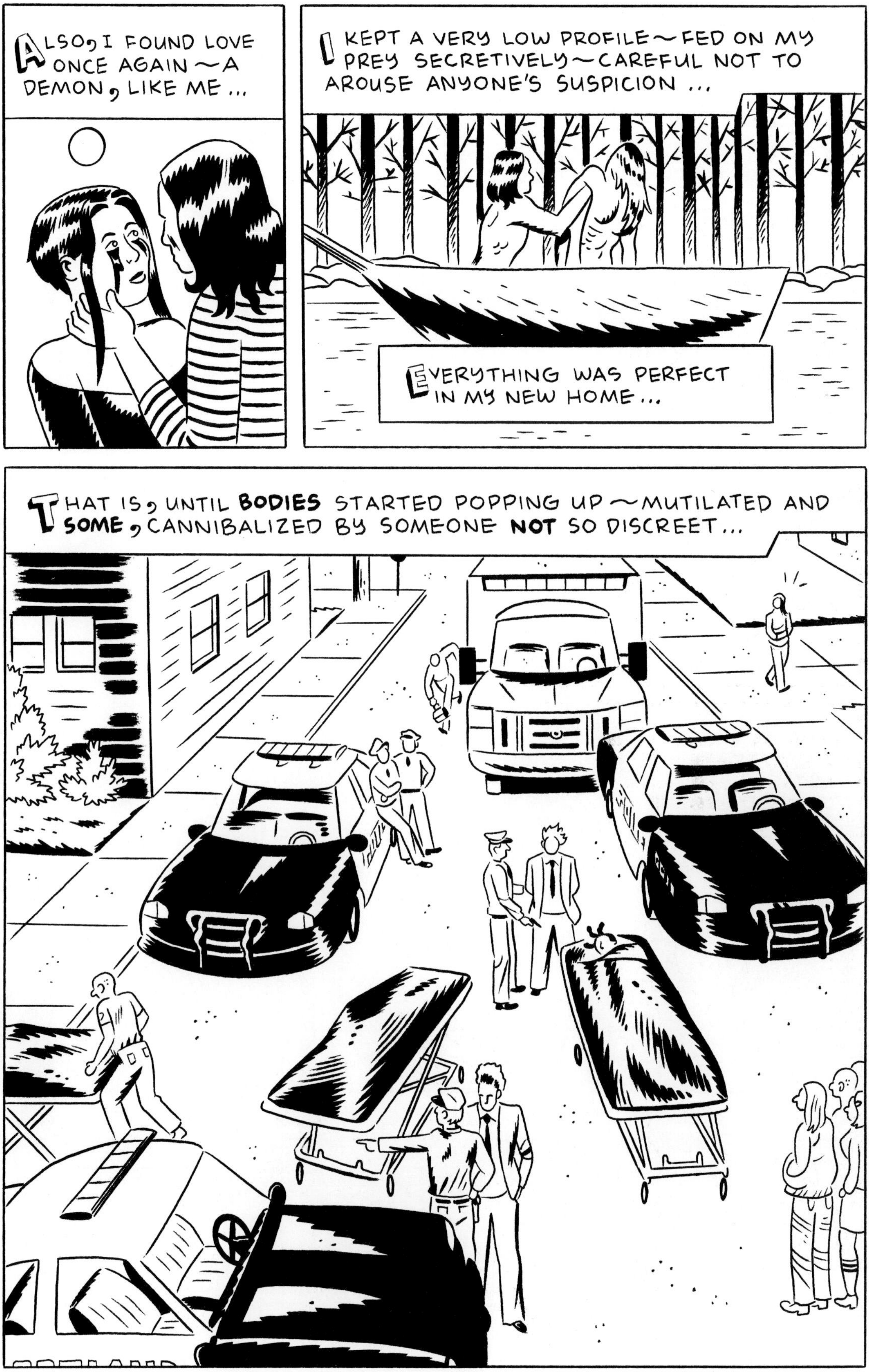
ALSO, I FOUND LOVE ONCE AGAIN ~ A DEMON, LIKE ME...
I KEPT A VERY LOW PROFILE ~ FED ON MY PREY SECRETIVELY ~ CAREFUL NOT TO AROUSE ANYONE'S SUSPICION ...
EVERYTHING WAS PERFECT IN MY NEW HOME...
THAT IS, UNTIL **BODIES** STARTED POPPING UP ~ MUTILATED AND **SOME**, CANNIBALIZED BY SOMEONE **NOT** SO DISCREET...

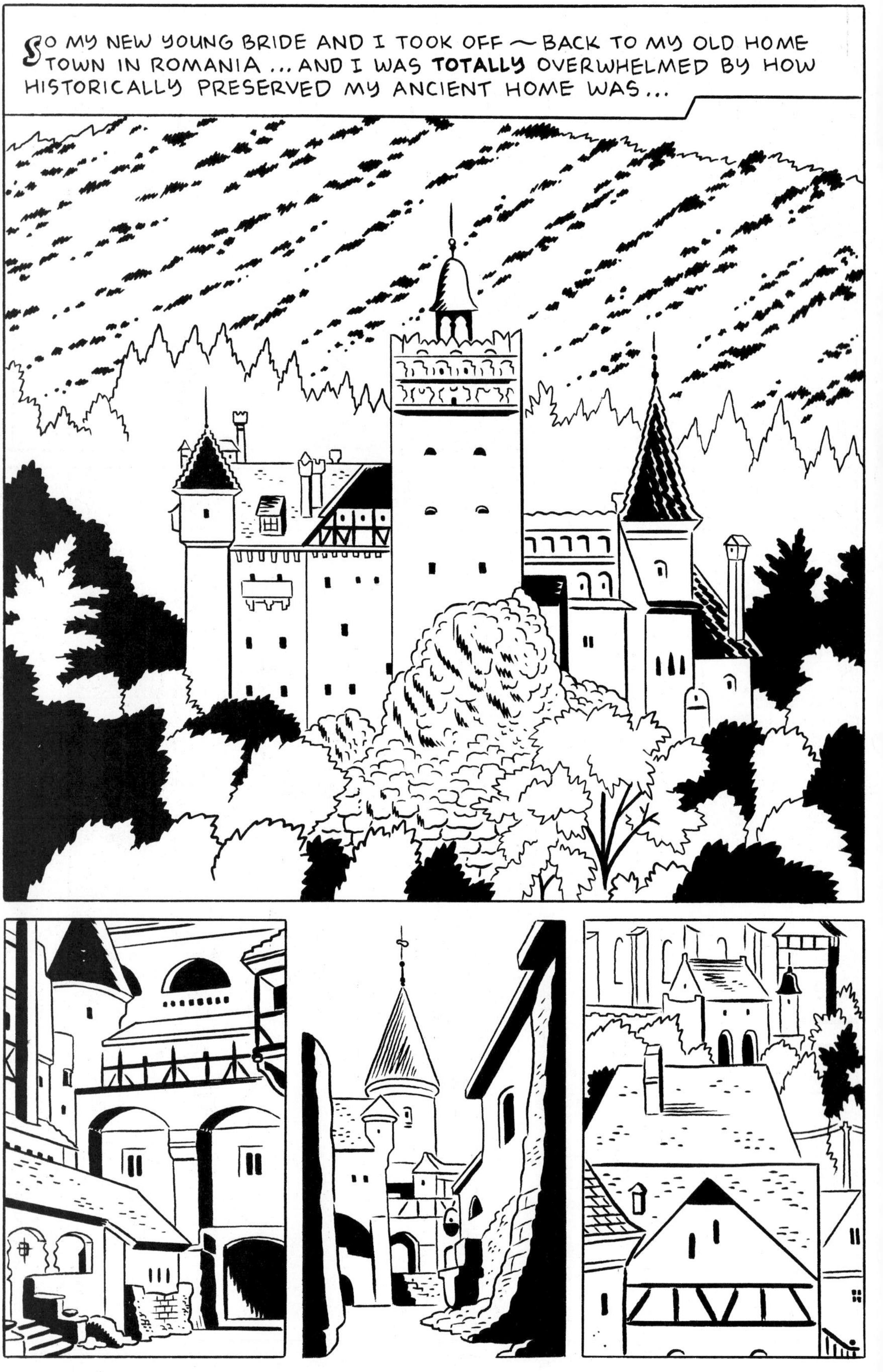
SO MY NEW YOUNG BRIDE AND I TOOK OFF ~ BACK TO MY OLD HOME TOWN IN ROMANIA ... AND I WAS **TOTALLY** OVERWHELMED BY HOW HISTORICALLY PRESERVED MY ANCIENT HOME WAS ...

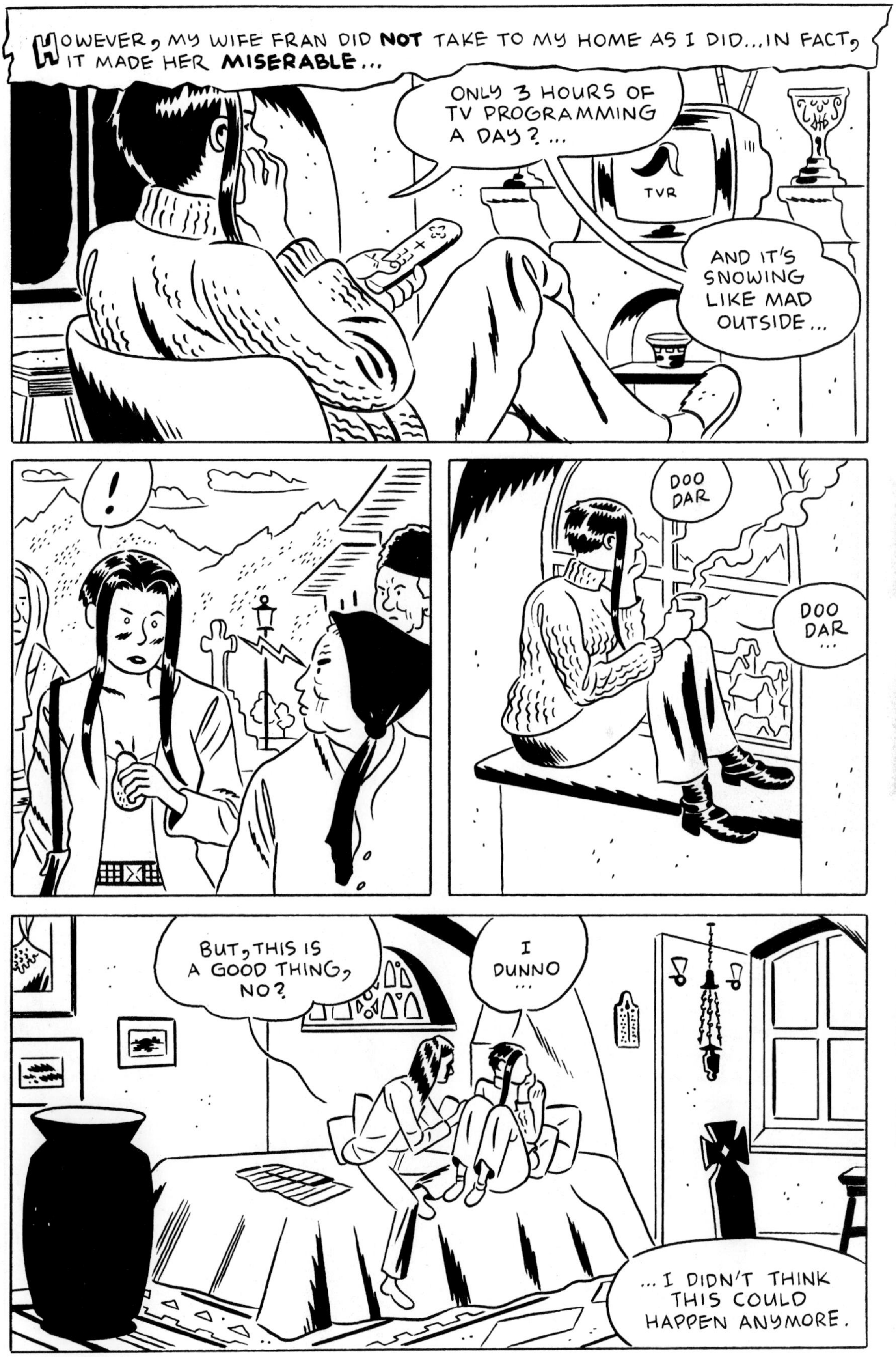
HOWEVER, MY WIFE FRAN DID NOT TAKE TO MY HOME AS I DID...IN FACT, IT MADE HER MISERABLE...
ONLY 3 HOURS OF TV PROGRAMMING A DAY?...
TVR
AND IT'S SNOWING LIKE MAD OUTSIDE...
!
DOO DAR
DOO DAR ...
BUT, THIS IS A GOOD THING, NO?
I DUNNO ...
...I DIDN'T THINK THIS COULD HAPPEN ANYMORE.

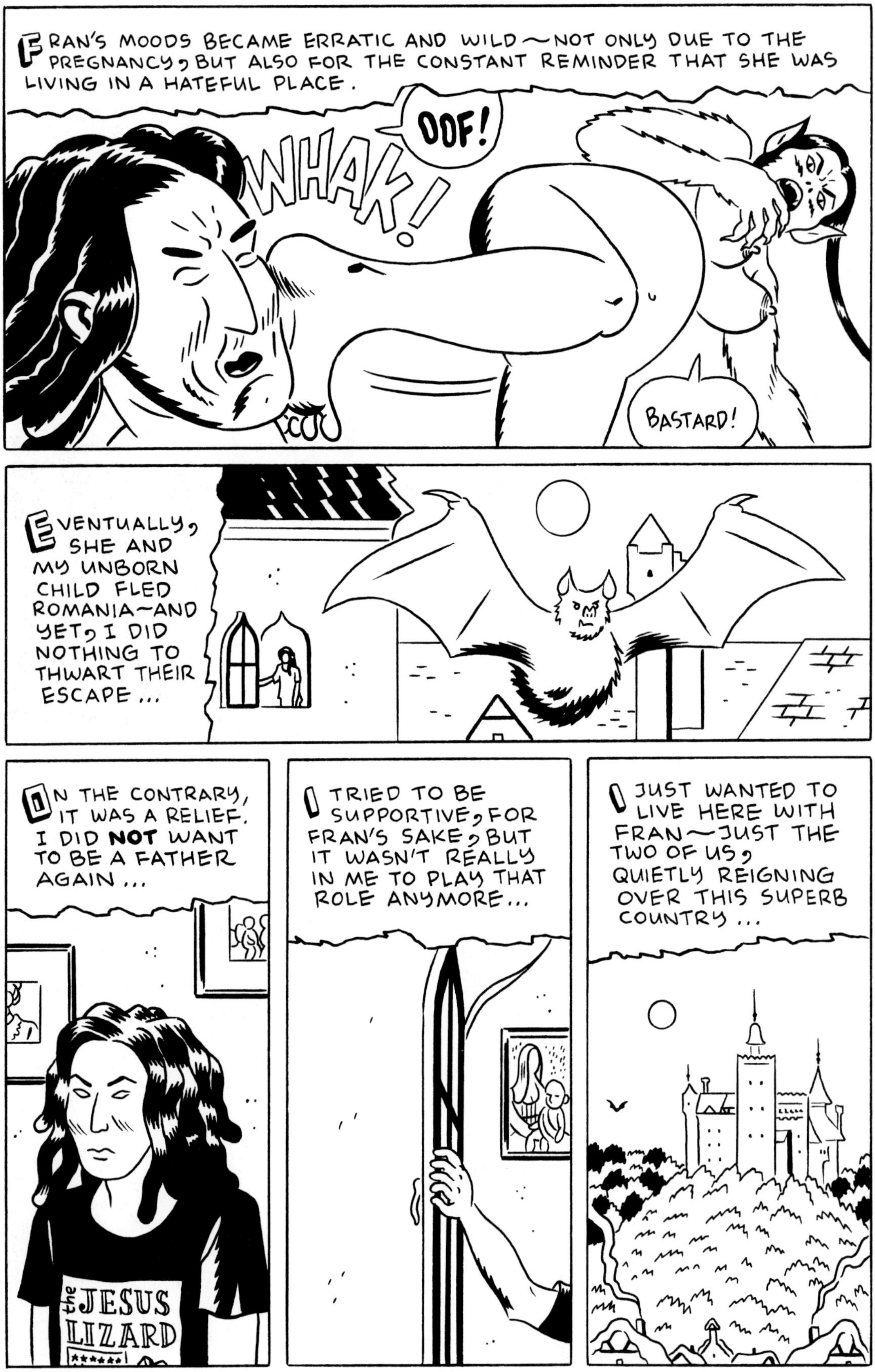
FRAN'S MOODS BECAME ERRATIC AND WILD~NOT ONLY DUE TO THE PREGNANCY, BUT ALSO FOR THE CONSTANT REMINDER THAT SHE WAS LIVING IN A HATEFUL PLACE.
WHAK!
OOF!
BASTARD!
EVENTUALLY, SHE AND MY UNBORN CHILD FLED ROMANIA~AND YET, I DID NOTHING TO THWART THEIR ESCAPE...
ON THE CONTRARY, IT WAS A RELIEF. I DID **NOT** WANT TO BE A FATHER AGAIN...
the JESUS LIZARD
I TRIED TO BE SUPPORTIVE, FOR FRAN'S SAKE, BUT IT WASN'T REALLY IN ME TO PLAY THAT ROLE ANYMORE...
I JUST WANTED TO LIVE HERE WITH FRAN~JUST THE TWO OF US, QUIETLY REIGNING OVER THIS SUPERB COUNTRY...

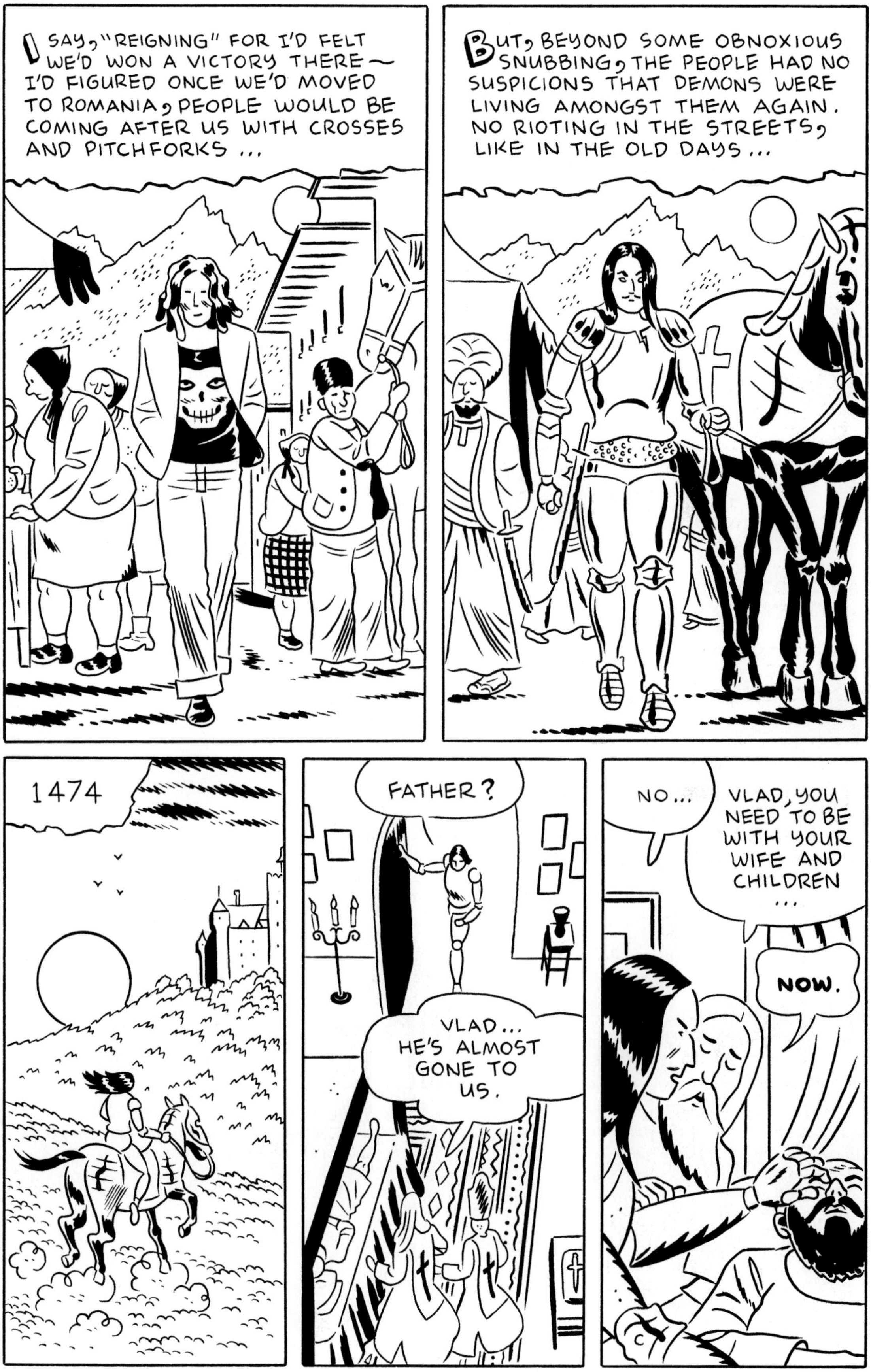
I SAY, "REIGNING" FOR I'D FELT WE'D WON A VICTORY THERE~ I'D FIGURED ONCE WE'D MOVED TO ROMANIA, PEOPLE WOULD BE COMING AFTER US WITH CROSSES AND PITCHFORKS ...
BUT, BEYOND SOME OBNOXIOUS SNUBBING, THE PEOPLE HAD NO SUSPICIONS THAT DEMONS WERE LIVING AMONGST THEM AGAIN. NO RIOTING IN THE STREETS, LIKE IN THE OLD DAYS ...
1474
FATHER?
VLAD... HE'S ALMOST GONE TO US.
NO...
VLAD, YOU NEED TO BE WITH YOUR WIFE AND CHILDREN ...
NOW.

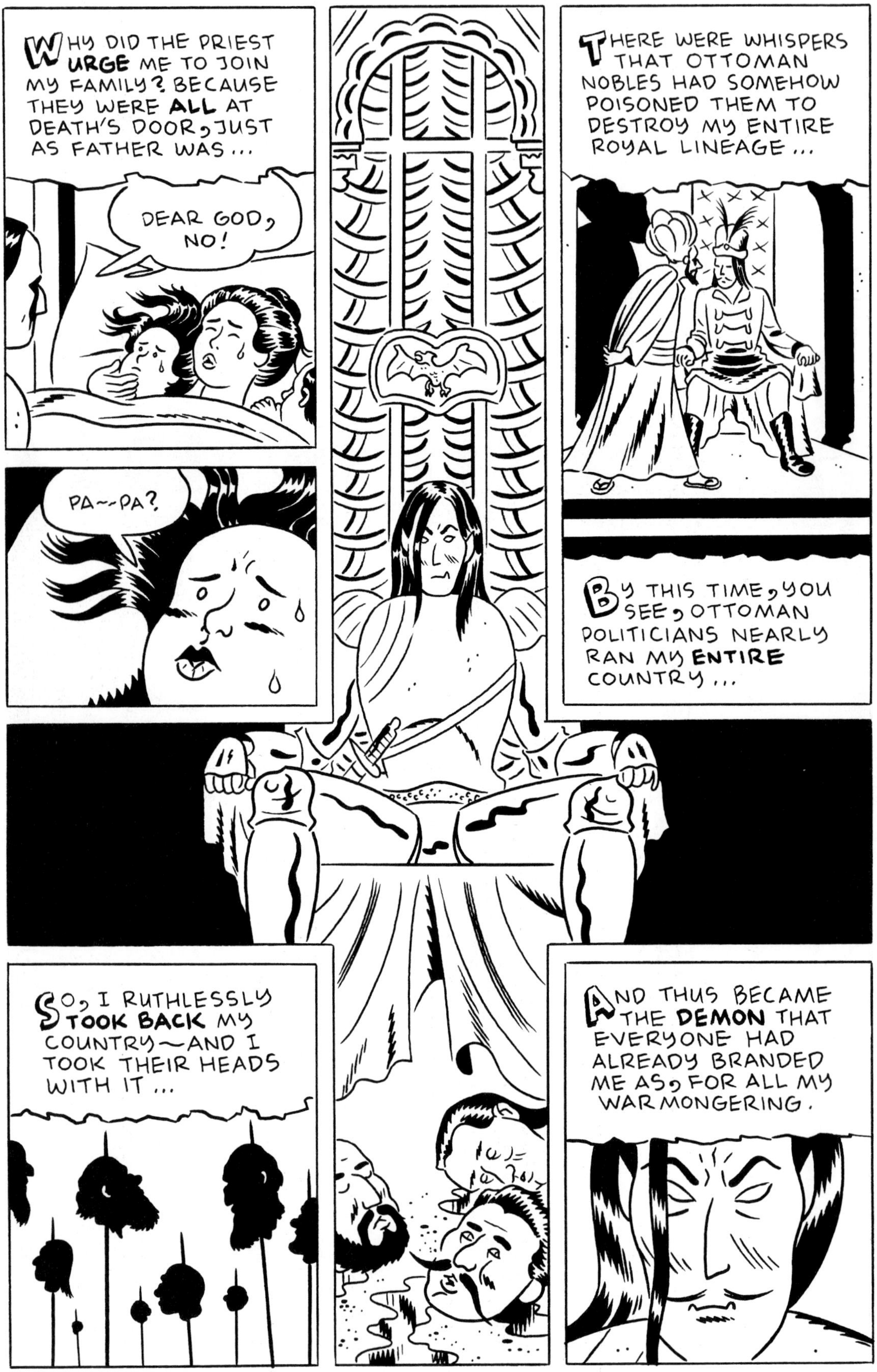
WHY DID THE PRIEST URGE ME TO JOIN MY FAMILY? BECAUSE THEY WERE ALL AT DEATH'S DOOR, JUST AS FATHER WAS...
DEAR GOD, NO!
PA--PA?
THERE WERE WHISPERS THAT OTTOMAN NOBLES HAD SOMEHOW POISONED THEM TO DESTROY MY ENTIRE ROYAL LINEAGE...
BY THIS TIME, YOU SEE, OTTOMAN POLITICIANS NEARLY RAN MY ENTIRE COUNTRY...
SO, I RUTHLESSLY TOOK BACK MY COUNTRY—AND I TOOK THEIR HEADS WITH IT...
AND THUS BECAME THE DEMON THAT EVERYONE HAD ALREADY BRANDED ME AS, FOR ALL MY WARMONGERING.

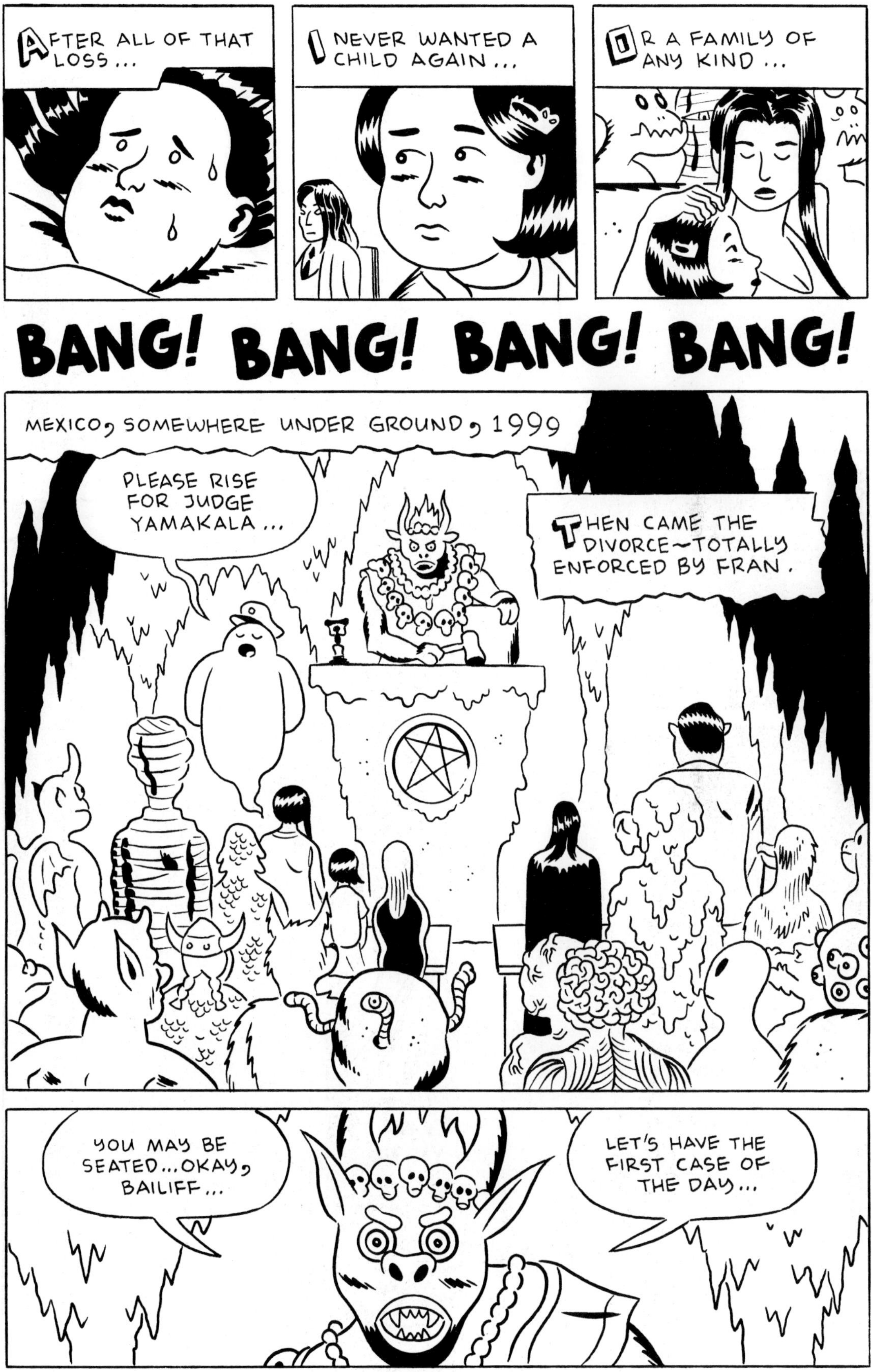
AFTER ALL OF THAT LOSS...
I NEVER WANTED A CHILD AGAIN...
OR A FAMILY OF ANY KIND...
BANG! BANG! BANG! BANG!
MEXICO, SOMEWHERE UNDER GROUND, 1999
PLEASE RISE FOR JUDGE YAMAKALA...
THEN CAME THE DIVORCE~TOTALLY ENFORCED BY FRAN.
YOU MAY BE SEATED...OKAY, BAILIFF...
LET'S HAVE THE FIRST CASE OF THE DAY...

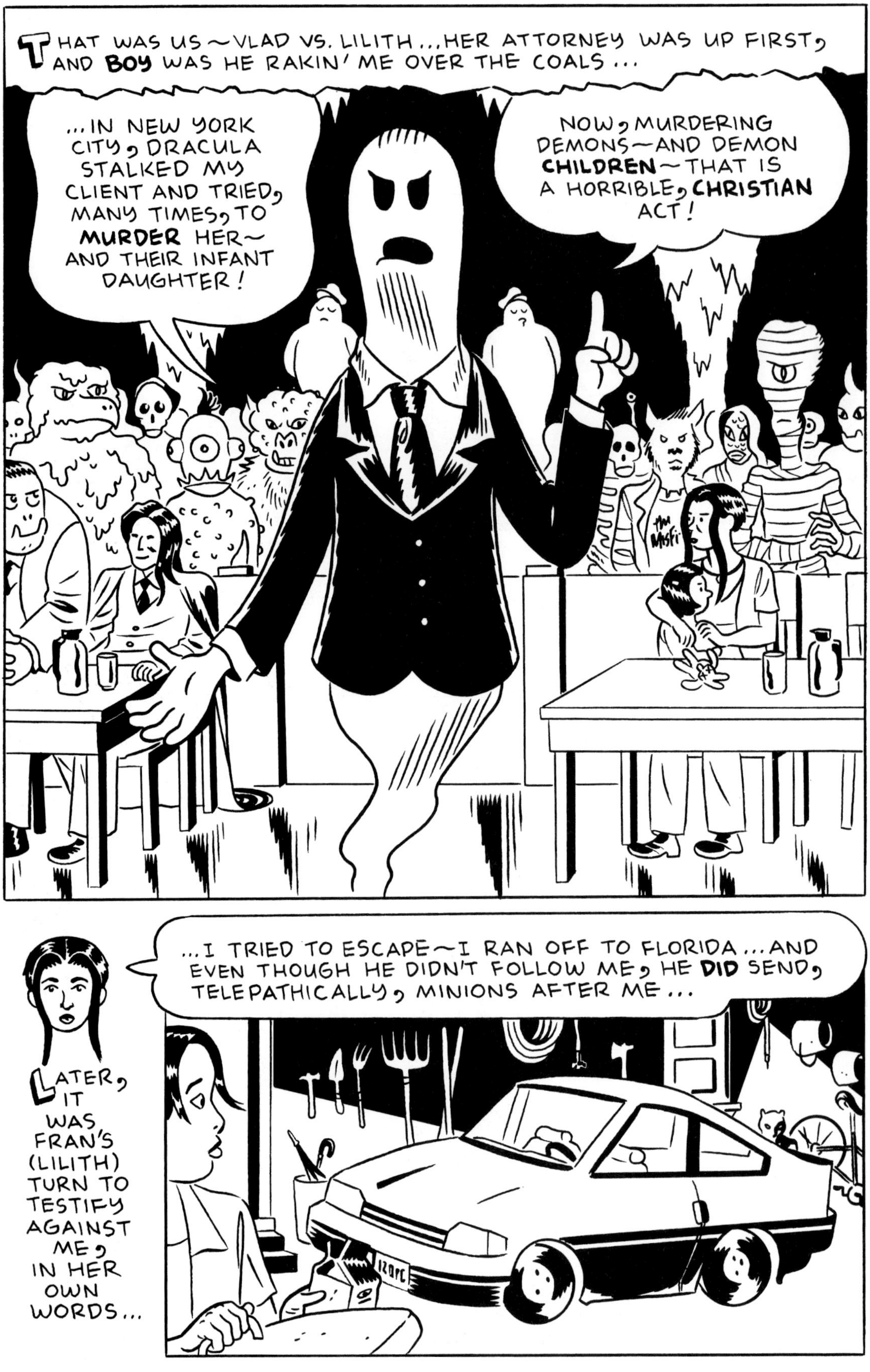
THAT WAS US ~ VLAD VS. LILITH ... HER ATTORNEY WAS UP FIRST, AND BOY WAS HE RAKIN' ME OVER THE COALS ...
... IN NEW YORK CITY, DRACULA STALKED MY CLIENT AND TRIED, MANY TIMES, TO MURDER HER ~ AND THEIR INFANT DAUGHTER!
NOW, MURDERING DEMONS ~ AND DEMON CHILDREN ~ THAT IS A HORRIBLE, CHRISTIAN ACT!
LATER, IT WAS FRAN'S (LILITH) TURN TO TESTIFY AGAINST ME, IN HER OWN WORDS ...
... I TRIED TO ESCAPE ~ I RAN OFF TO FLORIDA ... AND EVEN THOUGH HE DIDN'T FOLLOW ME, HE DID SEND, TELEPATHICALLY, MINIONS AFTER ME ...

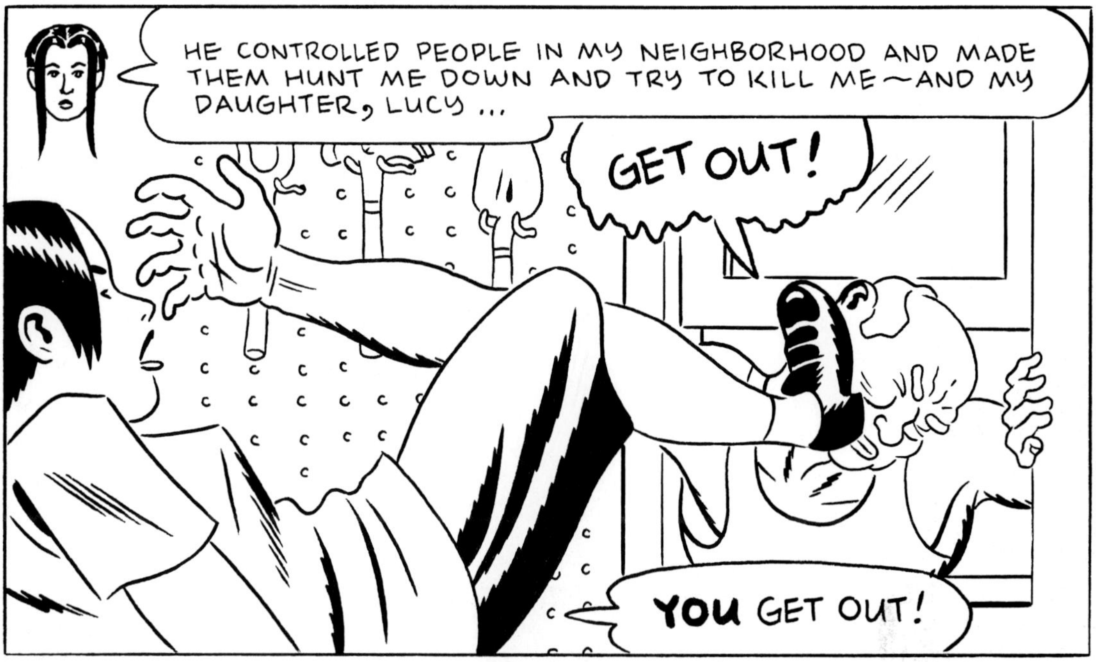
HE CONTROLLED PEOPLE IN MY NEIGHBORHOOD AND MADE THEM HUNT ME DOWN AND TRY TO KILL ME~AND MY DAUGHTER, LUCY ...
GET OUT!
YOU GET OUT!

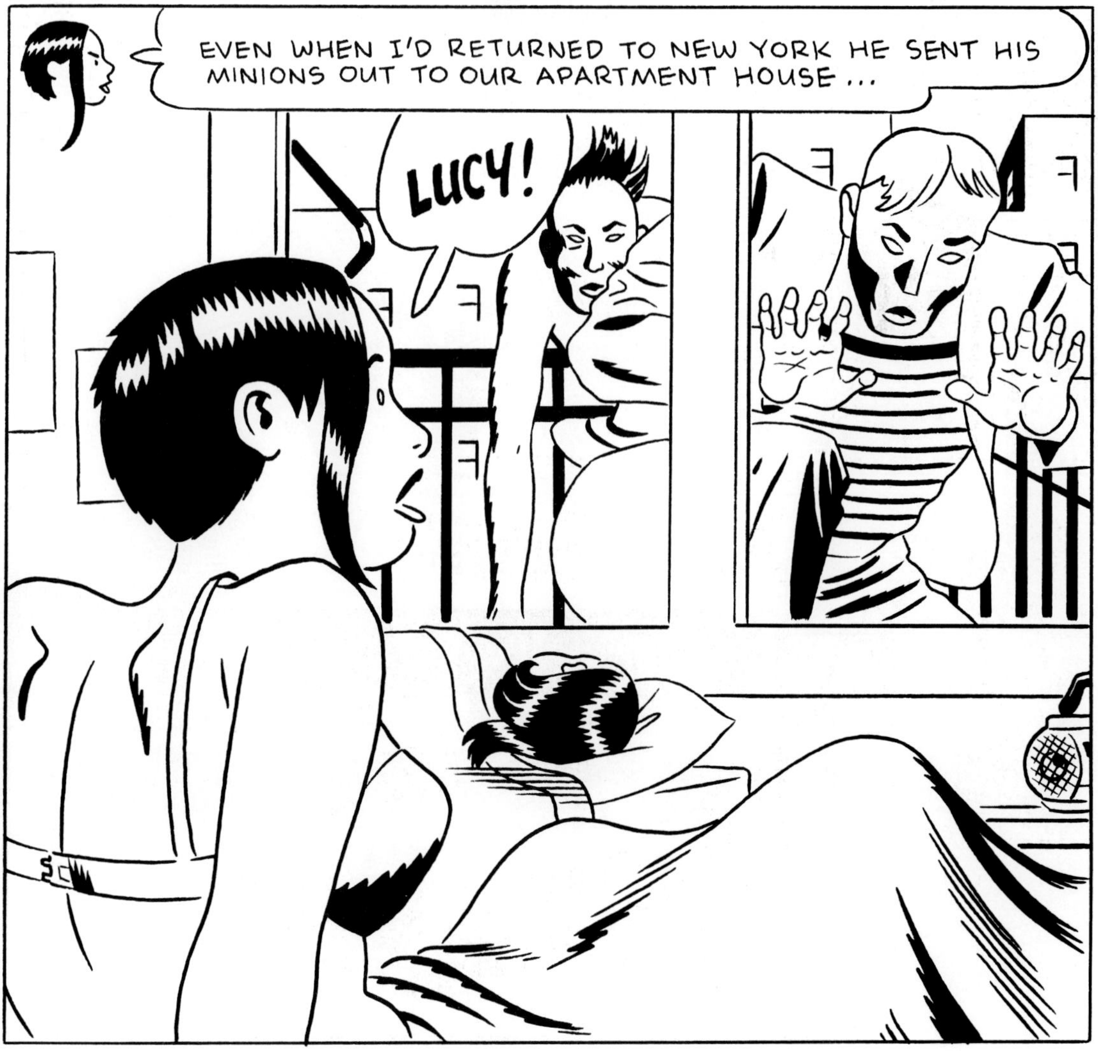
EVEN WHEN I'D RETURNED TO NEW YORK HE SENT HIS MINIONS OUT TO OUR APARTMENT HOUSE ...
LUCY!

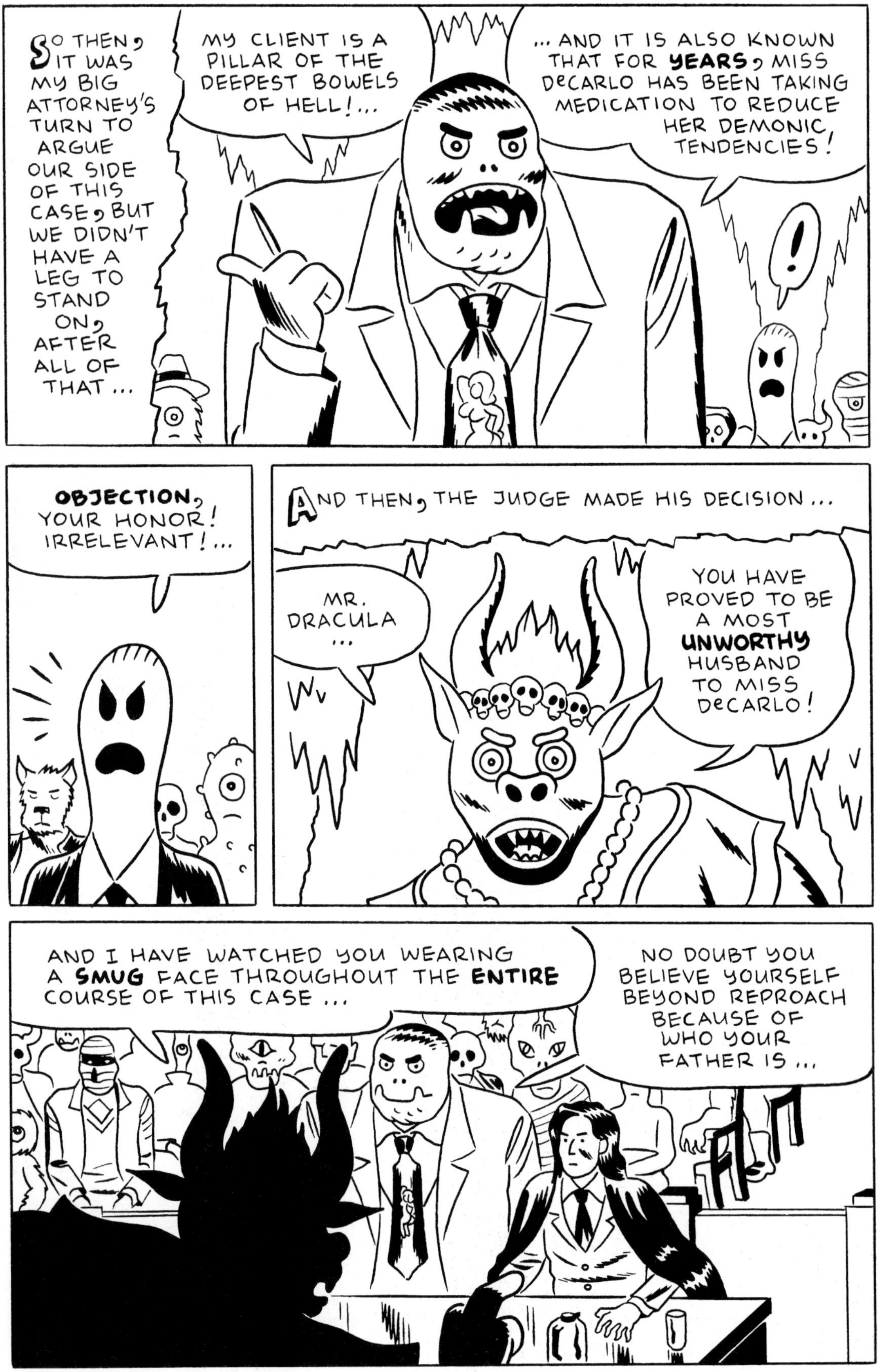

SO THEN, IT WAS MY BIG ATTORNEY'S TURN TO ARGUE OUR SIDE OF THIS CASE, BUT WE DIDN'T HAVE A LEG TO STAND ON, AFTER ALL OF THAT...
MY CLIENT IS A PILLAR OF THE DEEPEST BOWELS OF HELL!...
...AND IT IS ALSO KNOWN THAT FOR **YEARS**, MISS DeCARLO HAS BEEN TAKING MEDICATION TO REDUCE HER DEMONIC TENDENCIES!
!
OBJECTION, YOUR HONOR! IRRELEVANT!...
AND THEN, THE JUDGE MADE HIS DECISION...
MR. DRACULA...
YOU HAVE PROVED TO BE A MOST **UNWORTHY** HUSBAND TO MISS DeCARLO!
AND I HAVE WATCHED YOU WEARING A **SMUG** FACE THROUGHOUT THE **ENTIRE** COURSE OF THIS CASE...
NO DOUBT YOU BELIEVE YOURSELF BEYOND REPROACH BECAUSE OF WHO YOUR FATHER IS...

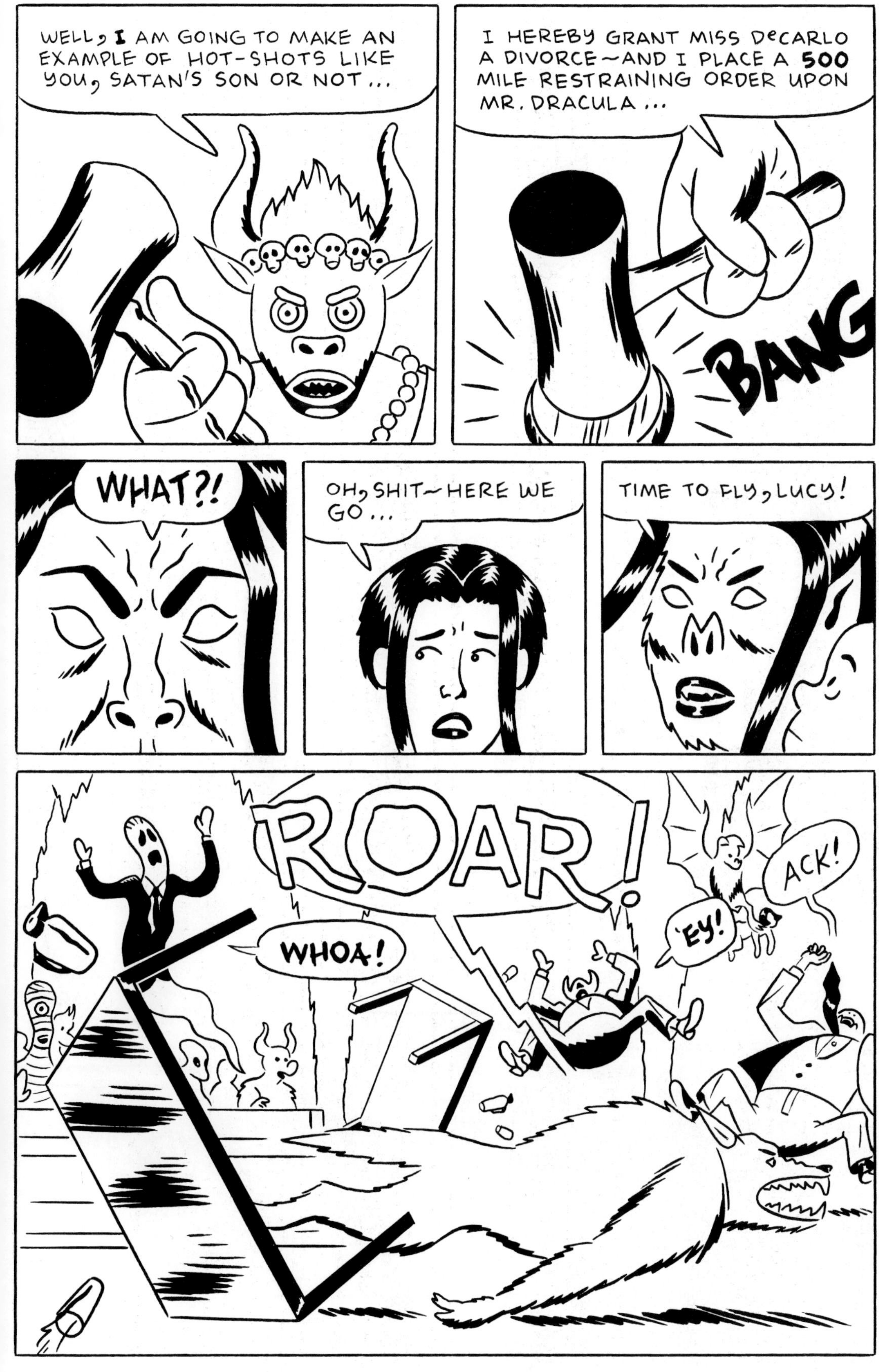
WELL, I AM GOING TO MAKE AN EXAMPLE OF HOT-SHOTS LIKE YOU, SATAN'S SON OR NOT...
I HEREBY GRANT MISS DeCARLO A DIVORCE~AND I PLACE A 500 MILE RESTRAINING ORDER UPON MR. DRACULA...
BANG
WHAT?!
OH, SHIT~HERE WE GO...
TIME TO FLY, LUCY!
ROAR!
WHOA!
'EY!
ACK!

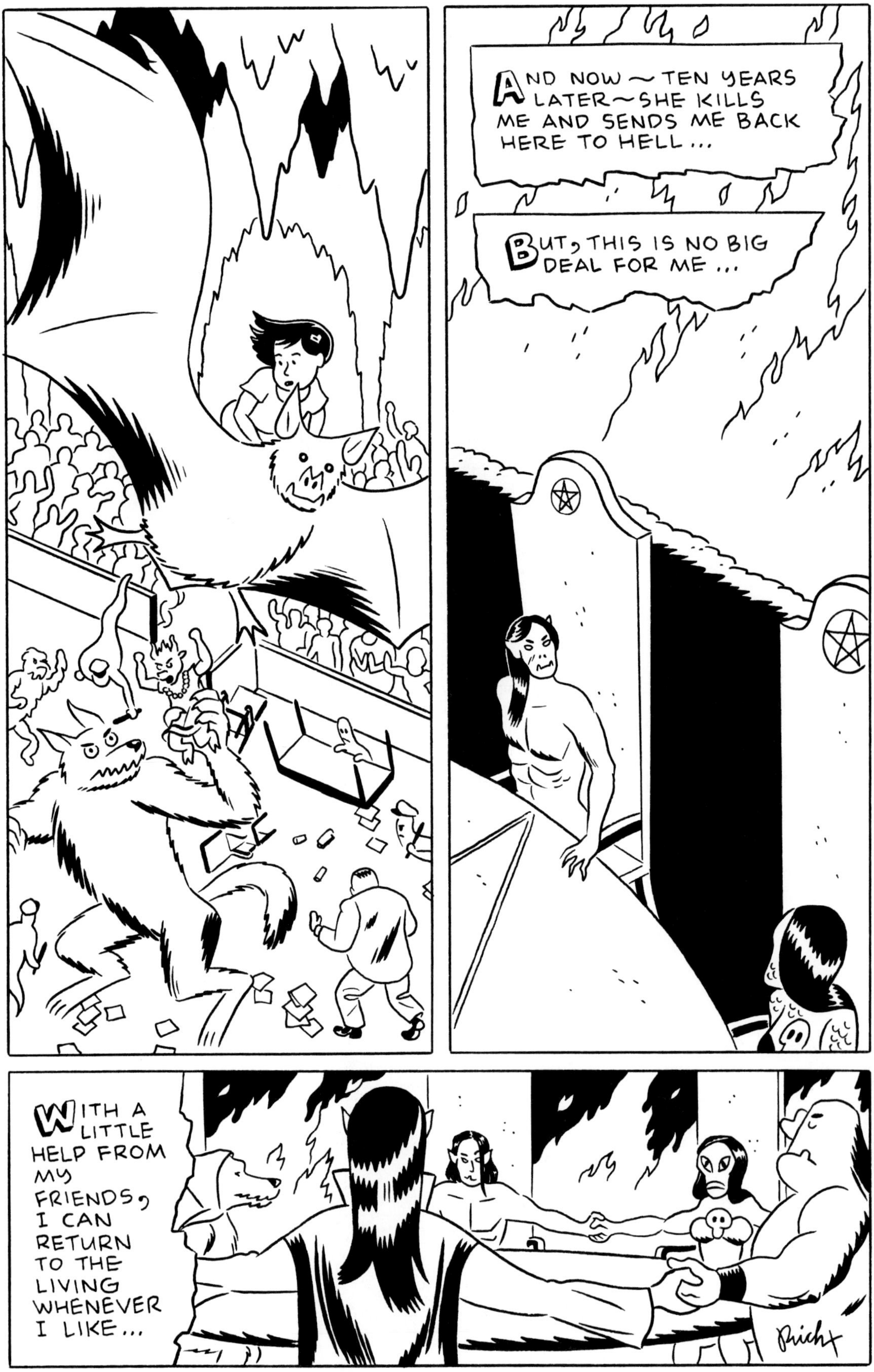
AND NOW ~ TEN YEARS LATER ~ SHE KILLS ME AND SENDS ME BACK HERE TO HELL...
BUT, THIS IS NO BIG DEAL FOR ME...
WITH A LITTLE HELP FROM MY FRIENDS, I CAN RETURN TO THE LIVING WHENEVER I LIKE...
Rich+

THE END ???

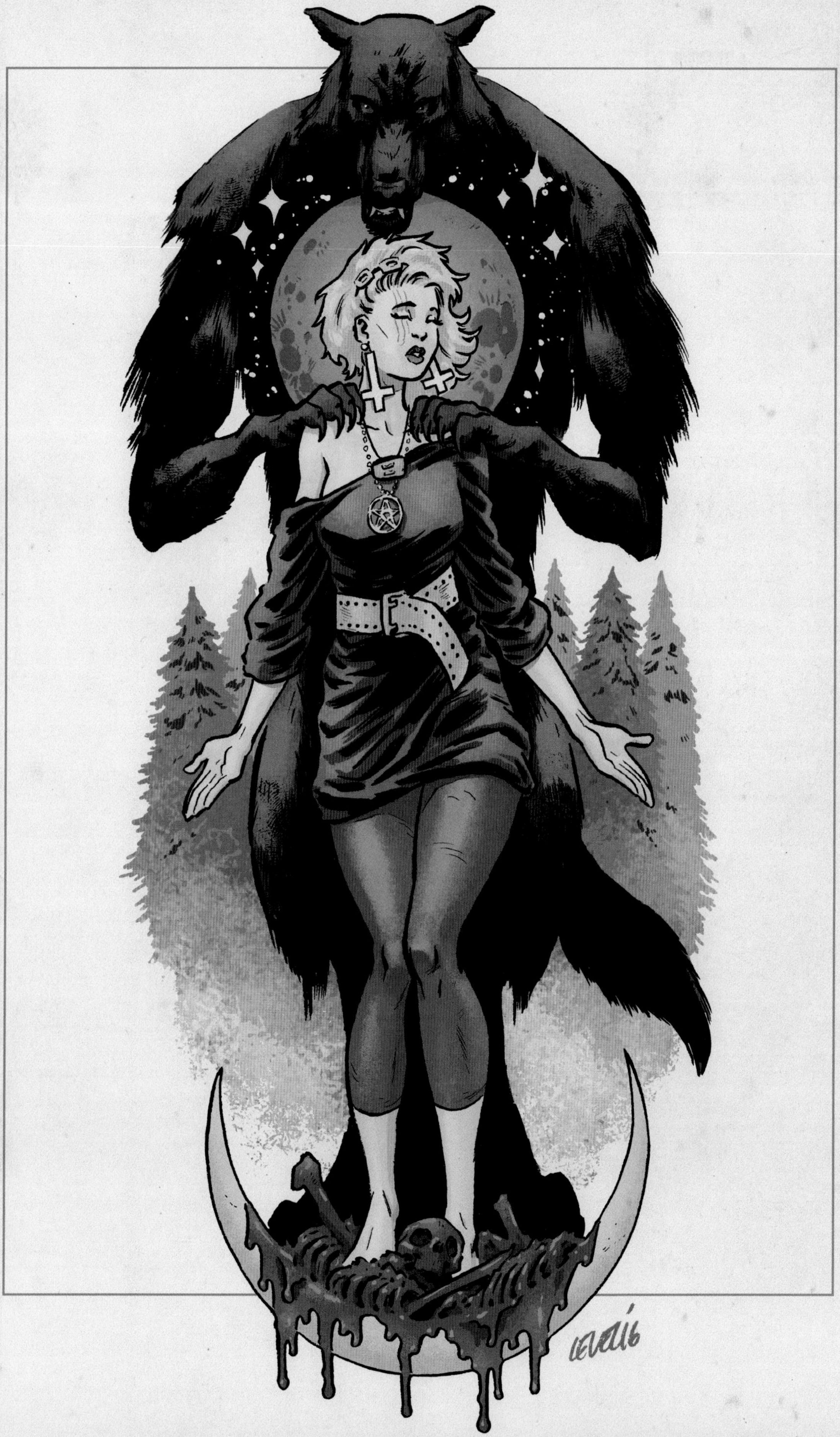

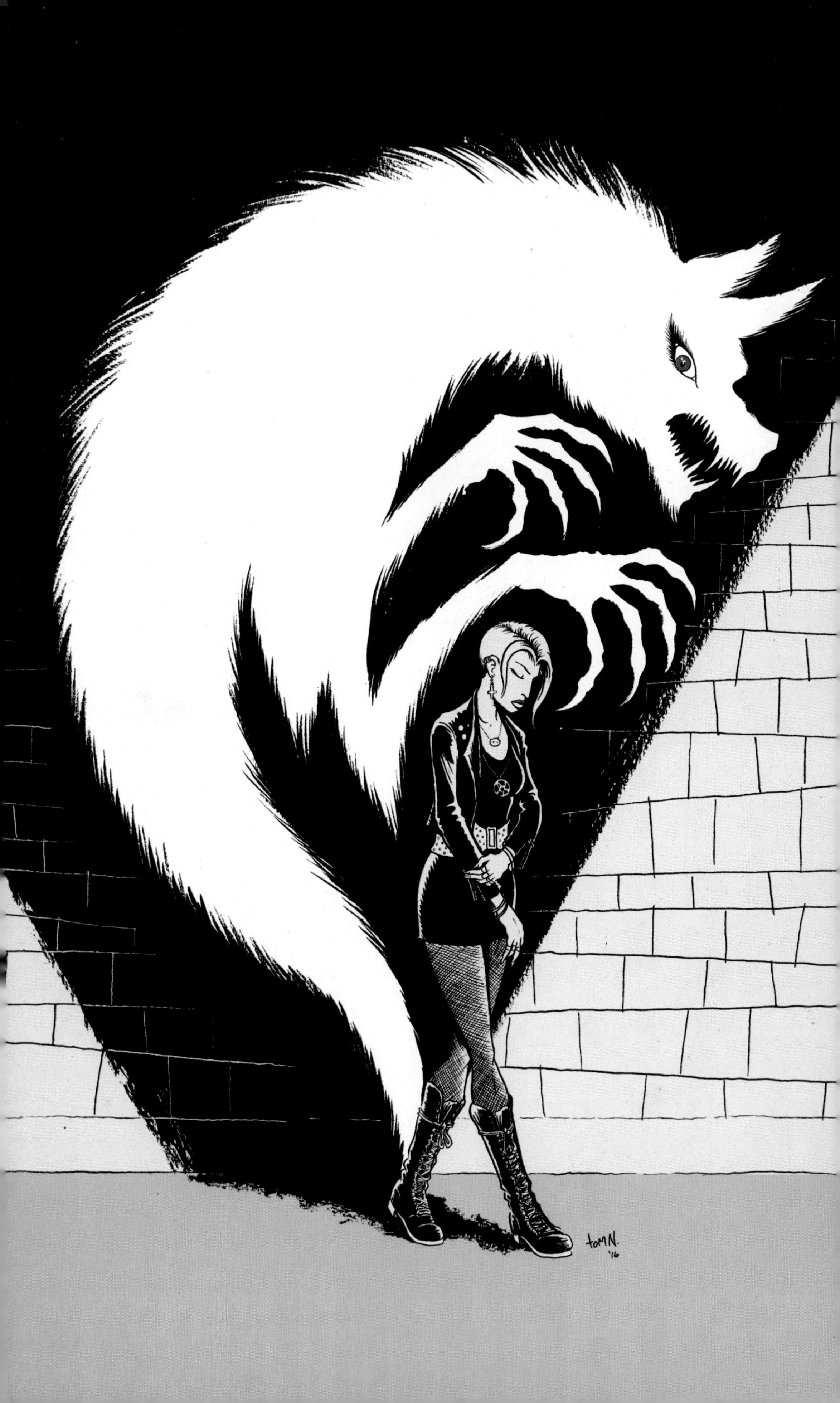

tom N.
'16

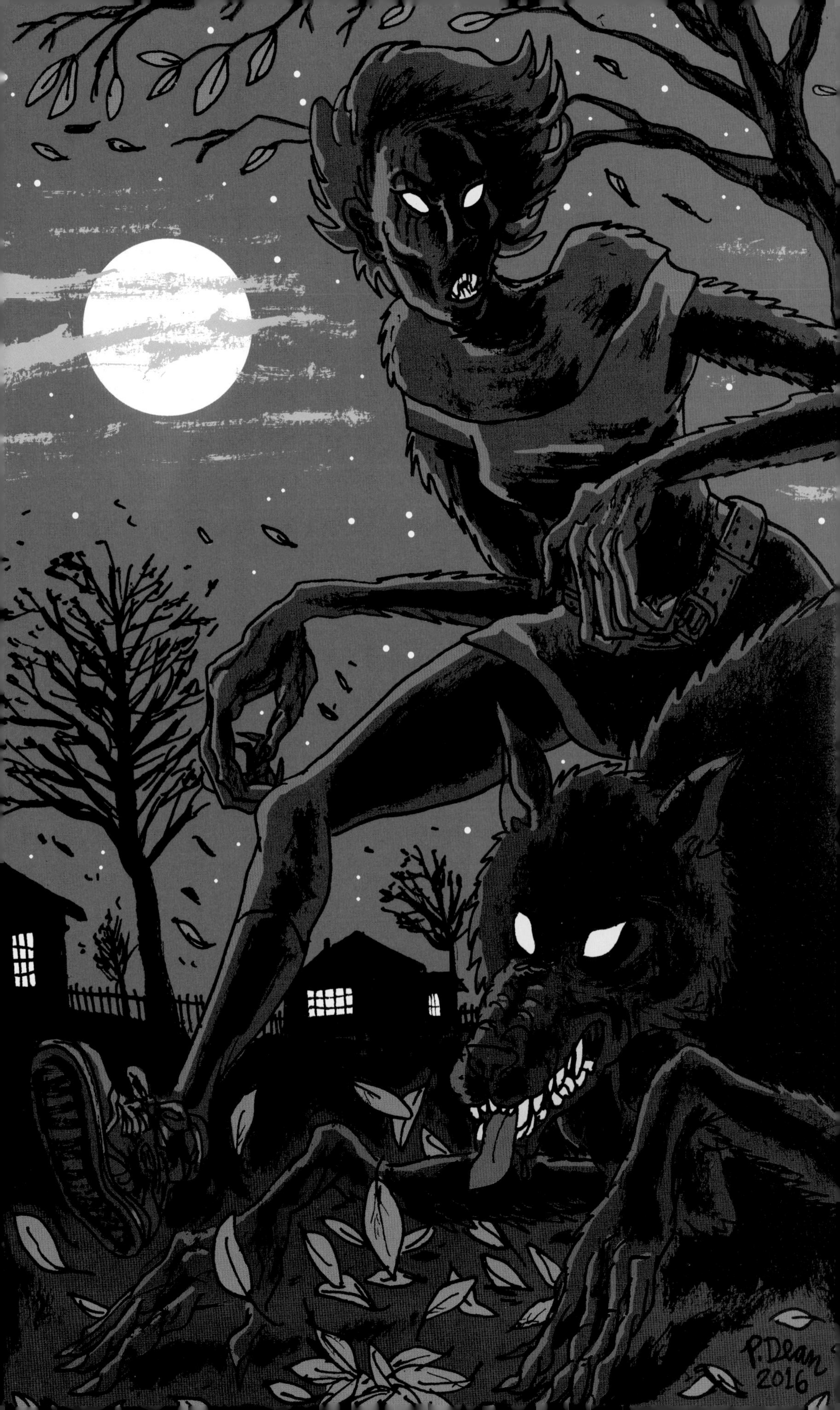
P. Dean
2016

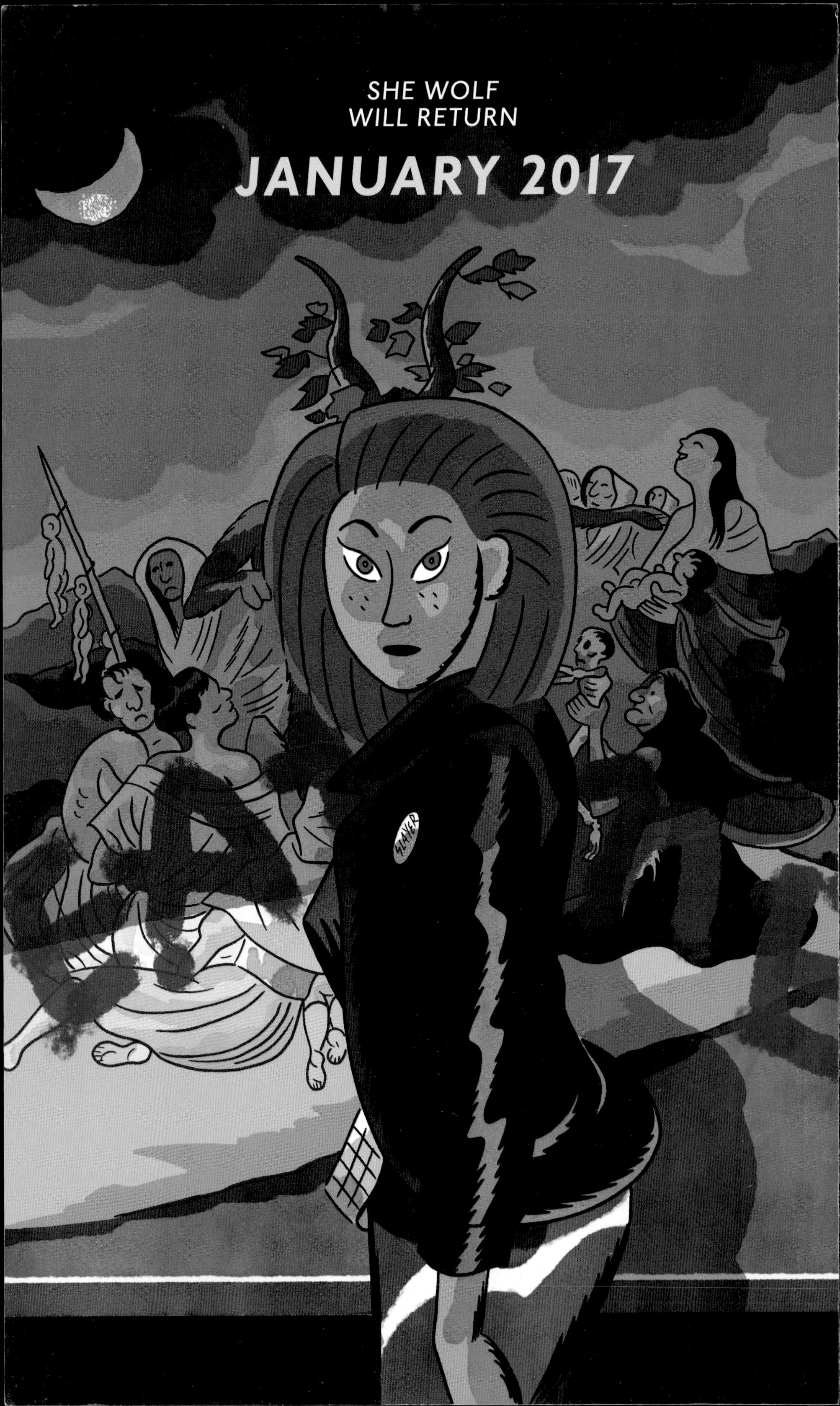
SHE WOLF
WILL RETURN
JANUARY 2017
SLAYER